Jacob L. [signature]
1970

The Life and Ministry of Our Lord

VOLUME SIX
BIBLE
SURVEY SERIES

the
Life and
Ministry
of Our
Lord

RAY F. ROBBINS

Convention
Press
Nashville,
Tennessee

© Copyright 1970 • Convention Press
Nashville, Tennessee

Library of Congress Catalog Card Number: 70-110607
Printed in the United States of America
35. F 70 R.R.D.

Illustrations by John White
Painting "Triumphal Entry" by Harold Minton

*To the millions of
faithful Christians in the churches
who know, worship, and serve
our living Lord*

Contents

Ray F. Robbins is professor of New Testament and Greek at the New Orleans Baptist Theological Seminary. A native of Flomaton, Alabama, he was awarded the A.B. degree from Mississippi College, the Th.M. and the Th.D. degrees from the Southern Baptist Theological Seminary, and the Ph.D. degree from the University of Edinburgh. He has done additional study at the universities of Oxford, Basel, Zurich, and Alabama. Before coming to his present position, he served as associate professor of religion at Howard College (now Samford University) from 1946 to 1952.

I

BETWEEN
THE
TESTAMENTS

JESUS CHRIST stands supreme in history. His name continues to command the love, reverence, and obedience of millions of people. With every century his name becomes more deeply imprinted upon history. Millions of adoring hearts around the world read about him, ponder who he was, reflect upon what he said, and marvel at what he did.

Our Lord lived on the earth. He participated in the nature and experiences of man. However, his life did not begin in the mystery of the incarnation and it did not end in the darker mysteries of Gethsemane and the cross. He voluntarily entered into the world from realms outside and above the world. He was before his historical manifestation (John 1:1), and he is personally present with his people now (Matt. 28:20).

In order to understand more fully this life of God expressed completely in Jesus Christ, it is necessary to see how God expressed himself through his people before Jesus' birth. The Old Testament records events of the working of divine providence through long stretches of history in the preparation of a chosen people. God expressed himself to and through these people in many ways. Some knowledge of the contents of the Old Testament is indispensable for an understanding of the Gospels.

God continued to reveal himself to his people during the period

1

after the close of the Old Testament. In order to understand the environment in which Jesus lived and to understand the reactions of the people to him and his message, it is necessary to know something of the Jews during this time. For this purpose we have included the first chapter in the study. This period is not as well known as the Old Testament or the New Testament, but it is very important for an understanding of the Gospels and the life of Jesus. Only by being acquainted with the religious, social, and political developments during the period can we understand the allusions to the life situations which the Gospel writers take for granted.

Following the presentation of the interbiblical period, this study will proceed to set forth in as clear and graphic a style as possible the great events of our Lord's earthly life and the scope and substance of his teachings. Insofar as it shall contribute to an understanding of the Gospels and to an apprehension of the life and teachings of Jesus, the object in view in its preparation will have been attained. It is hoped that the results derived from the study of this book will be the same as those Jesus pointed out as motives for his advent into the world: "That they might have life, and might have it abundantly" (John 10:10).[1] It is also hoped that for all those who study this book it may be true as Paul said: "We all, with unveiled face beholding as in a mirror the glory of the Lord, are being transformed into the same image from glory to glory, just as from the Lord, the Spirit" (2 Cor. 3:18).

To him, Immanuel, God with us, the Word made flesh, be glory in the church forever.

The Intertestamental Period

Between the time when the last Old Testament book was written and the first New Testament writer took up his pen, some tremendous changes had taken place. The Persian Empire had fallen and a Roman emperor was issuing a decree to be observed by the world. Nehemiah was no longer governor of the Hebrews of Judea; the Jews were ruled . by an Idumean king named Herod (Neh. 1:2). The high priest no longer held absolute authority but a great council, the Sanhedrin, exercised religious and political authority over the people. Israel was no longer a small remnant struggling to restore her ruined city in spite of poverty and surrounding unfriendly nations. Instead, there was a densely-populated country with terraced hills and crowded cities. These cities, bearing Greek names, were inhabited by rich merchants who had economic, social, and political strength in the Roman Empire.

The language of the religious leaders had changed, and the **people spoke Aramaic and Greek.** Their Scriptures were read in Greek. The intermarriage problems of Nehemiah's day had been solved by a policy of social exclusiveness. The former doctrinal and ecclesiastical unity of the Jews had given way to division which manifested itself in varied religious sects. These sects were vying with each other for the loyalty and support of the people. The hope of the coming of a king like the great David and realization of the promises made to Abraham had developed into a Messiah-concept which embodied a multitude of bizarre fantasies. The concepts included a hope that Israel would be restored to its former glory. The Jews' idea of messiah was both political and material in character and seemed to lack spiritual depth.

An Overview of the Period

To read meaningfully the important detailed information about the period between the close of the Old Testament and the birth of Christ, you will need to have some idea of the periods, people, and places in the story. (Key words and phrases will be set in bold type to keep you on your course in this chapter.)

HISTORY

The Persian Empire began to disintegrate in 424 B.C. The disintegration was hastened by Alexander the Great (336–323 B.C.), who was something of a missionary for Greek culture. Though his chief interest was conquest and fusion, he was humane and lenient in his treatment of the Jews. Alexander succeeded in conquering much of the world and scattering Greek culture. (Remember this fact when later you read of Hellenization of Judaism, which is the term used for the result of Greek influence.)

When Alexander died, his empire was divided among his five **generals.** Two of these figured in Palestinian history, **Seleucus** and **Ptolemy.** Eventually a power struggle between these two resulted in the defeat of Ptolemy when **Seleucus took Palestine** from him in 198 B.C.

Another significant point to remember is the rule of the brutal **Antiochus IV** (called Epiphanes). It was he who tried fiercely to coerce the Jews into embracing the Greek religion. His brutality and especially his desecration of the Temple are noteworthy, for they led to the **Maccabean revolt.**

The Maccabean period began when **Mattathias** refused to sacrifice a pig on the altar, killed those priests and soldiers who tried to make him do so, and fled to the hills with his five sons. Three of these sons succeeded their father as high priest-ruler—**Juddas, Jonathan, Simon.** During this time there was a period of Jewish independence, but it was over in 63 B.C. when the Roman period began. **John Hyrcanus,** grandson of Mattathias, began a dynasty of his own. The period which followed was a dark one for the Jews, for it finally ended in a civil war which claimed thousands of lives and opened the way for Rome to gain complete control of Palestine.

The **Roman period** began when **Pompey,** the Roman general, took Jerusalem, and the rule was in full force when Jesus was born. Herod was ruler of the Jews by the authority granted him from Rome.

SOCIAL-RELIGIOUS-POLITICAL STRUCTURE

Two major parties, a ruling body, a professional group, and a meeting place are also important to an understanding of this chapter and this entire study:

Sadducees.—This group of people were more interested in **politics** than they were in religion, though they are considered a religious party. They probably appeared first in Palestine during the Maccabean period. They always associated with the aristocrats and ruling classes. It is difficult to establish what their doctrine was since they concentrated their efforts on opposing the Pharisees. They accepted only the Pentateuch as inspired, resisted oral tradition, and did not believe in angels or the resurrection. They opposed Jesus primarily because they feared that his popularity with the common people would result in trouble with Rome.

Pharisees.—This group derived its name from a term that means separated ones. They were very careful about observance of all Jewish laws. They were very much in sympathy with **oral tradition,** feeling that it was necessary to help the people obey the law. They upheld the very **strictest form of Jewish worship.** They believed in the resurrection, in punishment and rewards in the afterlife, in angels, in the supremacy of the Pentateuch, and in divine sovereignty over history. They were a **religious party,** but they were not above "mixing in politics."

Scribes.—The Jewish interest in the law led to the development of this group who spent their time searching the law. They were professional **students and defenders of the Jewish law.** Their search led to the development of involved oral tradition which came to be more binding than the Scriptures. With cooperation from the Pharisees, this group finally reduced vital Old Testament religion to a sterile rabbinism.

Synagogue.—Much of the story of Christ centers around the synagogue. This institution may have begun to develop **as early as the Exile.** When the Jews were separated from their beloved Temple, they began to meet together to **read the Scriptures** in whatever form they existed at that time. When the synagogue came into its own, services were held there to read the Law and the Prophets, to pray, sing, and sometimes to discuss the Scriptures. The only requirement for establishing a synagogue or holding a synagogue service was the presence of ten men.

LITERATURE OF THE PERIOD

In addition to the Bible itself, the chief sources of our knowledge of the changes which took place within this period between the Old and New Testaments are the literary works that had their origin during this time or which reflect the causes or the results produced by the period.

Josephus.—The most informative writings on this period are **Josephus** and **First Maccabees** (in the Apocrypha of the Old Testament). Josephus was born in A.D. 37–38 and died sometime after A.D. 100. He was a carefully-educated son of one of the most eminent priestly families among the Jews. His first work was the *History of the Jewish War.* In the seven books of this work, he told the story of the Jewish insurrection against the Romans in A.D. 66–70 in which he took part. In his second work, *Antiquities of the Jews,* Josephus traced, in twenty books, the history of the Jews from the earliest time to the reign of Nero (A.D. 54–68).

The Life of Flavius Josephus was a sequel to *Antiquities of the Jews.* His primary object in this autobiography was to vindicate his conduct as the commander in chief in Galilee during the Jewish-Roman War. The fourth work of Josephus, *Against Apion,* consists of two books and is an explanation of Judaism. In this last work Josephus showed the excellencies of Judaism, while at the same time he showed the deficiencies of Hellenism. The importance of Josephus for the period between the Old and New Testaments lies in the fact that he is **often our only source of information of a period or an event.**

"Outside books."—The two terms used to designate other books on the period between the Testaments are Apocrypha and Pseudepigrapha. The apocryphal (hidden) books are **primarily those related to the history of the Maccabean revolt.** The Jews referred to them as "outside books" even though they were included in the Greek translation (Septuagint) of the Old Testament.

The most outstanding and informative apocryphal book is **First Maccabees.** Though not a part of our Bible, it is a **reliable history** of the events from the accession of Antiochus Epiphanes (175 B.C.) to the death of Simon the Hasmonean (135 B.C.). This work deals with the struggle of the Jewish people for religious orthodoxy, religious freedom, and political independence.

Pseudepigrapha is the term used to refer to a large group of books which were **not included in any translation of the Bible.** The term applies to material written as though it were the work of a well-known Old Testament person such as Enoch, Moses, and Ezra.

Actually the two terms—Apocrypha and Pseudepigrapha—are not clearly defined, for in recent years scholars have come to refer to all noncanonical works of this period as apocryphal.

Dead Sea Scrolls.—These scrolls were found in a cave in the **Qumran community,** a Palestinian community on the northeastern shore of the Dead Sea. These materials provide interesting information on **how a hermit-like society lived from about 140 B.C. to A.D. 68.** They lived ascetic lives in an effort to escape the corrupt life of the city and to seek to restore the ancient religion of their fathers. The **two Isaiah scrolls** found there are at least **two hundred years older** than the oldest ones available before the discovery. These Isaiah scrolls confirm the accuracy of the Isaiah copies that had been previously used by Bible translators.

For better understanding.—You have now had a sketchy overview of the main events, characters, and literature from the period between the Testaments. This reading has helped you to locate a few signposts. Now to prepare yourself for a meaningful study of the world into which the angel brought the glad tidings that a Savior had been born, you will need to take some of the side roads off the main thoroughfare of history. The material on pages 20–21 has been prepared to help you with this exploration.

The Early History of the Hebrews

"God, after He spoke long ago to the fathers in the prophets in many portions and in many ways." Thus, in the opening words of Hebrews, we are reminded that God has been speaking to his people from time to time in various ways to communicate the nature and character of the divine Being. In fact, from the beginning God has used the events of history to provide a setting in which to disclose himself as Creator, Redeemer, and Holy Spirit. The Bible is a record of historical events through which the living personal God chose to declare himself as dynamically and redemptively active in history.

In this unique salvation history, God has chosen to reveal himself through events, such as the creation, the calling of Abraham, the Exodus of the Hebrews from Egypt, the raising up of judges, the raising up of kings, the calling of prophets, the Exile, the restoration, the persecutions during the intertestamental period, the incarnation, and the creation and empowering of the church. God has not confined his revelation of himself to momentous occurrences. To those who have sympathetic imagination and intuitive insight, every event summed up in Christ and unfolding in the present provides the framework for this salvation history.

(A brief survey of the history of the Hebrews should disclose some of God's activity in this salvation history. However, it is not easy to find a starting point in what seems to be a cycle of history. For a brief résumé of Hebrew history, see appendix 1, p. 190. Careful reading of this material will enrich study of the intertestamental period.)

The Jews and Alexander the Great (336–323 B.C.)

The death of Philip II of Macedonia by the assassin Pausanias in 336 B.C. set the stage for Philip's son Alexander, who was only nineteen years old, to assume control of his army and his kingdom. Although a Macedonian in origin, Alexander was culturally a Greek. For several generations the Macedonian court had been deeply influenced by Greek ideas and had entertained Greek scholars and artists. When Alexander was thirteen years old, he became a pupil of the famous philosopher Aristotle. Through the influence of Aristotle, Alexander was convinced of the complete superiority of the Greek way of life.

After ascending the throne, Alexander immediately took steps to consolidate his position in the Greek states to the south. He also asserted his authority over the Hellenic League who, in its congress at Corinth, made him generalissimo of all the Greeks.

Having secured his position on his own borders, Alexander began the invasion of Persia. In 334 B.C. he crossed the Hellespont and entered Asia Minor, defeating the Persian army. The victory opened the way to the conquest of the whole of Asia Minor within a year. In 333 B.C., he met the Persian army again, led by Darius, decisively defeating Darius who fled for his life. Alexander then marched into Syria and captured Damascus.

At this point, Alexander thought it wise to subdue the territories to the south of Syria before going farther into Persia in pursuit of Darius. The city of Sidon welcomed Alexander; and, as a reward, the territory and the rights which had been taken away by Persia were restored. At Tyre Alexander met with opposition. Only after a seven months' siege was this island fortress taken in 332 B.C.

A STORY FROM JOSEPHUS

Josephus has told a long story of Alexander's meeting with the Jews when he conquered Persia. It is interesting but cannot be verified. With the available evidence, Alexander's dealings with the Jews must be left an open question. But without question, Alexander's influence was strongly felt in the developing Jewish history. His imprint is clearly visible in this period of Hebrew development.

It is true that Alexander's general policy broke down the barrier between the East and the West. In developing his provinces (satrapies), he fused the Orient with Western ideas, spreading Greek culture and art. The commerce and colonies which followed his conquests opened doors for improving social conditions. He introduced the Greek language and Hellenistic modes of thought. It was his fond dream to found a universal empire, which would be held together not merely by the unity of government, but also by the unity of language, customs, and religion. All the Oriental races were saturated with Hellenistic culture and the Jews were no exception. This slow and secret encroachment of Hellenism exposed separatist Judaism, as it had been interpreted by Ezra, to its greatest danger. These influences led many Jews, including the priests, to a religious syncretism (combination or fusion) whereby Zeus was identified with Jehovah. This was in flagrant disobedience of God's command.

The Jews and the Ptolemies of Egypt (321–198 B.C.)

Ptolemy I Soter	323–283 B.C.
Ptolemy II Philadelphus	283–247 B.C.
Ptolemy III Euergetes	247–221 B.C.
Ptolemy IV Philopater	221–204 B.C.
Ptolemy V Epiphanes	204–198 B.C.

Since Alexander had appointed no one to succeed him, rebellion and conflict broke out immediately after his death. His generals were able to put down these uprisings among the people. However, occasional warfare was waged among these generals for seven years. Alexander's conquered territory was divided among six of his generals. Four of these generals laid the foundations for four empires of which only two, Egypt and Syria, had any direct connection with the history of the Jews. Palestine was won by **Ptolemy Soter of Egypt.** Josephus quotes an account of Ptolemy's capture of Jerusalem written by Agatharchides, a Greek historian and geographer who lived in the second century B.C.

> There are a people called Jews, who dwell in a city the strongest of all other cities, which the inhabitants call Jerusalem, and are accustomed to rest on every seventh day; at which times they make no use of their arms, nor meddle with husbandry, nor take care of any affairs of life, but spread out their hands in their holy places, and pray till the evening. Now it came to pass, that when Ptolemy, the son of Lagus, came into this city with his army, these men, in observing this mad custom of theirs, instead of guarding the city, suffered their country to submit itself to a bitter lord; and their law was openly proved to have commanded a foolish practice. This accident taught all other men but the Jews to disregard such dreams as these were, and not to follow the like idle suggestions delivered as a law, when, in such uncertainty of human reasonings, they are at a loss what they should do.[2]

For some 125 years the Jews were ruled by the Egyptian monarchs (Ptolemies). During this time many **Jews** were **deported** or emigrated **to Egypt** from where they spread over Libya and Cyrene. These Egyptian Jews adopted the Greek language and were soon in need of having their Scriptures translated into Greek. During the reign of the **second Ptolemy, Philadelphus,** the **Septuagint** (usually written LXX) was begun to meet this need. This Greek translation became the Bible of Judaism not only in Egypt but in Asia and Europe as well and was the Bible used by the early Christians. Its use, however, accelerated the influence of Hellenism upon Judaism. During the years in which the Jews were subjects of the Ptolemies, the government of Judea was a combination of the city-state and theocracy. The high priest was not only the religious leader but the political leader as well. As long as he paid the annual tribute and kept the peace, he was left to rule the Jews in Judea.

The successor of Philadelphus was **Ptolemy Euergetes**. He also **treated the Jews with consideration**. They were allowed to practice their religion without interference and were allowed full freedom in the administration of their own affairs. The high priest, Onias II, precipitated a crisis by refusing to send the annual tribute to Euergetes. The problem was solved when the taxes were paid by a nephew of the high priest.

Ptolemy Philopater was Euergetes' successor. During his reign he visited Jerusalem and gave gifts and offered sacrifices in the Temple. He attempted to enter the holy of holies but was prevented by some supernatural terror. As a consequence of this experience, he wreaked his vengeance on the Jews in Alexandria.

Philopater was succeeded by his five-year-old son, **Ptolemy Epiphanes**. He was the **last of the Ptolemies to rule the Jews. During the Ptolemaic period Judaism was gradually permeated by the character, thought, culture, and ethical system of Hellenism.**

The Jews and the Seleucids of Syria (198–167 B.C.)

Antiochus III the Great	198–187 B.C.
Seleucus IV Philopater	187–175 B.C.
Antiochus IV Epiphanes	175–163 B.C.

In 198 B.C. the Syrian monarch, **Antiochus III the Great, defeated the Egyptians** and gained **control of Palestine.** The Jews welcomed Antiochus and gave him their support. Antiochus treated the Jews with kindness and settled thousands of them as colonists in various new cities which he founded. In 192 B.C. Antiochus found himself at war with Rome, and at the Battle of Magnesia (190 B.C.) suffered a crippling defeat. He was forced to pay an enormous indemnity and to hand over hostages, among them his own son, who would later become king as Antiochus IV Epiphanes.

Three years later Antiochus III died—a broken man. He was succeeded by his oldest son **Seleucus IV,** who, after an uneventful reign, was **murdered by** his chief minister. The young son of Seleucus IV was declared king. The news of Seleucus' death, however, had reached the ears of his brother Antiochus when he was on his way home from Rome. He immediately arranged for the disposal of his young nephew and proclaimed himself king.

After **assuming the kingship, Antiochus IV** was handicapped in three directions: he was in desperate need of money; his empire lacked cohesion and was in danger of breaking up; his neighbors—the Egyptians, the Romans, and the Parthians—were all ready to take advantage of Syria's weakness.

The **financial troubles** of Antiochus Epiphanes were met, at least partly, by **robbing** various **temples and shrines,** including the Temple in Jerusalem. He met the instability and potential disunity of his kingdom with a vigorous **program of Hellenization.** Such a policy had been pursued by his predecessors, but Antiochus IV devoted himself to the task with vigor.

The Jewish Struggle Against Hellenism (167–137 B.C.)

Mattathias	167–166 B.C.
Judas Maccabaeus	165–161 B.C.
Jonathan	161–144 B.C.
Simon	143–135 B.C.

The liberal Jewish party, led by the high priest Menelaus, introduced Gentile customs and set up Gentile schools in Jerusalem. Jewish lads, after the Greek custom, exercised in the nude in the city. The name of the city was changed to Antioch-Jerusalem. Jewish names were changed to Greek names. The legalistic-orthodox or conservative party, called the **Hasidim** (the pious), **opposed** these **inroads of Hellenism** and defended orthodox Jewish institutions. Eventually this division among the Jews resulted in open conflict.

The Hasidim were generally poor and disorganized, dispersed over a wide area. The heavy taxes by the king of Syria and the tithes and gifts required by the unsympathetic local governments were borne, for the most part, by the poor of the land, most of them Hasidim. Their economic plight and their orthodoxy, however, unified them against Hellenism. The **scribes** who were interested in the Law **encouraged the Hasidim** in their resistance movement. The Syrians looked upon this opposition to Hellenism as a divisive force. In a war between

Syria and Egypt, the Hasidim were sympathetic toward Egypt. Antiochus IV Epiphanes, who was successful, determined to strengthen
Hellenism, so he punished the city. He annihilated some rebels, placed
Hellenizers in control, entered the Temple, desecrated it, and took
gold and silver. Menelaus, Hellenistic high priest, was left in control
with hired soldiers to support him. The **Samaritans** were given the right
to **erect** a **temple to Zeus on Mount Gerizim.** Many Jews deserted their
faith. It was a dark day for the pious in Jerusalem.

The **Temple** in **Jerusalem** was **reconsecrated to Zeus Olympius.**
Swine's flesh, the chief offering of Greek sacrifice, was now offered in
honor of that god. The Hasidim called this act the **"abomination of
desolation"** (Dan. 11:31; Matt. 24:15; Mark 13:14). The observance of any part of the law was made a capital offense. The reading of the Law, circumcision, sabbath observance, and observance
of feasts of the Jewish year were strictly forbidden. Every copy of the
Hebrew Scriptures that could be found was defaced, torn to pieces,
or burned. These policies which promoted Hellenism and deprived
Judaism of the protection of the law only intensified the devotion of
the Hasidim to their law and their resistance to Hellenism. Many died
rather than comply with the desecrating sacrilege. The zeal by which
the Hellenizers sought to destroy the Hasidim evoked an indignant
reaction which brought into being an independent state.

Mattathias

In Modin an **influential priest** named Mattathias fell upon a liberal
Jew and slew him because he participated in a pagan feast. With the
help of his **five sons** (**John, Simon, Judas, Eleazar,** and **Jonathan**) and
others, he slew Antiochus Epiphanes' commissioner and his guards
and **fled into the hills.** Soon this little group was joined by many others
who were opposed to the program of Hellenism and its persecution. In
a short time about one thousand Jews were overtaken on a sabbath,
allowing themselves to be butchered without resistance so that they
might not break the law. After this occurrence, Mattathias proclaimed
that his followers could not attack but could carry on defensive warfare on a sabbath.

For about a year Mattathias led his guerrilla band through the
country of Judah. They **raided the villages and towns,** destroying the
heathen altars and the emblems of Hellenistic religion. They also
punished all liberal Jews who were captured, enforced circumcision,

reestablished Jewish worship, recovered many copies of the Law from the possession of their enemies, and killed the royal officers. After one year Mattathias succumbed to the hardships of the rebellion. He left the command of his guerrilla band to his third son, Judas, who was nicknamed Maccabaeus (this nickname possibly means "the Hammerer").

Judas Maccabaeus

Judas **rallied** all the **forces** who joined the revolt. For about six years he led the few thousand of his countrymen whom he had marshaled and equipped. He led his band in seven battles against large numbers of liberal Jews, Samaritans, and Syrians. He was successful in all of these except the last one.

During one campaign Judas **captured Jerusalem** and **restored the defenses.** He **repaired the Temple,** took away the polluted altar, constructed a new one, and rekindled the sacred flame. This **rededication** took place on **Kislev** (December 25, 165 B.C.), three years after its desecration. This occasion was subsequently celebrated by an eight-day **Feast of Dedication** known as Hanukkah (John 10:22).

After the death of Antiochus IV, Judas was recognized as **governor of Judea.** Thus in 162 B.C. **religious liberty** had been **achieved.** The arrangement was only temporary due to the change of power within the Syrian government and the death of Judas.

Jonathan

Demetrius Soter, successor to Antiochus, used Alcimus the high priest to sow discord among the patriots of Judas. The **Jewish nation** was **now divided** into three factions: the Maccabeans, the Hasidim, and the Hellenists. The **high priest** and **Hellenists were in power,** so opposition to the program of Hellenization was suppressed. The **Maccabean party elected Jonathan,** the youngest son of Mattathias, as its leader. Jonathan retired to the wilderness of Tekoa to wait for a favorable time to strike. **Death of the high priest** and the **rise** and **fall of Syrian leaders** finally placed **Jonathan in a bargaining position.** Each group tried to exceed the other in liberality of his offer. **Jonathan** evaded a decision until he had succeeded in getting **full control of Judea** and being **named high priest.** This began a breach between the Maccabees and the common people. **Jonathan's diplomacy backfired** and he was tricked, imprisoned, shackled with chains, and finally **slain.**

Simon

After the death of Jonathan, the Maccabean party turned to Simon, the oldest and **only surviving son of Mattathias.** He was recognized as **high priest** and **prince of Judea.** Claims on the Jewish nation for tribute, customs, and taxes were renounced. All offenses against Syria were forgiven. The Syrians surrendered Acra, their fortress in Jerusalem. Thus the year **143 B.C.** became recognized as the **year of independence of the Jewish nation.**

In recognition of Simon's service to the nation, he was granted absolute sovereignty and the office was made hereditary. In 137 B.C. **Simon** and **two of his sons were murdered** by his son-in-law, Ptolemy, a prominent leader of the Hellenizing faction. Simon's **only remaining son, John Hyrcanus I,** managed to **escape** and was acknowledged as his **father's successor.**

The Hasmonean Dynasty (135–63 B.C.)

John Hyrcanus I	135–106 B.C.
Aristobulus I	106–105 B.C.
Alexander Janneus	104–79 B.C.
Alexandra Salome	79–69 B.C.
Aristobulus II	69–63 B.C.

The death of Simon ended the leadership of the family of Mattathias. All five of his sons had met violent deaths while devoting themselves to the opposition of Hellenism. Judas and Eleazar died in battle. John was ambushed and killed. Jonathan and Simon met death by treachery. Mattathias and his five sons were all buried in the family tomb at Modin.

John Hyrcanus I

John Hyrcanus I was offered recognition on the condition that he consider himself subject to Syria and promise help in their military campaigns. The three factions among the Jews—the Maccabeans, the Hasidim, and the Hellenists—seem to have accepted these terms as satisfactory and all seem to have given allegiance to Hyrcanus. This political alignment was an important factor in Hyrcanus' reign.

Hyrcanus took advantage of **unsettled conditions in Syria** and asserted his complete independence. He immediately **fortified Judea** and began to **expand the territory** of the Jews in all directions. The territories beyond the Jordan, Samaria, and Idumea were brought under Jewish control. When Hyrcanus **captured Samaria, he destroyed the temple to Zeus** on Mount Gerizim which for two hundred years had been an offense to the Jews. Hyrcanus offered the Idumeans the choice of adopting the Jewish religion or leaving the country. Hyrcanus' father and grandfather had fought for the privilege of religious freedom. Now Hyrcanus took it away from those whom he conquered.

The **Hasidim** had been the main supporters of the Maccabean revolt. Their **spiritual descendants** were the **Pharisees** who were **Hyrcanus' chief supporters.** Before his death Hyrcanus broke with the Pharisees and supported the **Sadducees, the spiritual descendants of the Hellenists.** Thus, in about fifty years, the principles of Hellenism which the family of Mattathias had vigorously opposed were accepted by his descendants.

The rule of the **Hasmonean dynasty** from the time of John Hyrcanus I (135–106 B.C.) is a checkered course of intrigue and internal struggle. It was partially characterized by a **constant struggle** for power between the **Pharisees** and the **Sadducees.** Aristobulus I conquered the Ituraeans and caused those who did not flee to accept Judaism. Thus in subsequent years, though the population of Galilee was predominantly Gentile by race, it was Jewish in religion. **Alexander Janneus** was a ruthless soldier who murdered six thousand Jews in one fiasco at a Feast of Tabernacles. In a revolt he had at least fifty thousand **Jews slaughtered.** During Alexander's rule, the Pharisees called in the Seleucid ruler for help. A complicated struggle followed; and in the end, Alexander ruled over a territory almost as vast as Solomon's. But the Hasmonean power was about to come to an end. Alexandra Salome, wife of Alexander, allied herself with the Pharisees, so there was a rise of their power and a subsequent decline in Sadducean power during her reign. The biggest problem with Alexandra Salome's reign was the strife in her own family, particularly between Aristobulus II and Hyrcanus II.

Aristobulus defeated his brother **Hyrcanus** in battle, and the latter retired in favor of Aristobulus II. However, Aristobulus had his **problems** because of the rise in power of **Antipater,** father of the future Herod the Great and son of the Antipater whom Alexander Janneus had made governor of Idumea. Antipater stirred up trouble between the two brothers who were backed by the inevitable faction-makers, the Pharisees and Sadducees.

(For a fuller account of the Hasmonean Dynasty, see appendix 2, p. 196.)

At this point Rome, through its great general Pompey, interfered for the first time in the affairs of Palestine. Pompey heard of the troubles of the Hasmoneans while he was in Syria and sent his general, Scaurus, south to secure advantages for Rome. Scaurus succeeded in confirming the power of Aristobulus II for the time. The next year Pompey ordered representatives from the rival parties to appear before him. As a result, Pompey invaded and captured Jerusalem.

The Jews, Romans, and Herods (63 B.C.–A.D. 39)

John Hyrcanus II	63–37 B.C.
Herod the Great	37–4 B.C.
Archelaus	4 B.C.–A.D. 6
Philip	4 B.C.–A.D. 34
Antipas	4 B.C.–A.D. 39

All of the history of the period following the close of the Old Testament is of inestimable importance to our understanding of the period into which Christ came. However, our interest comes into sharper focus as we consider the period of the Jews, Romans, and Herods. These years—less than sixty before the coming of Christ and the time during and just after his death—can best be understood by looking to the events of Roman rule.

As a result of Pompey's conquest, the **Hasmonean kingdom became part of the Roman province of Syria.** Territory under Jewish control was reduced to Judea, Idumea, and Perea. Pompey set up Hyrcanus II as high priest and ethnarch over this territory, but withheld from him the title of king. Hyrcanus was no longer ruler of a kingdom but was high priest of a religious community, personally responsible to the Roman governor, to whom his people had to **pay annual tribute.** Antipater was appointed procurator of Judea, a position he held until poisoned by one of his rivals.

Herod the Great

In the years preceding the birth of Jesus there were revolutions and counterrevolutions both in Rome and Palestine. When the smoke of uncertainty cleared, the new **king was Herod the Great.** By religion **Herod** was a **Jew;** by **race,** an **Idumean;** by **cultural** sympathies, a **Greek**; and by **political** allegiance, a **Roman.** He was ruthless to his inferiors and cruel to his family. He adopted a cunning policy of "playing along with" whichever ruler was in power at that moment. Like his father before him, he was **ready to change sides at a moment's notice** to gain his purposes.

The reign of Herod can be divided into three periods: (1) the consolidation of power (37–25 B.C.); (2) the period of prosperity (25–13 B.C.); (3) the period of domestic trouble (13–4 B.C.).

CONSOLIDATION OF POWER

Despite Herod's endeavors to please, he failed to win the confidence and trust of his subjects. Therefore, during the first nine years of his reign he attempted to consolidate his power both at home and abroad. One of Herod's first acts was to strip the well-to-do of their wealth, eventually putting some of them to death. Among the aristocrats were the Sadducees, who largely made up the Sanhedrin. By developing his government on the lines of a **centralized bureaucracy,** Herod dealt a **deathblow** to the **power of the Sanhedrin.** He appointed the high priest, thus breaking the hereditary principle on which it had been based and abolishing its lifelong tenure.

In keeping with his vacillating loyalties, Herod switched from Antony to Octavius when the former was defeated in battle. With great boldness he confessed his former loyalty to Antony and now pledged his friendship to Octavius. Duly impressed, Octavius accepted Herod's offer of support, confirmed him on the throne, and extended his kingdom.

THE PERIOD OF PROSPERITY

Herod's second reign was a time of public works. He engaged in enormous building projects. Yet, despite his lavish expenditure on building schemes, Herod was a **man of great business ability** whose powers of planning and organization raised the country to a peak of prosperity. As examples of this, we note especially a new scheme of irrigation he introduced to fertilize the lower Jordan Valley, and a new city and port built on the site of Strato's Tower. Caesarea, the city named to honor the emperor, had an excellent harbor which encouraged profitable overseas trade.

The crowning glory of Herod's building feats was the **reconstructed Temple.** Josephus describes the Temple as "the most notable of all the things achieved by him . . . great enough to assure his eternal remembrance." Work on the Temple was **begun in 20 B.C.,** the Temple proper being completed in eighteen months and the outer courts and porticoes in another eight. However, the process of building continued until the time of the procurator Albinus (A.D. 62–65), a few years before it was destroyed in the Jewish war against the Romans.

THE PERIOD OF DOMESTIC TROUBLE

Herod was a man with many family connections, including ten wives, fifteen children, and innumerable grandchildren. The last few years of Herod's life tell a sad story of domestic intrigues and family quarrels in which his jealousies and suspicions grew rapidly to the pitch of mania. Goaded on by his scheming sister Salome, he gave free rein to his vindictiveness and **killed many of his wives and children.**

Herod became seriously ill with a terrible disease which caused him great pain and finally brought him to a state of mental derangement. When his life began ebbing away, he altered his will for the third and last time. He appointed **Archelaus** king of **Judea; Antipas,** tetrarch of **Galilee** and **Transjordan;** and **Philip,** tetrarch of **Gaulonitis, Trachonitis,** and **Paneas.** In the year 4 B.C. Herod died. His body, decked in all his royal regalia, was taken with elaborate ceremony to its last resting-place in the fortress of Herodium and there was buried.

Archelaus

In accordance with Herod's last will, Augustus divided the kingdom among Archelaus, Antipas, and Philip. Archelaus was named, however, not king, but ethnarch of Judea.

Archelaus' reign lasted ten years. It was a rule of **revenge** and **bloodshed.** He did **rebuild Jericho** so that it became a showplace of the ancient world. In A.D. 6 he was deposed and banished by Augustus on a joint petition from the Jews and the Samaritans. After the banishment of Archelaus, **Judea became a Roman province** or, rather, a division of the larger province of Syria.

Like other such divisions of provinces, it had its own **governor** called a **"procurator."** The procurator was responsible for the collection of **taxes** and the administering of **justice.** He was, strictly speaking, only a subordinate ruler under the governor general of the province, yet he was usually left much to his own discretion and exercised considerable power. Caesarea was made the capital under the Roman governors. These governors often went to Jerusalem, especially at the time of the great festivals, when their presence there was needed for the sake of order. Of these procurators or governors, **Pontius Pilate was the sixth** in order and continued **in office for about ten years.** He was on a visit to Jerusalem at the Feast of the Passover when Jesus was arraigned before him.

Philip

Philip was the most peace-loving, respected, and popular of the Herodian princes. He ruled as tetrarch of the territory east of the Lake of Galilee. The territory included a mixed population, less Jewish than Greek. He rebuilt ancient Panium and renamed it Caesarea Philippi. It was to his dominions—"the coast of Caesarea Philippi"—that Jesus retired in order to be with his disciples.

Antipas

During the ministry of Jesus, Galilee was under the rule of Herod Antipas. As a ruler he was ambitious and sly, though not as able as his father. He carried on an extensive building program, including the city of Tiberias. He married Herodias, the divorced wife of his half-brother. Because John the Baptist condemned this marriage, Antipas had him beheaded (Matt. 14:1–12; Mark 6:14–24; Luke 9:7–9). Herodias was ambitious for her husband and persuaded him to go to Rome and ask for the title of king. When Antipas arrived in Rome, charges of rebellion were brought against him. Instead of receiving a kingship, he was banished.

We have seen in the story of post-Exilic Judaism the story of dreams that faded one after the other. There was the short-lived success of Judas Maccabaeus, the temporary lifting of the clouds in the time of Simon, the last of the five sons of Mattathias. Then for a generation the flower of Judaism blossomed and grew to full power. Yet, as we have noted, despite the great conquests of Alexander Janneus, faction fights weakened the unity of the people. As each party within Judaism appealed for foreign help against the other, the glory of Judaism faded. Not of this world was the promised glory to come.[3]

1. Unless indicated otherwise, all quotations are from the *New American Standard Bible, New Testament* © The Lockman Foundation, 1960, 1962, and 1963.
2. Josephus, *Against Apion*, I, 22.
3. Norman H. Snaith, *The Jews from Cyrus to Herod* (New York: Abingdon Press, n.d.), p. 88.

	JEWS	GREEKS		ROMANS
336 B.C.		336 B.C. Alexander, king of Macedon		
		334 B.C. Alexander in Asia		
		323 B.C. Death of Alexander the Great		
		PTOLEMIES	**SELEUCIDS**	
		323–283 B.C. Ptolemy I		
300 B.C.		283–247 B.C. Ptolemy II		
		247–221 B.C. Ptolemy III		
200 B.C.		221–204 B.C. Ptolemy IV	223–187 B.C. Antiochus III the Great	
		204–198 B.C. Ptolemy V		
		198 B.C. Antiochus III victorious over Ptolemy V		
			187–175 B.C. Seleucus IV	
		190 B.C. Roman army victorious over Antiochus III at Magnesia		
	167 B.C. Maccabean Revolt		175–163 B.C. Antiochus IV Epiphanes	
	167–166 B.C. Mattathias			
	165–161 B.C. Judas Maccabaeus			
	165 B.C. Redication of the Temple			
	161–144 B.C. Jonathan			
	144–135 B.C. Simon			

	JEWS	GREEKS		ROMANS
		PTOLEMIES	**SELEUCIDS**	
	135–106 B.C. John Hyrcanus I			
	106–105 B.C. Aristo- bulus I			
100 B.C.	104–79 B.C. Alexander Janneus			
	79–69 B.C. Alexandra Salome			
	69–63 B.C. Aristo- bulus II			63 B.C. Pompey in Jerusalem
	65 B.C. Herod and Aretas' march on Jerusalem			48 B.C. Battle of Pharsalia
50 B.C.	37 B.C. Herod becomes king			44 B.C. Death of Julius Caesar
	Before the end of Herod's reign: Birth of John the Baptist			31 B.C. Battle of Actium
				27 B.C. Octavius becomes Augustus. He rules until A.D. 14
	Birth of Jesus			
	4 B.C. Death of Herod the Great			
	4 B.C.–A.D. 6 Archelaus			
	4 B.C.–A.D 37 Philip			
	4 BC.–A.D. 39 Herod Antipas			

2

THE GOSPEL RECORDS

"WHEN the fulness of the time came, God sent forth His Son" (Gal. 4:4). When God saw that the time was right, he sent his Son into the world. God's salvation appeared among the people of Israel for the benefit of all men. "The Word [*Logos*] became flesh, and dwelt among us, and we beheld His glory, glory as of the Only Begotten from the Father, full of grace and truth" (John 1:14).

The Coming of Jesus

The story of the coming of Jesus, the Christ-event, can be told simply. Perhaps it would be well for us to look first at the facts surrounding his coming, citing no theological interpretations.

Jesus was born in Bethlehem of Judea during the reigns of Augustus Caesar and Herod the Great. At an early age he was carried to Nazareth in Galilee, the territory of Herod Antipas, where he grew up.

When he was twelve years old, he attended a Passover in Jerusalem. He was baptized in the river Jordan by the prophet John when he was about thirty years old. He soon attached to himself a few personal followers who were convinced that the new age foretold in the Old Testament had arrived. That is, the eschatological kingdom of God had made its appearance with the coming of the Messiah. These followers were called disciples (students, learners, pupils). With these followers, Jesus became a traveling prophet and teacher.

Our Lord went about preaching, teaching, and healing. His mighty works and his teachings aroused great enthusiasm among the common people. The keynote of his proclamation was the same as the prophet John's had been, "The time is fulfilled, and the kingdom of God is at hand; repent and believe in the gospel" (Mark 1:15). However, as time passed, his teachings encompassed the whole scale of human experience and all aspects of religious and moral truth. His popularity with the common people grew. In a short while, great crowds gathered to see and hear him. This response of the people frightened and antagonized the religious authorities. The two power groups, the high priests and the rabbis, with their followers, formed an alliance against Jesus.

Most of Jesus' ministry was in and around Galilee, with an occasional visit to Jerusalem. When he concluded his ministry in the vicinity of Galilee, he attended a Passover in Jerusalem. Here he was met with a tumultuous welcome by the common people. This reception goaded his enemies to action, and through the treachery of one of his followers, he was captured. The religious leaders, with cooperation from the Roman government, had him arrested while he was praying in an olive orchard near the Temple. His followers who were with him at the time deserted him and fled.

The Teacher from Nazareth was tried by a religious court and declared to be guilty of blasphemy. He was then tried by the Roman procurator Pontius Pilate (A.D. 26–36) because he was accused of instigating sedition against the Roman government (Luke 23:2). Though Pilate found him guilty of no crime, he was condemned to die on a cross just as though he were guilty. He was executed outside the city wall of Jerusalem and was buried near the execution site in a rockhewn tomb, which was officially sealed. Three days later the tomb was empty. Our Lord's followers testified that he was alive and had appeared to them. They told of how he appeared to them from time to time for forty days and then ascended into heaven. They were also convinced that he would return.

When the Gospel Was Spoken Only

The substance of the Jesus-event, or Christ-event, which afterwards formed the content of the Gospels, was circulated originally by word of mouth (sometimes called oral transmission). The disciples proclaimed Jesus—his words, his deeds, and the whole impression of his personality. What they proclaimed was the *kerygma,* a Greek word which means the substance or content of what is preached as distinct from the act of preaching. This word stressed the character and content of the message. The *kerygma* for the early Christians was the whole story of the coming of Jesus and the meaning of this story for man. It was not just the enumeration of certain facts about the life of Jesus. Rather, these facts were used as evidence of the truthfulness of the message itself. The proof of messiahship was the signs which God performed through Jesus, especially his death and resurrection. The message was that the final stage of God's salvation had been realized and was being announced to all men in the life and ministry of Jesus. It was a divine work.

Early Christians were first and foremost concerned with the proclamation of the Christ-event, the *kerygma.* The followers of Jesus had no distinctively Christian literature of any kind nor special buildings for worship. The only sacred books which they had were the Hebrew Scriptures. These Jewish Christians had believed before their conversion to Christianity that their Scriptures were inspired. Now, in the light of these recent events, their Scriptures had taken on a new significance. The hope of the coming of God's Messiah, which inspired so many of the Old Testament writers, had been fulfilled in Jesus.

These early Christians continued to study their Jewish Scriptures (Old Testament) and to attend synagogue services. The one distinctive thing about them was their witness of Jesus as the one whom God had chosen to be anointed as the King of God's kingdom (Messiah). They knew about his birth, life, teachings, death, resurrection, and ascension. They were convinced that in him God's plan for the world had reached its climax. They interpreted his whole life as a divine activity performed for the salvation of man. They were so convinced that Jesus was alive that their former state of despair gave way to a joyous and unflinching boldness.

As these early followers of Jesus met, they told the story of Jesus and interpreted its meaning. They called upon all who heard them to repent and be baptized in the name of him whom God had made both Lord and Christ. They proclaimed that through him the Holy Spirit was now available. Soon after Pentecost, Peter gave a brief summary of the gospel story in answer to the questions about the meaning of the events at Pentecost (Acts 2:5–39). This summary also illustrates how the early apostles shared the *kerygma.*

In Acts there are also other summaries of sermons preached by the followers of Jesus. These summaries reveal the character and content of the message shared by the primitive church (the *kerygma*). These condensed sermons vary slightly, but they reveal a remarkably similar pattern. They supplement one another and give a comprehensive view of the character and content of the message that was preached before the New Testament was written.

The principal elements in Peter's "preached message" may be summarized as follows:

- The fulfilment of prophecy (Acts 2:16; 3:18,24)
- Some historical facts concerning Jesus, especially his death and resurrection (Acts 2:22–31; 3:13–15; 4:10; 5:30; 10:37–41)
- Christ's exaltation evidenced by the presence of the Holy Spirit in power (Acts 2:33; 5:32)
- Christ's second advent (Acts 3:20–21; 10:42)
- An offer of forgiveness (Acts 2:38–39; 3:19,26; 4:12; 5:31; 10:43)

The principal elements of Stephen's *kerygma* included the fulfilment of prophecy and the death of Christ. In his defense, he reached the climax of his message by declaring that his accusers were acting like their fathers (Acts 7:52–53). Their fathers had killed those who had proclaimed the coming of the Righteous One.

The condensed sermons and brief summaries of Paul's preaching in Acts and in his epistles reveal the same elements as found in the preaching of Peter and Stephen. C. H. Dodd examined the brief statements of Paul's *kerygma* as found in 1 Corinthians 15:1–7; 1 Thessalonians 1:10; Romans 1:1–4; 2:16; 8:34; 10:8–9; and Galatians 1:3–4; 3:1; 4:6. He concluded that "preaching" as Paul knew it and practiced it can be summarized in propositions something like those listed below:

(1) The prophecies are fulfilled, and the new age is inaugurated by the coming of Christ.
(2) He was born of the seed of David.
(3) He died according to the Scriptures, to deliver us out of the present evil age.
(4) He was buried.
(5) He rose on the third day according to the Scriptures.

(6) He is exalted at the right hand of God as Son of God and Lord of the quick and dead.

(7) He will come again as Judge and Savior of men.[1]

Thus in assemblies and less formal groups the followers of Jesus proclaimed the gospel message. Out of these testimonial gatherings small groups of people were formed who were persuaded by these followers that the final stage of God's plan of salvation had been realized in Christ. At first these people were known as "followers of the Way" (Acts 9:2; 16:17; 18:25–26; 19:23; 22:4; 24:14,22). Later they were called "Christians" (Acts 11:26). These groups developed into churches.

The central affirmation of these churches was that the promised Redeemer had come in the person of Jesus Christ. The new age foretold in the Old Testament had arrived. They supported this affirmation with a recital of the story of Jesus. He had inaugurated God's new age. They warned that God's judgment on the unrepentant was coming and pleaded with their hearers to repent. They pleaded with these unrepentant ones to confess their sins and accept the "way" of God. They proclaimed that God was acting in Jesus to establish the new age and to reconcile man to himself (2 Cor. 5:19).

This proclamation of what God had done in Christ was called the gospel. The Greek word translated "gospel" was first used to designate a reward or present given to a person who brought good news. It later was used to designate the good news itself. It was a message intended to rejoice the hearts of those who heard it. In the New Testament, the word "gospel" always refers to what God did for the salvation and transformation of the life of man in Jesus Christ. The gospel is Jesus Christ himself, in all that he represented and was, and in all that he accomplished through his death and resurrection. Jesus Christ is both the source and the substance of the good news. The word "gospel" became identified with the story of what he was, taught, did, and suffered. This is the only usage of the term in the New Testament. At a later time in the second century, the word "gospel" was used to refer to any one of the documents which recorded the story of Jesus' coming.

For several years after the death of Jesus, when his apostles and companions were alive and could give their personal testimony, there was no need for preserving in writing the story of what Jesus had said and done. In fact, oral and written tradition competed with each other for authority within the church for decades.

It was only after the voices of the companions of Jesus fell silent that the oral tradition was completely replaced by the written accounts. During the last half of the second century, the Christians began to feel the rightness of recognizing the four Gospels as having the authority of Holy Scripture. These four which had attained general acceptance were acknowledged to be a part of God's written revelation.

In *The Church History of Eusebius,* iii, 39, Papias, a Christian writer of Phrygia about A.D. 130, is quoted as saying: "I was never accustomed to consider materials from books of as much benefit to me as from a living and abiding voice." This statement implies that Papias set as high, if not a higher, value on oral tradition in regard to Christ's coming as he did upon the written Gospels with which he was acquainted.

Jesus himself wrote nothing. In the course of time, however, when the followers of Jesus increased and spread throughout the Mediterranean world and the number of firsthand witnesses grew smaller, it became necessary to record the story of Jesus. It is not certain just how long it was before the first account of the story of Jesus was written. The oldest of the canonical accounts, the Gospel of Mark, was probably written about A.D. 65.

New Testament scholars have given themselves to a diligent study of this period between the time of Christ's earthly ministry and the time when the Gospels were written. Some have called the results of this type of study form criticism or tradition criticism. This study does not attempt to detract from the fact that the Gospels are divine in their origin. But by this method, New Testament scholars attempt to identify within the written Gospels those units of oral tradition which were in circulation before the story of Jesus was written down.

One of the oldest and most significant statements concerning the period before there was a written account of Jesus is a statement of Papias:

> This also the presbyter said: Mark, having become the interpreter of Peter, wrote down accurately, though not indeed in order, whatsoever he remembered of the things said or done by Christ. . . . He followed Peter, who adapted his teaching to the needs of his hearers, but with no intention of giving a connected account of the Lord's discourses, so that Mark committed no error while he thus wrote some things as he remembered

them. For he was careful of one thing, not to omit any of the things which he had heard, and not to state any of them falsely.

This statement is good evidence that the Gospel of Mark consists primarily of Peter's testimony. Also, about A.D. 180, Irenaeus (Bishop of Lyons and theologian, born in Asia Minor) stated that after "their departure [i.e., the death of Peter and Paul] Mark, the disciple and interpreter of Peter, also transmitted to us in writing those things which Peter had preached."

These quotations from two of the earliest Christian writers support Paul's statement to the Thessalonians that he had given them traditions "by word" and "by letter" (2 Thess. 2:15). He also instructed the Thessalonians to "keep aloof from every brother who leads an unruly life and not according to the tradition which you received from us" (3:6).

All of this information points to the fact that the whole story of the historical Jesus and the meaning of this story for man was of prime importance to the first Christians. Different Christians told the story of Jesus with varying emphases and details. They were concerned with the converting of those outside the church and with the instruction of Christians. New Testament scholars use a variety of names for the forms which they are able to identify in the canonical Gospels, but they agree to a remarkable degree on the forms themselves.

Form criticism has its weaknesses and failures by the very nature of its inquiry. However, it has made some important contributions to New Testament study. It has focused attention upon the early oral period and upon the preservation, transmission, and shaping of the gospel tradition in the life of the church. It has emphasized the fact that the early church was a living, active organism. It has demonstrated that the words of Jesus were treasured as oracles. It has also shown that the narratives concerning Jesus were circulated as single detached units, each complete in itself, before they were combined in an inspired, canonical account.

The Written Sources

Luke introduced his account of the Jesus-event by telling of his method of research. He revealed his carefulness as a scholar. He said that he knew of "many" previous attempts to give an account of the events surrounding the coming of Jesus, and that he was now undertaking to provide an accurate, systematic record based on examination

CAP. XL.

CAP. XXXIX.

КАТА ΙΩΑΝΝΗΝ

The Word Became Flesh

1 Ἐν ἀρχῇ ἦν ὁ λόγος, καὶ ὁ λόγος ἦν πρὸς τὸν θεόν, καὶ θεὸς ἦν ὁ λόγος. 2 οὗτος ἦν ἐν ἀρχῇ πρὸς τὸν θεόν. 3 πάντα δι' αὐτοῦ ἐγένετο, καὶ χωρὶς αὐτοῦ ἐγένετο οὐδὲ ἕν. ὃ γέγονεν 4 ἐν αὐτῷ ζωὴ ἦν, καὶ ἡ ζωὴ ἦν τὸ φῶς τῶν ἀνθρώπων· 5 καὶ τὸ φῶς ἐν τῇ σκοτίᾳ φαίνει, καὶ ἡ σκοτία αὐτὸ οὐ κατέλαβεν.

6 Ἐγένετο ἄνθρωπος ἀπεσταλμένος παρὰ θεοῦ, ὄνομα αὐτῷ Ἰωάνης· 7 οὗτος ἦλθεν εἰς μαρτυρίαν, ἵνα μαρτυρήσῃ περὶ τοῦ φωτός, ἵνα πάντες πιστεύσωσιν δι' αὐτοῦ.

8 οὐκ ἦν ἐκεῖνος τὸ φῶς, ἀλλ' ἵνα μαρτυρήσῃ περὶ τοῦ φωτός. 9 Ἦν τὸ φῶς τὸ ἀληθινόν, ὃ φωτίζει πάντα ἄνθρωπον, ἐρχόμενον εἰς τὸν κόσμον. 10 ἐν τῷ κόσμῳ ἦν, καὶ ὁ κόσμος δι' αὐτοῦ ἐγένετο, καὶ ὁ κόσμος αὐτὸν οὐκ ἔγνω. 11 εἰς τὰ ἴδια ἦλθεν, καὶ οἱ ἴδιοι αὐτὸν οὐ παρέλαβον. 12 ὅσοι δὲ ἔλαβον αὐτόν, ἔδωκεν αὐτοῖς ἐξουσίαν τέκνα θεοῦ γενέσθαι, τοῖς πιστεύουσιν εἰς τὸ ὄνομα αὐτοῦ, 13 οἳ οὐκ ἐξ αἱμάτων οὐδὲ ἐκ θελήματος σαρκὸς οὐδὲ ἐκ θελήματος ἀνδρὸς ἀλλ' ἐκ θεοῦ ἐγεννήθησαν.

14 Καὶ ὁ λόγος σὰρξ ἐγένετο καὶ ἐσκήνωσεν ἐν ἡμῖν, καὶ ἐθεασάμεθα τὴν δόξαν αὐτοῦ, δόξαν ὡς μονογενοῦς παρὰ πατρός, πλήρης χάριτος καὶ ἀληθείας. 15 Ἰωάνης μαρτυρεῖ περὶ αὐτοῦ καὶ κέκραγεν λέγων, Οὗτος ἦν ὃν εἶπον, Ὁ ὀπίσω μου ἐρχόμενος ἔμπροσθέν μου γέγονεν, ὅτι πρῶτός μου ἦν. 16 ὅτι ἐκ τοῦ πληρώματος

of that which had already been written. Many had set themselves to the task of putting the early oral gospel into written form. Luke's "many" is too comprehensive a term to be limited to Mark and Matthew. It likely means that when Luke wrote, there were in existence Christian documents in historical form beyond the number which have survived as the "Scriptures."

Luke also stated that, previous to writing, he had carefully traced the entire course of events embraced in his history. His purpose to present facts in an orderly and well-arranged fashion, perhaps even in their true chronological relationship, is evident from his use of the phrase variously translated "in consecutive order," "in order," or, perhaps better, "organically" or "continuously" (Luke 1:3). This phrase denotes orderly succession, or at least continuity of narration as opposed to a fragmentary treatment of the subject. These other accounts to which Luke referred probably were not dominated by any chronological consideration.

Apparently these numerous accounts were brief reports (written fragments) of our Lord's words and acts, taken down from the lips of those who had been "eyewitnesses and servants of the Word" (Luke 1:2). Also, there may have been fairly complete manuscripts of the accounts of Jesus' life. Probably the process of committing the *kerygma* to writing began about twenty years after the close of our Lord's earthly ministry. The earliest Christian writings were likely excerpts or collections of Old Testament passages which were regarded as having been fulfilled in Jesus. These were books of testimonies.

Years later, Luke and the three other Gospel writers used these written accounts and testimonies as sources. New Testament scholars have endeavored to determine these sources in the Synoptic Gospels (Matthew, Mark, and Luke). This study is known as Source Criticism. These scholars are not able to determine conclusively the exact number and extent of these sources, but the Four-document Theory of B. H. Streeter as developed in his book, *The Four Gospels: a Study of Origins,* has been widely accepted. According to this theory, the sources for the canonical Gospels are: Q, L, M, and Mark. There are other scholars who think that more than these four sources can be detected in the Synoptic Gospels. The letter "Q" refers to "sayings" sources (the letter begins the word **Quelle** which means source). "L" refers to material appearing only in Luke. "M" designates the material that is peculiar only to Matthew. All three of the Synoptic Gospels seem to have been composed chiefly out of earlier documents and oral tradition. To suggest this possibility does not rule out their divine origin. It simply helps us understand how God worked to bring us his word. (See pp. 42–44 for a fuller discussion of these four sources.)

The Canonical Gospels

For Christians, the written accounts of words and deeds of Jesus soon took their place as authoritative, alongside the Old Testament. In the second century the books in which these words and deeds were written were recognized as having the same sacred and authoritative character as the Hebrew Scriptures. These books became known as the "Gospels." We have these accounts because, before they were written, the message of what God did in Jesus Christ, the *kerygma* itself, was already a living force in the world. The four Gospels bear witness to the life and ministry of our Lord.

However, strictly speaking, there is but one gospel. Four books each record one and the same story. The earliest recorded use of the word "Gospels" to refer to the written accounts of the Christ-event is by Justin Martyr (about A.D. 140). Near the close of the second century, Irenaeus argued for the necessity of four Gospels. Many other accounts had been written by this time. However, most of these are full of legendary details and fanciful stories with very little historical basis. Therefore, they were not accepted as canonical (a part of the Bible itself). These accounts tell about Jesus' infancy, childhood, passion, and resurrection. They are known as extracanonical or Apocryphal gospels. They are not regarded as a part of God's inspired written revelation. These are available in English in *The Apocryphal New Testament* by M. R. James and in the *New Testament Apocrypha* (vols. 1 and 2) by Edgar Hennecke (English translation edited by R. McL. Wilson). Only four accounts of the story of Jesus have been accepted as inspired and authoritative. These are, in two possible orders of writing: Mark, Luke, Matthew, and John; or Mark, Matthew, Luke, and John.

These Gospels are not lives of Jesus, memoirs, biographies, romances, folk tales, or primarily literary products. They are a unique literary form developed to present a unique message. The fact that they tell nothing of the physical appearance of Jesus, give no careful dates, largely omit the events of thirty years of his life, and do not follow him from place to place in his public work is evidence that the writers were not writing "the life of Jesus."

However, the Gospels do not give a neutral account of what happened. Rather, they relate the work of God in the life of Jesus, and they present the event as an offer of salvation to men. The four Gospels are documents of the church and are to be preserved and used by the church in the proclamation of the gospel. They contain the church's memory and testimony about Jesus. They were written to be used to pass on the knowledge of Jesus and the elements of Christian morality. They were not bare chronicles but accounts that proclaim the good news of what God did for man in Jesus Christ.

Each of the Gospel writers had his own special point of view, which guided his selection, arrangement, and presentation of what he told on behalf of the church. A leading motive guided his general procedure, shaping the account from whatever source it was drawn. Unquestionably, the Spirit of God guided the Gospel writers in their selectivity and interpretation. Each writer presented the story of God's redemptive work for men through Jesus Christ.

It is obvious that these four Gospels separate into three and one. The first three (Matthew, Mark, and Luke), set side by side, yield the same general view or outline. This common view has given the name "synoptic" to these three Gospels. Even though they give fragmentary records of Jesus' life, they show remarkable agreement in the incidents and sayings selected and in the general order in which these matters are presented.

The Fourth Gospel stands alone. The writer's purpose was to interpret Jesus as the Christ, the Son of God, rather than to tell the story of his earthly life (John 20:31). The writer did not begin his account with narrative but with the most profound theology. Instead of recording teachings in parables and direct sayings, the writer gave long discourses. Some of these are mystical in character and are difficult to understand. The Gospel of John deals with theological concepts such as life, light, truth, way, witness, and glory.

THE EARLIEST ACCOUNT—MARK

The Gospel of Mark was probably written about A.D. 65 in Rome and was based on Peter's sermons and witness of the Christ. The date of Peter's death is uncertain. He probably suffered martyrdom during Nero's persecution which followed the fire in Rome in July, A.D. 64. This fact, along with other considerations, leads to the conclusion that Mark was the earliest of the canonical Gospels; and it remained the pattern Gospel for all the other Gospel writers. According to Papias, this Gospel was written by John Mark to preserve those fragments of Peter's preaching which told the story of Jesus.

Mark is not mentioned by name in the Gospels. (Many Bible students believe Mark to have been the "young man" of Mark 14:51.) He is mentioned several times in other New Testament writings (Acts 12: 12,25; 13:13; 15:37–39; Col. 4:10; 2 Tim 4:11; 1 Pet. 5:13). He was first named in Acts 12:12. Here the writer says that Peter, after his miraculous escape from prison, "went to the house of Mary, the mother of John who was also called Mark." This statement indicates that Mark's house was in Jerusalem, in which case he could have had opportunities of hearing and seeing part of the story he related.

Mary, the mother of John Mark and a relative of Barnabas, was a woman of some importance in the church in Jerusalem. Her house was a place where the early Christians gathered. Therefore, it is probable that Mark's boyhood was spent in close contact with the apostles. This would have afforded him opportunities to hear many of the stories about Jesus. He was probably converted to Christianity by Peter, who called him "my son" (1 Pet. 5:13). Mark started with Barnabas and Paul as their "helper" (Acts 13:5) during their first missionary effort, and he visited with them on the island of Cyprus. When the group reached Pamphylia, Mark left them and returned to Jerusalem (Acts 13:13).

This "drop out" action by Mark was the cause of a dispute and separation between Paul and Barnabas when they were planning a second missionary effort (Acts 15:36–41). Mark's name does not appear again in Acts, but persistent nonbiblical tradition assigns him a ministry in Egypt and credits him with the founding of the church in Alexandria. Later in their ministry, Paul and Mark were reconciled. During Paul's first imprisonment in Rome, Mark was with him (Col. 4:10; Philem. 24). Mark was also with Peter when he wrote his first epistle (1 Pet. 5:13). During Paul's second imprisonment in Rome, he was anxious to have Mark with him for he said: "He is useful to me for service" (2 Tim. 4:11).

The traditional view of the early church is almost universal that John Mark was a companion of Peter in his last years. At what time Mark attached himself to Peter cannot be ascertained. The New Testament furnishes little information on this point, but historical sources outside the Bible allude to their association, furnishing distinct notices of companionship between them. These same sources indicate that Mark wrote his account of the story of Jesus as a record of Peter's preaching.

Mark wrote his Gospel in Greek chiefly for Gentile Christians. The book contains few quotations from the Old Testament. Explanations of Jewish words and customs are given (Mark 7:3). The Second Gospel preserves vivid details, often omitted by the others, that draw attention to the human difficulties of Jesus' work (Mark 3:20–21; 8:23–25; 14:34).

Mark's Gospel has a narrower range than the others, beginning as it does with the ministry of John the Baptist and saying nothing about the birth and early life of Jesus. Its ending also is abrupt. Mark has a higher percentage of narrative (as compared with the teaching element) than is true of Matthew and Luke, and its narrative style is unusually graphic.

Mark appears to have aimed at a simple narrative of Jesus' ministry. However, his account is very remarkable for the minuteness and vividness of its description. He omitted the Sermon on the Mount, the Lord's Prayer, all the parables except four, and all the longer discourses except that on the second coming of Christ. Yet in vividness, fulness, and picturesque detail, Mark's Gospel surpasses the other Synoptic accounts. Many details appear to have come from an eyewitness. The inclusion of these details is probably due to Peter's repeatedly telling the story to Mark. In his account, Mark seems to have developed in greater detail Peter's description of our Lord: "God anointed Him [Jesus] with the Holy Spirit and with power, and . . . He went about doing good, and healing all who were oppressed by the devil; for God was with Him" (Acts 10:38).

Mark's account of the gospel may be outlined as follows:

• Preparation for the ministry (1:1–13)
• Jesus' ministry in Galilee (1:14 to 7:23)
• Jesus outside of Galilee (7:24 to 8:26)
• Jesus' warnings of tragedy (8:27 to 10:52)
• Jesus in Jerusalem (11:1 to 12:44)
• Jesus' apocalyptic discourse (13:1–37)
• Jesus' arrest, trial, and death (14:1 to 15:47)
• Jesus' resurrection (16:1–8)

The oldest and best Greek manuscripts end with Mark 16:8, probably in the middle of a sentence. The last word in the oldest copies of the manuscript is the preposition translated "for."

> There is no parallel in ancient literature for a book to end, as does the Greek of Mark 16:8, with a conjunction such as *gar* (for). Moreover this gospel obviously intended to exalt the strong Son of God whom Mark and his readers believed would yet come "in clouds with great power and glory." It is incredible . . . that Mark intended such a conclusion.[2]

Two endings undoubtedly have been supplied by later hands. The *New American Standard Bible, New Testament* supplies both of these endings. Both in vocabulary and style, these two endings are unlike the rest of the Gospel. Possibly the original was damaged and the ending Mark wrote was torn off. If Mark had continued his narrative or, if he wrote it and it was later lost, he, like Matthew, probably would have given the account of Jesus' journey into Galilee.

THE ACCOUNT FOR JEWISH CHRISTIANS—MATTHEW

Like the other three accounts, this Gospel is anonymous as far as the text itself is concerned. However, tradition has connected this account with the apostle Matthew or Levi (Matt. 9:9–17; Mark 2:14–22; Luke 5:27–32). Papias stated that Matthew wrote in the Hebrew language. Most scholars today conclude that this tradition which goes back to Papias is not reliable. It seems obvious to this writer that the present Gospel of Matthew was composed in, not translated into, Greek. This seems clear from the Gospel writer's use of Greek sources. It is possible that the writing referred to by Papias was the document "Q" (see "The Document Q," p. 42). Also, the apostle Matthew may have written two independent works, one in Aramaic and the present one in Greek. On the other hand, those who would argue against Matthew as author have at least one strong point. It seems unusual that an original apostle and eyewitness would have depended on Mark for so much of his material. With the present evidence, one cannot be dogmatic about authorship.

> Scholars are far more convinced that Mark and Luke wrote the Gospels bearing their names than that the first Gospel was written by Matthew. What is at stake is a church tradition, not the genuineness or value of the Gospel of Matthew.[3]

We have but scanty knowledge concerning the Matthew to whom tradition has ascribed the authorship of the First Gospel. Although one of the twelve, Matthew's activities as an apostle evidently were not significant enough to mention in the Gospels. After the mention of his call to be an apostle, he is unnoticed in the Gospel accounts except for the mere mention of his name (Matt. 10:2–4; Mark 3:16–19; Luke 6:14–16; Acts 1:13). It is chiefly as the reputed author of this Gospel that Matthew excites our interest. He seems to have been known as Levi before being called to be a disciple. Afterwards he was known in Christian circles as Matthew (which means "gift of God").

The Gospel of Matthew probably was written between A.D. 80–90 in Antioch of Syria or in Phoenicia. It is strongly Palestinian-Jewish, written primarily for use among Christians who formerly had been Jews. Matthew wrote as though he expected his readers to be well acquainted with Judea, its geography and natural productions. Such acquaintance could only have been expected of the Jews. By a simple record of what our Lord taught, did, and suffered, Matthew sought to redeem his Master's memory from reproach, to disarm the prejudices of his countrymen, and to set forth the true character of the Messiah. More generally, the book may be regarded as an exposition of the "kingdom of heaven," a phrase occurring thirty-three times in this Gospel and in no other.

By the time of Matthew's writing, the church and synagogue were in vigorous conflict. The writer wished to show that the Jewish Scriptures were the possession of the church. He also sharply contrasted Christian and Jewish ethics.

The writer of the First Gospel had at least two objectives in view. First, he wanted to show how Jesus had fulfilled the deepest hopes and aspirations of the Law and the Prophets. He repeatedly stressed this fulfilment by quotations from the Old Testament. His writing evidences a conviction that Jesus was the expected Messiah of the Jewish people and that prophecy pointed to him as the Lord's Anointed. There are sixty-eight quotations from the Old Testament, taken from sixteen different books, in addition to the innumerable echoes of phrases and words. Of all the New Testament writers, only the author of Revelation cited the Old Testament more frequently. Matthew no doubt intended to show that the Jewish prophecies had been fulfilled in the work of Christ and the beginning of the church.

Second, the author of Matthew evidently wanted to emphasize the teachings of Jesus. He included much such material which Mark had omitted. A large part of his book, like Mark's, deals with Jesus' ministry in Galilee. But he amplified Mark's narrative by the introduction of large bodies of connected teachings. This leads to some changes in narrative details when compared with Mark. The Gospel of Matthew is the most complete of the Synoptic Gospels and is best arranged for teaching purposes. It was regarded most highly by the early church fathers. They alluded to it and quoted from it more frequently than any other Gospel.

The material in the Matthew account is arranged around five great discourses of Jesus. The framework is made clear by the repetition of the similar formula at the end of these discourses; that is, "It came to pass, when Jesus had ended these sayings" (7:28; 11:1; 13:53; 19:1; 26:1).

These five sections are:

- The Sermon on the Mount (5:1 to 7:29)
- The charge to the apostles (10:5–42)
- The parables (13:1–52)
- The discourse on humility and forgiveness (18:1–35)
- The apocalyptic discourse (24:1 to 25:46)

THE ACCOUNT FOR GENTILE CHRISTIANS—LUKE

There is nothing in this work to indicate who was its author. However, the earliest traditions of the church all bear witness that the author of the Third Gospel was identical with the author of Acts. Uniform ancient tradition ascribes both to Luke. In the opening words of the Acts, the writer spoke of a "first account" concerning "all that Jesus began to do and teach" (1:1). Both of these writings were dedicated to Theophilus (Luke 1:3; Acts 1:1). It seems certain that this "first account" refers to the Gospel of Luke. The identical authorship of these two books is all but universally conceded. The name Luke is mentioned only three times in the New Testament (Col. 4:14; Philem. 24; 2 Tim. 4:11). In three sections of Acts the writer used the first person plural (we) to describe the events (16:10–17; 20:5 to 21:18; 27:1 to 28:16). This language seems to indicate that the writer was using his own diary. Therefore, there is strong evidence that the author was Luke, the "beloved physician" and companion and worker with Paul (Col. 4:14; 2 Tim. 4:11).

Some scholars have connected Luke with the authorship of this Gospel by pointing out certain terms which, they claim, would have been used only by one trained as a physician. Other scholars do not think the language clearly supports this argument. However, most of them agree that the writer probably was "the beloved physician" mentioned in the Epistle to the Colossians. If Luke was the author of the Third Gospel, he was the only Gentile writer of any book of the Bible.

All serious New Testament students testify to the gracefulness of Luke's style. An old tradition says that he was a painter. This tradition is at least true to the extent that he was an artist in words, with artistic skill preserving for us a picture of Jesus. He often used more classical words instead of the simple words used by Mark and Matthew.

Jerome (i.e., Hieronymous, about A.D. 340–420) was a monk and scholar of the Roman Catholic Church, translator of the Latin version of the Bible known as the Vulgate. He recorded a tradition that Luke was a native of Antioch of Syria and a member of the church there. In Luke's missionary sympathies and universalism, we discover the Antioch spirit at its best. Were it not for this tradition, however, we might more easily suppose that Luke was the "man of Macedonia," and that he lived in Philippi (Acts 16:9).

The Gospel of Luke probably was written between A.D. 70–85. In support of this date, we consider these facts: The city of Jerusalem was destroyed by the Romans in A.D. 70 and there seems to be an allusion to that event in Luke (21:20–27). This destruction took place during the Jewish-Roman War of A.D. 66–70, which seems to have been the occasion for the break between the church and the synagogue. After this break, Christianity was loosed from the shackles of Judaism; and it soon became a universal movement. In his account of events, Luke portrayed a world religion, which had risen above racial and provincial limits. He portrayed a movement which was a fulfilment and not a subversion of Roman civilization with its universal state. His sympathies were universal. One example of the inclusiveness of Luke's account is the fact that he traced Jesus' genealogy back to Adam, the universal man, rather than to Abraham, the father of the Hebrews.

Luke presented Jesus as the ideal man and as the Savior of all classes of men. He recorded that Jesus passed through all the stages of a normal human life, from infancy through boyhood to manhood (Luke 2:40,52). The Gospel writer made it clear that Christ is the Savior of all mankind: the poor, the rich, women, Gentiles, Jews, Samaritans, publicans, sinners, harlots, lepers, and shepherds.

The close association of the author of the Third Gospel with Paul naturally accounts for signs of Pauline influence in Luke. A very early tradition says that Luke's Gospel contained the substance of Paul's teaching, as that of Mark contained the substance of Peter's preaching. While this suggestion may be exaggerated, it must be noted that there is a striking correspondence between the general scope of Luke's Gospel and the Pauline teaching of grace, forgiveness, and justification.

We cannot be certain about the place where this account was written. Some manuscripts of the Greek New Testament have a footnote suggesting that it was written at Rome. Other manuscripts assign it to Alexandria. Jerome stated that it was written in "the parts of Achaia." We cannot, then, be dogmatic about the place where it was written.

Luke's account of the Jesus-event contains the following:

- Preface (1:1–4)
- The advent of Christ (1:5 to 2:52)
- Jesus' preparation for his ministry in Galilee (4:14 to 9:50)
- Jesus' journey to Jerusalem (9:51 to 19:28)
- Jesus' ministry in Jerusalem (19:29 to 21:38)
- Jesus' death and resurrection (22:1 to 24:53)

THE FOURTH ACCOUNT—JOHN

The difference between John and the other three accounts (Synoptics) has been felt from the earliest time. Clement of Alexandria (about A.D. 150–215, Christian theologian) quoted from an older source and described the difference well: "John, perceiving that the bodily facts had been set forth in the other Gospels, composed a spiritual Gospel." Clement might well have referred to John's as a theological Gospel. The Fourth Gospel probably was written between A.D. 80 and A.D. 95 in Ephesus. Many traditions connect it with the apostle John's later life in Ephesus.

Like the other three Gospels this account is anonymous. It makes no claim about authorship. Since the second century, the authorship of this Gospel has been debated. One tradition says that John the apostle wrote it. Another tradition says that he did not write it. However, questions about authorship do not affect the message of the book. The author was an Aramaic-speaking Jew. He was familiar with Jeru-

salem and the Temple rites. He had some geographical and topo-
graphical knowledge of the land. The Gospel contains numerous
indications, often delicate and unobtrusive, of the nationality, date, and
position of its author:

1:14,16,21,35–39	13:23–25
4:25	19:15,21,26–27,35
6:14–15	20:2–10,30–31
12:13,34	21:1–25

The mention of time, persons, and places seems to indicate that the
writer was an eyewitness. Perhaps his name was John. Eusebius says
that "there were two persons in Asia that bore the same name, and
. . . there were two tombs in Ephesus, each of which, even to the
present day, is called John's."

The main importance of the Johannine account of the gospel story
is found in the teachings that it gives us. The main current which
flows through it is the incarnation. It is the story of Jesus Christ, the
incarnate Son of God. It stresses the eternal aspects of Christ's person
and ministry.

It has already been pointed out that the writer was not simply writing a life of Jesus; he was interpreting our Lord's person and mission.
The theme is outlined in the prologue (1:1–18). The writer's motive
is summed up in his final word (20:31). It was this purpose which
determined his selection of deeds and discourses and the grouping of
the chosen "signs" as he looked back upon the events.

The writer's objective was to declare who Christ was and to tell
how he came out of the very life of God in order to bring God into
the very life of man.

The writer of the Fourth Gospel was more interested in teaching
than he was in history. History and interpretation are interwoven. The
discourses of Jesus are treated more fully and his actions less fully
than in the Synoptic Gospels.

John's Gospel is developed around a series of seven mighty works
of Jesus which are called "signs." After the prologue in 1:1–18, these
signs are:

- 1:19 to 3:36   Jesus is the fulfiller of the Old Testament and
  the giver of the New. New life comes by the
  creative power of the Son of God.

- 4:1–54   Jesus was not limited by time and space.
- 5:1–47   There is a unity of being and activity between God and Jesus. Both God and Jesus have the power of life because they are one.
- 6:1–71   Jesus is the source, sustenance, and protector of life.
- 7:1 to 10:42   Jesus is the Light of the world.
- 11:1–57   Jesus is the resurrection and the life.
- 12:1 to 20:31   Jesus is Immanuel, "God with us." As man he suffers and dies; as God he lives.

The Four Gospels

These four books contain the information which serves as a basis for our study of the life and ministry of our Lord. But let us remember that these Gospels are not primarily intended to present a purely historical biography of Jesus. Each is a selection from the vast material available to demonstrate the divine purpose which guided the author.

These four Gospels are not objective history, if ever such was written. They are what all history must be—interpreted history. They combine the record of facts with the Christian evaluation of those facts.

However, these accounts give us a good source of historic fact, fixed and impregnable. The Gospels are reliable sources of knowledge about Jesus. The Christ who is exhibited in them is historical. This does not mean that we have from them as good a biographical knowledge as we might wish. Each of the Gospels presents materials in a different way and with religious aims in view. Therefore, when we try to establish a chronological account of the life of Christ, we have to be selective. This may result, and probably does, in a sense of greater understanding of some aspects of Jesus' life than about others. In fact, from the Gospels we learn nothing of Jesus' life after his earliest childhood until he began his public ministry. Except for the report of a visit to Jerusalem when he was twelve years old, there is no record of his activities until his baptism. However, some facts regarding Jesus of Nazareth can be ascertained. As we look at these facts in their historical context and search for their theological significance, we can increase our understanding of the life and ministry of our Lord. We look to the four Gospels in the written revelation from God to find the main facts of his life and death and the rise of the community that bears his name.

While we are supremely interested in the accounts of the historical Jesus, we remember that his life and death were different from that of all others; therefore, they must have a greater significance. His life was historical, but in him the eternal God revealed himself to the world. He is suprahistorical; he is more than history. He is as historical as Alexander the Great, Caesar Augustus, or Herod the Great. He also is a contemporary living person who is the living revelation of God. He *is* God (John 1:1). He *was* God incarnate (John 1:14).

The purpose of these Gospel writers was to bear witness to Jesus, in whom both the writers and their first readers already believed. These books show what these people considered important. Their faith found its basis in him and what he had done. They used the facts of his life and death in support of the claim that a righteous God willed men to be righteous. They also based their faith in what they understood to be historical events. Back of this faith in historical events lay, of course, the conviction that it was God who was at work in and through Jesus. The accounts and interpretations which the Gospel writers have left us are a part of the inspired written revelation of God to man.

ENRICHMENT READING FOR CHAPTER 2

The Document Q

THE LETTER "Q" (for *Quelle,* which means source) is used by scholars to designate the "sayings source," or sources, used by Matthew and Luke which do not appear in Mark. Other names given this source are "double tradition" and "Logia." There is widespread agreement among scholars that "Q" was composed largely of detached sayings of Jesus. It probably contained little narrative and no Passion story.

This material amounts to about 272 verses. According to the British scholar T. W. Manson, "Q" falls into four sections:

*   Jesus and John (Matt. 3:7–12,16–17; 4:1–11; 8:5–10,13; 11: 2–11,16–19; Luke 3:7–9,16–17,21–22; 4:1–13; 6:20–49; 7: 1*b*–10,18,22–35)
*   Jesus and his disciples (Matt. 7:7–11; 8:19–22; 11:25–27; 13:16–17; Luke 9:57–62; 10:2–16,21–24; 11:9–13)

- Jesus and his opponents (Matt. 12:22–30,38–42,43–50; Luke 11:14–26,27–28,29–32,33–36,37–52; 12:2–12,22–34)
- Jesus and the future (Matt. 5:13; 6:24; 10:37–38; 13:31–33; 22:1–10; 23:37–39; Luke 12:35–48,49–59; 13:18–21,22–30, 34–35; 14:15–24,25–27,34–35; 16:13,16–18; 17:1–6,22–37)

The Document L

The letter "L" is used to designate the material appearing only in the Gospel of Luke. It is composed of narrative and teachings. It adds many details to the Passion account. "L" probably represents some of the research which Luke did while he was staying with Paul in Caesarea during Paul's imprisonment there (Acts 23–26). Most scholars agree that this material can be listed somewhat as follows (all the references are in Luke):

- Birth stories (1–2)
- John and Jesus (3:1–6,10–14,18–20,23–38)
- The rejection at Nazareth (4:16–30)
- Mighty works (5:1–11; 7:11–17,36 to 8:3)
- Lessons (9:51–56; 10:1,17–20,25–37,38–42; 11:1–8,53 f.; 12:1)
- Warnings (12:13–21; 13:1–9,10–17,31–33; 14:1–6,7–14, 28–33)
- Parables of the lost (15)
- Teachings (16:1–12,14–15,19–31; 17:7–10,11–21; 18:1–8, 9–14; 19:1–27)
- Jerusalem (19:37–44; 21:11b,18,25b,26a,28,34–36; 22:14 to 24:52, less Marcan passages)

The Document M

The letter "M" is used to designate the material peculiar to the Gospel of Matthew. It is composed of Old Testament texts, narrative, sayings, teachings, and parables. This material is listed as follows (all references are in Matthew):

1:1 to 2:23	39a,41,43,45,	8:1,5a,17
3:14–15	47–48	9:13a,26–36
4:13–16,23–25	6:1–20,34	10:2a,5–8,16b,
5:1–2,5,7–10,13a,	7:6,12b–16a,20–	22–25,40–42
14,16–24,27–	23,28a	11:1,14–15,28–30

12:5–7,11–12,17–   17:6–7,13,24–27   24:10–12,20,30
  23,36–37,40   18:3–4,10,12–14,   25:1–46
13:14–15,18,24–   16–20,21–35   26:1,25,44,50,
  30,35–53   19:1a,9–12,28   52–54
14:28–33   20:1–16,28–32   27:3–10,19,24–
15:12–13,22–25,   21:1–16,28–32   25,36,43,51b–
  30–31   22:1–4,33–34,40   53,62–66
16:2b–3,11b–12,   23:1–11,13–22,   28:2–4,9–10,11–
  17–28   24–33   20

The Document Mark

According to B. H. Streeter in his book, *The Four Gospels: a Study of Origins,* pages 150 ff., there are some 661 verses in the text of Mark. Matthew uses over 606 of these verses either in whole or in part. Luke uses about 350 verses of Mark. The substance of over 90 percent of Mark's verses is contained in Matthew; the substance of over 50 percent in Luke. There are only 31 verses in Mark that are not used by Matthew or Luke. These verses are: 1:1; 2:27; 3:20–21; 4:26–29; 7:3–4,32–37; 8:22–26; 9:29,39b,48–49; 11:11a; 13:33–37; 14:51–52.

These data indicate that Mark wrote prior to Matthew and Luke and that both of them used Mark as a source. This conclusion is strengthened by the way Matthew and Luke used Mark. The order of events in Mark is always followed by Matthew or Luke; that is, they do not agree together against Mark's order. When Matthew departs from Mark's order and arrangement, Luke normally follows it. When Luke departs from Mark's order and arrangement, Matthew normally follows it. The same is true with regard to the wording; that is, Matthew and Luke do not agree together against Mark's words. Both Matthew and Luke use more than half of Mark's actual words. Matthew and Luke often improve on Mark's unpolished and rough Greek. These facts provide strong evidence that the Gospel of Mark was used by Luke and Matthew as a fundamental source for their record of the Jesus-event.

---

1. C. H. Dodd, *The Apostolic Preaching and Its Developments* (London: Hodder and Stroughton Limited, 1936), p. 28.

2. Henry E. Turlington, *The Broadman Bible Commentary,* Vol. 8 (Nashville: Broadman Press, 1969), p. 262.

3. Frank Stagg, *The Broadman Bible Commentary,* Vol. 8 (Nashville: Broadman Press, 1969), pp. 72–73.

3

THE EARLY HISTORY OF JESUS

The Date of Jesus' Birth

WHEN JESUS was born, the Roman world used a calendar reckoning time from the founding of the city of Rome (A.U.C.; i.e., *anno urbis conditae*—in the year of the founded city). This calendar was used for more than five hundred years after Jesus' death. Sometime during the sixth century, an eminent scholar and monk named Dionysius Exiguus proposed that a Christian calendar should be adopted. He proposed that Christians should date everything from the birth of Jesus Christ. His idea met with immediate and almost universal acceptance among the Christians. Its general acceptance was much slower. Although early introduced into southern Europe, the Christian calendar did not appear in English history until the end of the seventh century. It was not until the fifteenth century that it came into general use throughout the world.

In calculating the change from the A.U.C. calendar to the B.C.-A.D. calendar, Dionysius made a mistake of several years (B.C.—before Christ; A.D.—*Anno Domini*—in the year of the Lord). The available data seem to place Jesus' birth sometime between 4 B.C. and 6 B.C. Scholars have used eight items to try to calculate the date of Jesus' birth, only three of which are of much help in determining the precise time of the event. These data are:

- The death of Herod the Great (Matt. 2:19)
- The entrance of John the Baptist upon his ministry (Luke 3:1–3)
- The building of the Temple by Herod the Great (John 2:20)
- The census of Caesar Augustus (Luke 2:1)
- The appearance of the star in the east (Matt. 2:2)
- The slaughter of the infants in Bethlehem (Matt. 2:16)
- The language of the heavenly host (Luke 2:14)
- The entrance of Jesus upon his ministry (Luke 3:23)

THE DEATH OF HEROD THE GREAT

Matthew stated that Jesus was born before the death of Herod the Great (Matt. 2). The evidence from secular records, histories, inscriptions, and coins seems to indicate that Herod died between the 13th of March and the 4th of April A.U.C. 750 or 4 B.C. The reign of Herod Antipas and the reign of Herod Archelaus demand the year 4 B.C. as the time for the death of Herod the Great. Matthew does not tell us how long before the death of Herod that Jesus was born. The account of the flight into Egypt gives no exact information as to its duration. All that we can conclude is that Jesus was born before Herod died. Herod died in 4 B.C.; therefore, Jesus was born in 4 B.C. or earlier.

THE ENTRANCE OF JOHN THE BAPTIST UPON HIS MINISTRY

Luke wrote:

> In the fifteenth year of the reign of Tiberius Caesar, when Pontius Pilate was governor of Judea . . . the word of God came to John, the son of Zacharias, in the wilderness. And he came into all the district around the Jordan, preaching.
>
> —3:1–3

Caesar Augustus died in A.D. 14 and Tiberius became emperor at that time. The "fifteenth year" of Tiberius' reign would seem to indicate that John the Baptist's ministry began in A.D. 29. However, Augustus associated Tiberius with him in his reign two years before his death. Was Luke calculating from A.D. 12, when Tiberius really began his reign, or from A.D. 14 when Augustus died? It seems likely that he reckoned from A.D. 12 which would indicate that John began his ministry in A.D. 26 or 27. We are not told how long John had been preaching and baptizing before Jesus was baptized. If Jesus "was about thirty years of age" when he was baptized, and if John's ministry began in A.D. 26, Jesus must have been born about 5 or 4 B.C. (Luke 3:23).

THE BUILDING OF THE TEMPLE BY HEROD THE GREAT

According to John, Jesus attended a Passover in Jerusalem near the beginning of his ministry. At this Passover the Jews told him, "It took forty-six years to build this temple" (John 2:20). Herod began the building of the new Temple in 20 B.C. If we add to this twenty the "forty-six years" as stated by the Jews, again we get A.D. 26. If Jesus was then about thirty years of age, it would again seem that he was born during the time from 6–4 B.C.

There is also difference of opinion about the day and the month of Jesus' birth. The church fathers who mentioned it in their early writings disagree. Some claim that it was on May 20, others April 19 or 20, others September 29, and others September 20. Clement of Alexandria (about A.D. 150–215) dated the birth of Jesus on November 18. The Eastern churches celebrated his birth on January 6. The first mention of December 25 as the date of Jesus' birth was made by a Latin chronographer in A.D. 354. He wrote: "In the consulate of Caesar and Paulus, the Lord Jesus Christ was born on December 25, a Friday, and the 15th day of the New Moon."

Tradition is of little help in determining the month and day of Jesus' birth. The only satisfactory guide is what we find in the Gospels. In Luke 2:8 we learn that the shepherds were "keeping watch over their flock by night." The presence of the shepherds on the hills at night seems to indicate that it was not winter. The season of pasturage in Judea was between March and November, and shepherds would not be watching their flocks by night at any other time. The evidence available is too meager and indefinite to permit one to be dogmatic as to the exact day or month of the birth of Christ.

The Supernatural Birth of Jesus

According to Matthew 1:18–25 and Luke 1:26–38, Jesus was born of Mary, a virgin, through the special action of the Holy Spirit. This was the grandest event in the annals of time. These Gospel narratives teach clearly that the Holy Spirit was the agency of the

conception. They represent Jesus as having been born through the immediate influence of the divine Spirit. This does not mean that Christ
came into being at this time (John 1:1–2; Rom. 8:3; Gal. 4:4). His
life did not begin when he was born. His birth was an advent. Over
and over Jesus himself declared not that he had *become,* but that he
had *come.* His conception was a miracle. It was distinct from all other
conceptions. It was unique. The Gospel narratives describe the way
by which God became an integral part of human existence.

The whole New Testament testifies to the miracle of the incarnation. It is nothing less than the coming of God in the form of a human
being. This affirmation of the unique, purposeful work of God in
sending Christ into the world is essential to the gospel story. It does
not, however, negate the fact that Jesus was both God and man. He
was a human being and lived a truly human life while, at the same
time, he was the eternal Son of God.

The doctrine of the incarnation is not that God masqueraded as a
man. He is presented in the Gospel accounts as a man. He came into
the world as a real human being, though his conception was supernatural. He was subject to the laws of human development. He was
liable to hunger and thirst, infirmity and pain, even to mental limita-
tion and suffering. His manhood, therefore, was real and no illusion.

Incarnation does not mean simply that Jesus had a human body
and a divine spirit. It is not that he was half-God and half-man, but
neither one nor the other completely. It is not that he was a good
man whom God promoted to the rank of God. He was the *Logos*
(Word) made flesh. He was the God-man. The doctrine of the incarnation is that the humanity of Jesus was completely united with God,
and that everything he said and did as a man was at the same time
the word and activity of God. It was the union of the divine and the
human, a truth which is beyond the ability of our finite minds to
understand.

In Donald Baillie's book, *God Was in Christ,* he shows that all of
God that can be expressed in humanity was revealed in Jesus. This
is a great wonder. Men have tried for centuries to probe this mystery.
No theory has proved completely satisfactory. Paul stated the truth
without trying to explain it. He affirmed that "although He existed
in the form of God, [he] did not regard equality with God a thing
to be grasped, but emptied Himself, taking the form of a bondservant,
and being made in the likeness of men" (Phil. 2:6–7).

The Announcements of the Birth of Jesus

The mother of Jesus was from Nazareth in Galilee. Though of lowly condition, she was possibly of King David's line. Nothing is known of her previous history except that she had been betrothed to Joseph, a carpenter, who was himself of royal descent.

Betrothal was not only considered as sacred as marriage but as being virtually a part of it, so that it could not be made void except by a legal process of divorce. However, this process of divorce could be conducted without publicity. The most approved custom regarding betrothal required that there should be an interval of several months between betrothal and the completion of the marriage rites. Sometimes the interval was for years. There was no formal marriage ceremony following the betrothal, only a marriage feast when the bride was taken home to her husband's house. This betrothal relationship was that which existed between Mary and Joseph when an angel visited her.

Near the end of the reign of Herod the Great, the angel Gabriel was sent to Mary with a message. He said to her, " 'Hail, favored one! The Lord is with you' " (Luke 1:28). Mary was startled and troubled by this unexpected appearance and address of the messenger. The angel calmed her fears, saying: " 'Do not be afraid, Mary; for you have found favor with God. And behold, you will conceive in your womb, and bear a son, and you shall name Him Jesus' " (Luke 1: 30–31). The name was selected because of the significance of its root meaning. "Joshua," or "Jesus," is equivalent to "savior" or "deliverer." The child was to be so named because he was the one who would save his people from their sins.

This announcement awoke in Mary's mind a doubt in the very face of seeming impossibilities. The angel gave her an explicit answer, " 'The Holy Spirit will come upon you, and the power of the Most High will overshadow you; and for that reason the holy offspring shall be called the Son of God' " (Luke 1:35).

Conscious of the miracle wrought upon her by the creative power of God, Mary traveled about one hundred miles to the hill country of Judah. Mary's cousin Elizabeth, the wife of Zacharias, lived here. The meeting of these two women was accompanied by divine mysteries which were hidden from all the world. Mary probably remained with Elizabeth for about three months (Luke 1:39–45,56).

Soon after Mary returned to Nazareth, she encountered her first

was conception accomplished prior announcement, or after she agreed to it?

great trial because of her condition. Though Joseph does not seem to have been an unkind or suspicious man, he undoubtedly soon became aware of Mary's condition. He was shocked and disturbed because it violated his previous impressions of Mary's character. He was reluctant to bring her to open shame, and therefore determined to put her away without assigning any cause. God communicated to Joseph in a dream; and, as a result, he took Mary at once under his protection.

The Birth in Bethlehem

According to Matthew 2:1–12 and Luke 2:1–15, Jesus was born in Bethlehem, which is located about five miles south, southwest of Jerusalem. The town's prominence in the Old Testament rests on its associations with David (1 Sam. 17:12,15; 20:6,28; 16:1–13; etc.). Bethlehem was the promised birthplace of the Messiah (Mic. 5:2; John 7:42). Members of the house of David who returned with Ezra and the exiles were resettled in their own city and their inheritance restored (Ezra 8:1–2; Neh. 7:26; 11:3,20). Bethlehem remained the center for the house of David.

The occasion for Jesus' birth in Bethlehem was a decree by Caesar Augustus for a general census. The purpose of the census was partly to obtain correct statistics and partly to prepare the way for general and systematic taxation. Apparently, Augustus allowed each province to proceed with the enrolment according to existing practices. Among the Jews it was customary to go to one's ancestral city for the registration. Joseph and Mary made the three-day journey for his enrolment from Galilee where he lived to Bethlehem in Judah, because he was descended from King David. It is noted that Quirinius, a high Roman official, was given the assignment of the census in Syria (Luke 2:2).

The census brought many people to Bethlehem, and the inns were soon filled. These inns were for the most part very crude, consisting of a series of thatched rooms built around a courtyard. The occupants were compelled to furnish their own food and provide the pot in which to cook their food in the courtyard, their own bedding, and wood.

When Joseph and Mary arrived, the only available place for them was one of the cattle stalls, probably under the inn. It was in one of these stalls that Jesus was born and laid in a manger (Luke 2:7). Luke probably intended for us to see in this incident that the importance of this birth was not recognized by man.

The Announcement by the Angels

The birth of Jesus was an event of universal and eternal significance. In the incarnation God entered human life and provided in Jesus a fresh start for man. The first Adam came into being by a creative act of God. The second Adam came into being in the same way. Jesus entered into world history in accordance with its divinely-constituted laws and took his place in a historic relation to the human family. As a regenerating force, he penetrated the great heart of mankind. All things are to be begotten anew in him, and from him history took a new departure.

The angelic chorus ascribed glory to God because Christ's coming into the world marked the culmination of the divine self-revelation to the human family (Luke 2:13–14). The song of the angels was a twofold message: glory to God and peace on earth to the men of good will. News of this birth resounded to God's glory in heaven and inaugurated a new era on earth. Luke probably intended the accounts of this angelic chorus to remind his readers that the importance of this birth was recognized by heaven.

The Visit of the Shepherds

According to Luke 2:8–20, the first earthly worshipers of the Christ child were the shepherds from the hillside. These shepherds probably lived in Bethlehem and were keeping watch over their sheep near the village. It was customary to keep the sheep as near the village as possible. (There is now a small hamlet about a mile east of Bethlehem called "The Village of the Shepherds.")

Shepherds generally were despised by orthodox Jews because their occupation did not allow them to follow all the prescribed religious observances. They were exposed to the elements. They were often unwelcome because they smelled like sheep. They were poor, unlearned, and plain men, with no gifts to bring. They were, however, among the simple trusting people who were "looking for the consolation of Israel." It was to these shepherds that the first announcement of Jesus' birth was made. The wonder with which the shepherds' story was greeted anticipated the deeper and more abiding wonder to come.

The Circumcision of Jesus

Mary and Joseph complied with all the requirements of the law at the time of Jesus' birth. According to Luke 2:21, the religious ceremony of circumcision was performed on Jesus on the eighth day after his birth. This rite was presumably performed in the home occupied by Joseph and Mary in Bethlehem. By this sign of the covenant between God and Israel, Jesus was made a party to the covenant which God established with Abraham (Gen. 17:10–14). It was an act of initiation into the covenant community of Israel. It represented subjection to all the conditions of the law and acceptance of the privileges and obligations of the covenant. The name "Jesus" was given to him at this time in obedience to the command of God (Luke 1:31). It was a heroic and sacred name in Hebrew history. "Jesus" is the Greek equivalent of the Hebrew "Joshua," which means "the Lord is salvation." Therefore, it was not its historic associations which gave the name its significance, but its prophetic import (Matt. 1:21).

The Presentation in the Temple

In the case of a firstborn male child, the law required, any time after the first month, the payment of a five-shekel offering for the redemption of the child (Ex. 13:1–2,11–15). Forty days after a birth the law required the purification of the mother (Lev. 12:1–8). According to Luke 2:22–38, when Jesus was forty days old he was presented in the Temple in Jerusalem and the rite of purification for Mary was performed. Apparently these two ceremonies were performed for Jesus and Mary at the same time. The redemption of the firstborn did not require a visit to the Temple, but it seems that parents residing near Jerusalem went to the Temple for the rite. The regular offering for the purification of a mother was ordinarily a lamb (Lev. 12:6). However, in cases of poverty, provisions were made to substitute a pigeon or a turtledove for the lamb (Lev. 12:8). According to Luke 2:24, this substitution was made in Mary's case, indicating that Joseph and Mary were poor. Luke's chief interest in this visit to the Temple lay in the predictions of Simeon and the praise of the prophetess Anna (Luke 2:25–39). "Simeon's brief hymn of praise . . . is as beautiful as any of the psalms of praise in the Old Testament. The thought underlying its wording is of a slave who is instructed by his master to keep watch through the long, dark night on a high place to wait for the rising of a special star and then announce it. After wearisome hours of waiting, he at last sees the star rising in all its brightness. He announces it and is then discharged from keeping watch any longer." [1] Apparently Jesus was unrecognized at this time except by those two devout persons who were supernaturally enlightened and, therefore, realized that in Jesus God's salvation had come.

The Visit of the Magi

According to Matthew 2:1–12, sometime after the birth of Jesus, Magi (wise men) from the East came to worship him. When they arrived, Jesus was no longer in the stable but was in a house (Matt. 2:11). It is probable that, after Jesus' birth in the stable, Joseph made some arrangements for a house where the family lived for some time. There is no way of determining how old Jesus was when the Magi arrived. It is possible that he was a year old. (It is highly unlikely that Jesus was visited by the Magi while he was in a stable as so much Christmas art and legend depict.)

The nationality of the Magi is not disclosed. It is stated that they came "from the East" (Matt. 2:1). They were probably priests from Persia, Arabia, or Babylonia. There were many Jews in Babylonia, and these men may have been Jews. Tradition has been busy with this story. Later generations have had much to say about these Magi and their history after they made their memorable journey. Their names according to unreliable legend were Gaspar ("white"), Melchior ("light"), and Balthasar ("the lord of the treasury"). However, we do not know of a certainty how many there were, where they were from, or what their names were. These men possessed unusual knowledge of the strange star that guided them to the newborn King.

Astrology was studied extensively in Persia. Whether the star was a comet or a regular star we are not told. Many attempts have been made to identify it with some conjunction of planets. The word that Matthew uses, however, is "star" not "stars." It is best to confess that the star's appearance was a miracle.

The Magi found, no doubt to their surprise, that the great event was unknown in the capital of Judaism. They inquired of Herod where they could find and worship the newborn King. Naturally Jerusalem was thrown into a state of excitement by the arrival of the distinguished strangers in search of an infant Messiah. So Herod convened the chief priests and scribes and inquired of them where the Christ should be born. Anxious for the safety of his throne, Herod planned to use for his own advantage the information which the Magi might obtain concerning the abode of the child from whom he thought he had much to fear in the future. To the Magi, Herod pretended that he himself desired to do honor to the coming king. However, through the inspiration of a dream, the Magi returned to their own country without revisiting Jerusalem.

Because of Matthew's emphasis on the kingdom, his purpose in including this story in his account probably was to show the inevitable conflict between the earthly and the heavenly kingdom. The Magi's visit pointed up a conflict between the Messiah, who is truly King of Israel, and Herod the king who saw his position threatened. Their coming pointed to the unique and royal role of the newborn child.

Flight to Egypt

According to Matthew 2:13–18, Herod was determined to destroy Jesus. He had ascertained what time the star appeared and had calculated the age of his infant rival. He had hoped, on the return of the strangers, to learn the name and abode of the one who might cause him or his dynasty serious trouble. He waited impatiently for the message they were to bring. When it became apparent that the Magi had eluded his cruel purpose by a secret departure, his rage knew no bounds. Herod would not allow even his own sons to be rival contenders for his throne and had already killed several of them. He resolved to destroy this new rival.

At this same time, Joseph was warned in a dream; and he took Jesus and Mary and fled into Egypt. The nearest part of Egypt was not far from Bethlehem, and there were many Jewish communities there. Herod's plan to have the young child slain was now enlarged. He sent soldiers to the village of Bethlehem with orders to put to death all the male children there from two years of age and under. We are not told how this cruel order was carried out. Bethlehem was a small village, and this massacre may not have included more than twelve or fifteen children.

The "slaughter of the innocents" is not mentioned by Josephus, the Jewish historian. However, there were so many cruelties which marked the end of Herod's reign that the historian could not include them all. There is a possible reference to this massacre in a composite book written around A.D. 7–29, entitled *Assumption of Moses*. This book is independent of all Christian tradition; therefore, it gives a Jewish, non-Christian witness to the acts of Herod. In 6:2–5 it says:

An insolent king shall succeed them (the Hasmonaeans), who will not be of the race of the priests, a man bold and shameless, and he shall judge them as they shall deserve. And he shall cut off their chief men with the sword, and shall destroy them in secret places, so that no one may know where their bodies are. He shall slay the old and the young, and he shall not spare. Then the fear of him shall be bitter unto them in their land.[2]

This allusion to the slaying of the *young* by Herod may be a reference to the slaughter of the infants in Bethlehem.

We have no certain record of the length of Joseph's sojourn in Egypt. He was simply told to remain there until he was instructed further. The stay could not have been long, probably not more than three or four months. The record indicates that Joseph, Mary, and Jesus remained in Egypt until the death of Herod, which took place in 4 B.C.

The Child Brought from Egypt to Nazareth

In Matthew 2:13–23 we are told that after the death of Herod, Joseph brought Mary and the child back to Israel. Matthew saw in this departure from Egypt a fulfilment of the prophecy in Hosea 11: 1. "When Israel was a child, I loved him, and out of Egypt I called my son" (RSV). Here is one of the clearest and most striking instances of Matthew's use of prophecy. At the time these words were written by Hosea, they referred to the bringing of the children of Israel out of Egypt by Moses (Ex. 4:22–23). These words of the prophet certainly found fulfilment also in God's calling Jesus from Egypt. Matthew saw in this event a parallel with the Exodus, when Moses the prophet and lawgiver led "God's Son" (his people) out of Egypt. Matthew stated that Jesus is the second and greater Moses whose advent is foretold in Deuteronomy 18:15. Many early Christians saw striking parallels between Moses and Jesus.

Apparently Joseph desired to make his home in Bethlehem, but when he learned that Archelaus had succeeded his father, Herod the Great, in Judea, he went to Nazareth in Galilee.

Galilee (which is from the Hebrew word "circle") originally was called "Galilee [circle] of the nations [Gentiles]" (Isa. 9:1, RSV). In the first century its population was mainly Jewish, although Gentile elements still remained. The region was very fertile, and it had a large population. Josephus stated:

Their soil is universally rich and fruitful, and full of the plantations of trees of all sorts, insomuch that it invites the most slothful to take pains in its cultivation, by its fruitfulness: accordingly, it is all cultivated by its inhabitants, and no part of it lies idle. Moreover, the cities lie here very thick; and the very many villages there are here, are everywhere so full of people, by the richness of their soil, that the very least of them contain above fifteen thousand inhabitants.

Josephus also mentioned that there were 240 cities and villages in Galilee. According to this information, the population would have been over three million in an area of about one hundred square miles.

Galilee was ruled by Herod Antipas, and he was evidently not likely to be a threat to the life of Jesus. Jesus spent the "silent years" of his life in Nazareth of Galilee. In this fact Matthew seems to have seen a fulfilment of prophecy, though no written prophecy to that effect has been found (Matt. 2:23). It seems reasonable to suppose that he interpreted freely the meaning of perhaps more than one portion of the Scriptures.

The Childhood of Jesus at Nazareth

At least ten years of Jesus' life in Nazareth are passed over in silence by the Gospel writers. His growth and development are mentioned in Luke 2:40. This is the only scriptural reference to Jesus from the beginning of his stay in Nazareth until his twelfth year. We could wish that the Gospel writers had given us some experiences from the family of Joseph and Mary in their humble home in Nazareth. However, the authors of the four Gospels were not writing biographies —they were writing Gospels. We can only conclude that information related to this part of Jesus' life is not necessary for our understanding of what God did in Christ.

The apocryphal Gospels, those which were not included in the Bible, are full of stories and legends of the feats performed by Jesus during his early years. These accounts are not trustworthy. Luke's summary in 2:40 indicates that the humanity of Jesus was a reality. He was subject to all the laws of human growth and development during these years. He had ideal development in physical, mental, moral, and spiritual growth. The laws which regulate the development of manhood in other individuals had their full and natural operation in the life of our Lord.

Jesus also had his place in the historical development of the Chosen People and of the world. Though his growth and development were at all points in accord with God's plan, they were at the same time related to the facts of nature around him. No doubt his development was in some degree influenced by his condition in life—his employments, his companions, and the instructions which he received. He doubtless attended synagogue school and learned to read like other male Jewish children. There is the clearest evidence that he was taught the Law and the Prophets.

The humanity of Jesus has always been a stumbling block to many persons and groups. The first real theological threat to the Christian movement came when certain persons denied that Christ had come in the flesh. This belief was known as Docetism. Some of those who held to this doctrine denied that Jesus actually had a physical body. They claimed that this just *seemed* to be true. Other Docetists claimed that the divine Christ came upon the human Jesus at his baptism and left him before the crucifixion. This teaching was already present when the Gospel of John was written. And it was such false teachings that John refuted in his epistles.

We must not attempt to interpret Jesus as man only; neither must we attempt to interpret him as God and not man. The Gospel writers never attempted to present him as God or as man—they presented him as the God-man. This was an essential part of the incarnation.

The Boy Jesus in Jerusalem

In Luke 2:41–51 we have the only incident in the life of Jesus recorded in the four Gospels from the time of his going to Nazareth until the beginning of his ministry. This incident, his visit to the Temple, indicates Jesus' interest and progress in the religion of his nation. He did not come to destroy the Law and the Prophets but to fulfil them.

Apparently Luke used this one incident from the life of Jesus to show that he followed the regular religious program of Jewish male children in his growing to manhood. In 2:40 and again in 2:52 Luke indicated the fact of Jesus' growth. Involved in the growth of a Jewish male at the time of Jesus' boyhood were these events:

- On the eighth day after birth he was circumcised and given his name (Lev. 12:3).
- After forty days he was presented in the Temple (Lev. 12).
- When he was three years old, he was given the fringed garments (Num. 15:38–41; Deut. 22:12).

- At five years of age he began to learn portions of the Law.
- At the age of six or seven he was sent to the elementary school. This was connected with the local synagogue, and since the manual of instruction was the Book of the Law, it was known as "the House of the Book."
- At ten years of age he began the study of the Mishna (a compilation of traditional interpretations).
- After his twelfth birthday, a Jewish boy became bar mitzvah (a son of the law). At that time he entered upon all the privileges and responsibilities of an Israelite, including attendance at the Feast of the Passover.
- At the age of thirteen years he wore, for the first time, the phylacteries which the Jews always put on at the recital of the daily prayers. He also was now responsible for the practice of the commands. His childhood was over, and he left the House of the Book and began his preparation for his proper lifework.
- At eighteen it was time for marriage.

It was commanded in the law that each year every male Israelite should attend the three great feasts: Passover, Pentecost, and Tabernacles (Ex. 23:14–17; Deut. 16:1–8; 1 Sam. 1:3,21). The Passover was the most solemn and important of the feasts, and most Jews preferred to attend this feast. After the Exile, these requirements were not enforced; so a choice could be made. When Jesus was twelve years old, he attended a Passover in Jerusalem with Mary and Joseph. Mary's attendance at the feast was an act of devotion not commanded by the law.

When the week of sacred solemnity was over, the train of Galileans started on their homeward journey. Mary and Joseph set out with the others, not knowing that they were leaving Jesus behind. Only when the caravan halted at the end of the first day's march was Jesus' absence noticed by his parents. Joseph and Mary returned to Jerusalem, and on the third day they found him taking advantage of his opportunities to learn from the rabbis in the Temple courts. To Mary's rebuke he replied in words of profound significance which strike the keynote of his life: " 'Why is it that you were looking for Me? Did you not know that I had to be in My Father's *house?*' " (Luke 2:49).

In recording Jesus' statement, Luke did not give the noun. Did Jesus say house, business, affairs, or things? The translators must supply some noun to complete Jesus' statement. The point of the statement, however, is that not only had Jesus become bar mitzvah (son of the law); he now had become intensely aware of being "Son of God." From his early years, Jesus was aware of a special filial relationship to God. He not only felt he had to be obedient to the law; he had to be obedient to the God of the law.

Luke's is the first recorded saying of Jesus. He must have known, partly at least, the secret of his mission. Nevertheless, he returned to Nazareth and resumed his simple life. For the next eighteen years he worked as a carpenter in Nazareth (Mark 6:3). These were not wasted years because Jesus continued to grow. He was subject to all the laws and conditions of human nature. The time also served as a preparation for the work which the Father had given him to do.

This Temple incident is the last time Joseph is mentioned in the story of Jesus, though the Gospels indicate that four other sons were born to Joseph and Mary: James, Joses, Judas, and Simon. Also, daughters were born to them, though we do not know the number and names of them (Mark 6:3). Apparently Joseph died before Jesus began his public ministry. There is an ancient tradition that Joseph was older than Mary. When Joseph died, Jesus, as the oldest son, took up the trade of Joseph and provided for the family. During this time, "Jesus kept increasing in wisdom and stature, and in favor with God and men" (Luke 2:52).

The Forerunner Appears

After Jesus' visit to Jerusalem when he was twelve years old, eighteen years elapsed before he began his ministry of redemption. All four of the Gospel writers agree that Jesus' call was in some way connected with John the Baptist's preaching and with the revival which that preaching had started.

For hundreds of years the voice of a prophet had not been heard. Just before the silent years between the Testaments, a prophetic voice had announced that a herald, an antitype of Elijah, would come and prepare the way for the time when "the great and terrible day of Jehovah come" (Mal. 4:5, ASV). An angel of the Lord had renewed this announcement to Zacharias as he offered incense in the Temple (Luke 1:17). Thirty years later (Luke 3:1–3), John the Baptist received a special command from God to begin his preaching.

The expression "the word of God came to John" is similar to the ones used in relation to the inspiration of the prophets of the Old Testament (Jer. 1:2,4,11,13, etc.). All three Synoptic writers indicated that the appearance and preaching of John were the fulfilment of what had been prophesied in the Old Testament concerning a forerunner (Isa. 40:3–5). The figure in Isaiah is taken from the ancient custom of sending forward a body of men to build or repair the road over which some great person would travel. This prophecy seems to have had an immediate reference to the return of the Jews from captivity. The writers of the Gospels, however, saw its higher fulfilment in the coming of the God-man. It continues to have meaning today, for the road is to be made in the hearts of men that Christ may enter and dwell there.

The Jews believed that Elijah would return to be the herald of the Christ. John the Baptist denied that he was Elijah (John 1:21). When Jesus was questioned, he said: "If you are willing to accept it, he is Elijah who is to come" (Matt. 11:14, RSV). It required the explanation of Jesus to open the eyes of his disciples on this subject. (Read Matt. 17:10–13.) John's resemblance to Elijah was twofold.

He looked like Elijah because they both wore the same kind of rough clothes (2 Kings 1:8; Matt. 3:4). Furthermore, they both had the same message of stern rebuke and demand for repentance (1 Kings 18:21; 21:20; Luke 3:7–14).

John's message was new and startling: "Repent, for the kingdom of heaven is at hand" (Matt. 3:2; see Mark 1:15). The Greek word for repent, *metanoeo,* means to change one's mind. It came to mean such a radical change of mind as to reverse completely one's life direction, to be converted.

The phrase "kingdom of heaven" which John used occurs in the New Testament only in Matthew (thirty-two times). Four times the phrase "kingdom of God" occurs in Matthew. Both phrases mean the effective rule of God over his people. The reign of God was about to invade the earth, and men must reverse their life's direction and be cleansed in order to be prepared for the kingdom.

The burden of John's message was "the wrath to come" (Luke 3:7). At last, the era, so often foretold in prophecy, was at hand. John proclaimed that the new era was not to be ushered in by a political victory over Israel's enemies (as they expected), but by a judgment upon Israel herself. The judgment would be so thorough that every unrepentant Israelite would be destroyed. John summoned all who heard him to prepare for the appearance of another (Mark 1:7).

John thought of "the wrath to come" as an essential part of the rule of God. There would be a judgment, and justice would be the order of the day. Evildoers would by no means escape the penalty of their deeds. Repentance was necessary, and this repentance had to be real; it had to issue in a change of conduct. In this coming judgment only what was good would be preserved, and all that was worthless would be destroyed in the fire. The agent in this coming crisis was to be the Messiah. To show his reverence for the one who was coming, John said that he was not worthy to fasten the Messiah's shoes—a job which normally would have been done by a servant.

John's ethical teaching was radical and revolutionary. In Luke 3:10–14 we find illustrations of the practical application of John's teachings. The principle running through the three answers in these illustrations is that each person must conquer the temptation of greed and practice love and kindness. He did not ask any of his hearers to forsake his profession; he only required that each do his duty in his calling.

John required those who came repenting to submit to the rite of baptism. This rite had unusual importance as preparation for the coming kingdom. It probably was customary that Gentile proselytes to Judaism be baptized. "There was a Jewish proselyte baptism in the first century, and the likelihood is that it was practiced before John's time. . . . It is not likely that orthodox Judaism would have adopted a Christian rite. Since Christianity was cradled in Judaism, no problem would be faced in the development of baptism from Jewish practice." [3] What was unusual about John's baptism was that he was baptizing Jews. This was a radical demand that John made of those who came to repent. His examination of baptismal candidates must have been searching and practical.

Jesus' Baptism

Jesus was about thirty years old when he understood that it was time for him to begin the work for which he had come into the world (Luke 3:23). He presented himself to John and requested baptism. Jesus' baptism is a problem which has exercised the minds of men since the first century. In fact, John himself recognized the problem (Matt. 3:14). John's baptism was a rite of repentence, designed to symbolize the cleansing of penitents (Mark 1:4; Luke 3:3). Jesus did not need repentance! And John recognized this. Why should this sinless one be baptized with a rite which was a mark of repentance and the symbol of cleansing from sin? The explanations for this problem have been many and varied. The early church fathers struggled with the dilemma. The writers of the Apocryphal Gospels gave several explanations. The only explanation given in the New Testament is the one given by Jesus to John, " 'Permit it at this time; for in this way it is fitting for us to fulfill all righteousness' " (Matt. 3:15). No explanation of Jesus' baptism is without its difficulties. Possibly, he was baptized as a deliberate act of self-identification with sinful men whom he had come to save. "Here [in Matt. 3:14] it is simply indicated that Jesus' baptism was willed by God and conformed to his order. It is only later that the profound meaning of this act may be grasped—that by this act Jesus identified himself with his people, took on himself their guilt, and received with and for them the baptism of repentance. The messianic meaning of this act is to be seen from the rest of the story." [4]

Jesus never used his divine nature to make unmeaningful his human nature. When he was eight days old, he was circumcised, signifying the putting away of the defilement of the flesh (Luke 2:21). During his ministry he paid the Temple tax though, as the Son of God whose house the Temple was, he could have claimed exemption (Matt. 17: 24–27). In the same way, Jesus' baptism was his own choice to identify himself with the penitents.

The Hebrew word "Messiah" and the Greek word "Christ" mean "anointed." In New Testament thought, the descent of the Spirit at Jesus' baptism constituted the "anointing" of Jesus as God's Messiah (Acts 10:38). In the Old Testament, kings, priests, and prophets were anointed for their ministry. In 1 Samuel 16:13 the writer said that David was anointed by Samuel with the results that the "Spirit of Jehovah" came "mightily" upon him. In Isaiah 11:1–2 it is recorded that the "shoot out of the stock of Jesse" was to have a special endowment of the Spirit, for the "Spirit of Jehovah shall rest upon him" (ASV). These Scriptures were fulfilled at Jesus' baptism when the Holy Spirit descended upon him. This does not mean that Jesus did not possess the Spirit before his baptism. The Spirit is presented here as an active power which came upon Jesus to anoint him and give him power and guidance for his work. At his baptism Jesus was equipped for the work which he was called to do. His baptism was a solemn consecration to his office as Messiah.

The Jews had a term, *bath-kol* or "daughter of a voice," which they used to refer to God's spoken messages from heaven. The voice to Jesus at his baptism was the voice from God. The words of the heavenly voice were the same as parts of Psalm 2:7 and Isaiah 42:1. In Psalm 2 the reign of God's anointed was proclaimed. Isaiah 42: 1–6 contains the first of a series of prophecies about the Suffering Servant of the Lord. This Suffering Servant, chosen by God to carry true religion to the Gentiles, would suffer rejection, indignity, and death. This voice from God at his baptism was the call for which Jesus had been waiting. He was God's anointed who would rule in the kingdom of God. He would rule through suffering. This voice expressed both appointment and approval. " 'Thou art my beloved Son, in whom I am well pleased'—that swept the last hesitation from Jesus' soul, and the messianic vocation was accepted. And with the vision came the endowment for messiahship; the sense of power flooded his soul. The Spirit of God, which had been brooding over creation from the first [Gen. 1:2], haunting the dreams of saints [Ps. 139:7], and breaking out intermittently in the words of prophets [Isa. 61:1], was now focused and concentrated to one burning point in Jesus' soul; and he came up from the water, the power of God unto salvation." [5]

The Temptations of the Messiah

Mark's brief narrative (1:12–13) gives the nucleus of the story of Jesus' temptations. A much more extended account is given by Matthew and Luke (Matt. 4:1–11; Luke 4:1–13). We must not suppose that these accounts relate all the temptations that Jesus experienced in the desert or later. He was "tempted in all things as we are, yet without sin" (Heb. 4:15).

The Synoptic writers all stated that Jesus' temptations took place in the wilderness (desert). The Wilderness of Judah is an area about thirty miles long and fifteen miles wide. It is west of Jericho and north of the Dead Sea. This region is a land of precipices, burnt hills, bare gorges, and deep ravines. Wild animals infest the region. Little natural food is available. The traditional site of the temptations is on a mountain just west of Jericho called Quarantania. This mountain is about eight miles from the traditional place of Jesus' baptism.

The story of these temptations must have come from Jesus himself, since he was alone when they occurred. Why did Jesus tell it? There are at least two reasons for which Jesus gave an account of the ordeal to his disciples. First, he may have shared this experience in order to offer encouragement to his disciples in their own times of temptations. And second, Jesus may have told this story because the struggle of the desert days and nights marked his soul forever, and he could never forget the experience.

These temptations were directed toward Jesus in his divine calling as the Son of God and the Suffering Servant. He was not being tempted to do things which would be regarded as antisocial or immoral. The strongest and subtlest temptation is to do what appears to be good. The experience in the desert brought into focus Jesus' own conception of his ministry. His victory in this struggle indicated the method and pattern which he would follow in his messianic work. The decisions which he made in refusing to follow the line of the tempter foreshadowed the inevitability of his death.

The temptations of Jesus were the sequel to his baptismal experience. He had dedicated himself to God's cause and had received the anointing of the Spirit. He was now fully conscious of a unique and special vocation and of his possession of the accompanying exceptional powers. How was he to use his power? As Messiah, how would he claim his kingdom? What kind of Messiah would he be? To what extent was he to conform to popular expectation that there would come a conquering political Messiah who would restore Israel's glory?

A variety of messianic expectations were to be found in Jesus' day. The Zealots would have achieved national deliverance by force and thus reveal a Messiah. The Pharisees did not approve of revolution. They felt that when God so willed it the Messiah would come. They expected him to be a son of David who would fulfil the law. Both of these groups expected a Messiah who would be concerned with national and political matters. However, some scribes were expecting a "more other-worldly, transcendental, and universalistic type." [6] Most Jews of Jesus' day were expecting a Messiah of one form or the other. But it is safe to say that not many Jews, if any, were expecting the kind of Messiah that Jesus would prove to be.

The temptations picture the clash between what Jesus knew himself called by God to do and what many of the people were going to demand. For forty days (a figure of symbolic significance) he pondered the work which he had been given to do. He wrestled with perplexities which crowded in upon him. God had called and anointed him for his work. He was to bring the kingdom of God among men. But how? He had come to redeem the world. But how? It was inevitable that the messianic expectations which prevailed among his contemporaries should present themselves to him.

THE FIRST TEMPTATION

One of the beliefs current in Jesus' day concerning the messianic age was that it would be a time marked by a miraculous abundance of material goods. The Messiah was expected to bestow bread from heaven, so the people thought, just as Moses had done (John 6:30–31). The most popular picture of the messianic age was that of a great banquet, "a feast of fat things" (Isa. 25:6–8, ASV).

"Satan's words, 'If you are the Son of God,' were not necessarily calculated to cast doubt. Rather the design of the words [those heard at his baptism] was to prompt Jesus confidently to make certain demands upon God. But sonship is not manifested in demands but in obedience." [7] Probably the point of the temptation was not to satisfy Jesus' own hunger by performing a miracle to save himself. If he had been thinking of himself, he could have walked back to a village to get bread. He undoubtedly was contemplating how to accomplish his work and to get his message across to men. He knew the desperate need of the great multitudes. Since he was the Son of God, should he not use his power to satisfy their hunger? Jesus probably knew what it was to be hungry and had a deep sympathy for the poor. The hungry people craved a kingdom built on bread (John 6:31–34). Surely this was their most pressing problem. How could the people worship God unless they were fed? What good did it do to tell them about God's love unless he satisfied their human need?

The question here involved the method Jesus would adopt for his messianic work. If he used his power to satisfy men's bodily needs, he would gain their affection and loyalty. He would then be able to lead them into the kingdom of God.

Jesus rejected the idea that men's allegiance was to be bought by a promise of better conditions. He resisted the suggestion of giving priority to men's physical needs and insisted on giving first place to spiritual needs. Jesus' reply to Satan was taken from Deuteronomy

8:3. This passage teaches that man's real life depends on more than bread; real life comes from obedience to God's word.

Let it be said, however, that neither this passage in the Old Testament nor the experience of Jesus recorded in Matthew can be used to force us from responsibility toward the hungry of our country and of the world. Jesus rejected the temptation to build a kingdom on bread, but he was filled with compassion for the hungry. He did not ever overlook men's physical needs. Jesus would have us to understand that strength for kingdom living springs not from physical sustenance but from obedient response to the will of God.

THE SECOND TEMPTATION

In the order of Matthew's record, the second temptation dealt with the methods to be used in establishing the kingdom. Jesus was transported mentally from the desert to the holy city (Matt. 4:5). There the devil "stood Him on the pinnacle of the temple." The pinnacle of the Temple was probably the southside of the outer court which was known as the "Royal Colonnade." Josephus said that it made one dizzy to look down from this portico.

The proposal in this temptation was for Jesus to go and cast himself down from this high point and rely upon God's providential action to save him from harm. Satan supported his appeal with a quotation from the Scriptures (Ps. 91:11–12). The whole psalm from which this passage was taken encourages reliance upon divine protection. The truth that God cares for his own lies at the very heart of God's revelation of himself. He does care for those who do his bidding. However, Satan misapplied this Scripture passage in order to justify presumption upon God.

Again Jesus was encouraged to gain the attention and applause of the people in an unworthy way and to conform to traditional expectations. The people expected the Messiah to show signs to attest his claims. The rulers and the multitudes continually demanded signs from Jesus during his ministry (John 2:18; 6:30, and so on). Paul, who knew the Jews, said: "Jews ask for signs" (1 Cor. 1:22). There was a legend among the Jews that when the Messiah came, he would come floating in the clouds and descend upon the Temple and reign.

Jesus must have turned over in his mind the question, Would not this feat convince the people that he had come from God? This suggestion, like the first temptation, was made on the assumption that

Jesus was the Son of God. We must remember that this temptation also occurred in the context of decisions about his messianic work and the methods he would follow. How could he get the people to listen to him? Would it not be permissible to use supernatural power to impress the people if he only wanted to help them? If the end was good, did the means really matter? Why not do something spectacular? Would not this convince the people that he was different from all other men and force them to listen to his message?

The challenge to act outside the limits of piety and sanity was met by Jesus with words from Deuteronomy 6:16. Jesus said, in effect, that to test God's good faith would be to show one's own lack of faith. When we possess faith, we do not act upon what God has said merely to see whether it is true. To thrust oneself into peril merely to furnish the occasion for testing God is not faith but presumption. Furthermore, Jesus knew that no transient impression made on men's senses would establish God's sovereignty in their spirits. Wonder is not faith! The only proof of authority that Jesus was willing to use was the evidence of the power of the Spirit of God in his life.

THE THIRD TEMPTATION

According to Matthew's records, the third temptation took place on the summit of some lofty mountain (Matt. 4:8). Luke's words, "in a moment of time," suggest a visionary experience (Luke 4:5). Luke also said that the devil claimed the power to bestow all the earthly power and glory which was viewed (Luke 4:6).

The Jews had an undying hope that one day Israel would rule the world. The Messiah would rally his people and lead them in a victorious campaign against Rome. This was the messianic ideal presented to Jesus in the third temptation.

We must remind ourselves that each of these temptations was in connection with Jesus' work as Messiah—to win the whole earth for God. The tempter now suggested that the easiest, quickest, surest way to accomplish this work was to come to terms with the world powers. Satan promised Jesus worldwide dominion if he would only prostrate himself in homage before him. Satan's line of reasoning was that becoming a king would be so easy if Jesus would compromise and give himself to the spirit of domination. Satan said, in effect: "Lower your standards, use my methods, and you cannot fail to succeed as Messiah." Perhaps he told Jesus that his way would bypass all the misunderstandings, hardships, sufferings, rejection, and the crucifixion.

Satan's third offer was also rejected by Jesus in terms taken from Deuteronomy 6:13. Jesus could make no compromise with evil. God must be his only resource. He must worship the God whose method is love, patience, humility, and suffering. Only suffering love can cast out the fear that tempts men to force and violence. In rejecting the earthly kingship, he accepted the lowly path of service and sacrifice. At the end of this path stood not a throne but a cross.

Jesus had fought his way through unacceptable alternatives to a clear vision of his messiahship. He never swerved from the truth brought into clear focus in the wilderness. It was clear to him that he must not buy men with bread, with magic, or with patriotic feeling. He must give himself.

> Jesus brushed aside all compromise and surrender and ordered Satan to go hence. . . . Death then faces Jesus at the very beginning. He must be willing to die for men before he can save men. So Jesus chose the high and stony path that led to Calvary, a lonely way and a weary one. His decision meant eternal conflict with Satan till he has conquered and the kingdoms of this world have become the kingdom of our Lord and of his Christ.[8]

1. Norval Geldenhuys, *Commentary on the Gospel of Luke* (Grand Rapids: William B. Eerdmans Publishing Co., 1951), p. 119.
2. *Assumption of Moses* in *The Apocrypha and Pseudepigrapha of the Old Testament,* translated by R. H. Charles (Oxford: At the Clarendon Press, 1913), p. 11.
3. Stagg, *The Broadman Bible Commentary, op. cit.* p. 91.
4. Suzanne De Dietrich, *Saint Matthew* (London: SCM Press, 1961), p. 23.
5. James S. Stewart, *The Life and Teaching of Jesus Christ* (Nashville: Abingdon Press, n.d.), p. 38.
6. Stagg, *New Testament Theology,* p. 46.
7. Stagg, *The Broadman Bible Commentary, op. cit.* p. 98.
8. A. T. Robertson, *Epochs in the Life of Christ* (New York: Charles Scribner's Sons, 1929), pp. 22–23.

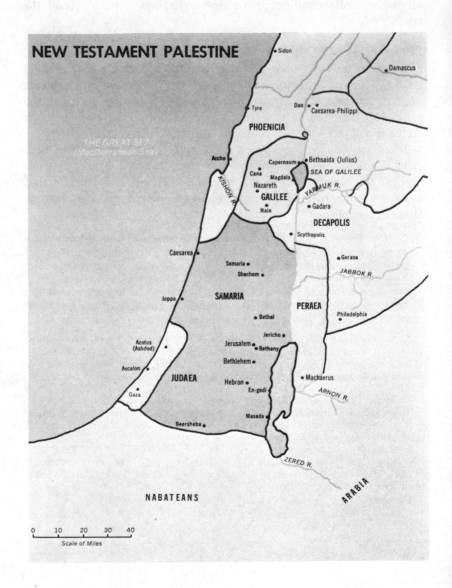

NEW TESTAMENT PALESTINE

Sidon

Damascus

Tyre

Dan

Caesarea-Philippi

PHOENICIA

THE GREAT SEA
(Mediterranean Sea)

Accho

Capernaum

Bethsaida (Julius)

Cana

Magdala

SEA OF GALILEE

Nazareth

KISHON R.

YARMUK R.

GALILEE

Nain

Gadara

DECAPOLIS

Scythopolis

Gerasa

Caesarea

Samaria

Shechem

JABBOK R.

Joppa

SAMARIA

PERAEA

Philadelphia

Bethel

Jericho

Azotus
(Ashdod)

Jerusalem

Bethany

Bethlehem

Ascalon

JUDAEA

Hebron

En-gedi

Machaerus

Gaza

ARNON R.

Masada

Beersheba

ZERED R.

ARABIA

NABATEANS

0   10   20   30   40

Scale of Miles

4

JESUS' PUBLIC MINISTRY
Part I
Judea (Early)

Introduction to the Public Ministry

IN THE preceding portion of this study, each section has had a unity of its own. Each topic admitted a certain logical compactness in its treatment. We now enter upon the narrative of the life and labors of Jesus, and the method of treatment will attempt chronological order. However, since the writers of the Gospels had little interest in chronology, it is difficult to establish an exact chronology for the events of Jesus' ministry. These writers did have a certain plan and structure which exhibited their conception of his ministry. Without overdue strain on the arrangement of materials in the Gospels, we will attempt a chronological study of Jesus' ministry. (The discussion of the ministry is divided into four parts to simplify study.)

According to the Synoptic Gospels, the public ministry of Jesus lasted about one and one-half years. These Gospels mention one visit to Jerusalem and one Passover. Their narratives suggest, though they do not assert, that Jesus' ministry was little more than one year long. However, the Fourth Gospel allows nearly four years for his ministry. John named three, possibly four, Passovers (2:13; 6:4; 11:55; possibly 5:1). He mentioned several visits to Jerusalem, involving a ministry of at least three full years. We shall attempt to fit the Synoptic

material into John's structure. We shall also rely upon the Gospel of
Mark for much of our relative chronology. In general, we shall follow
the sequence of events given in the *Harmony of the Gospels* by A. T.
Robertson.

It was once thought possible to so combine the four Gospels as
to retain the contents of each in its usual order and to produce by
the combination one harmonious and self-consistent narrative. This
plan frequently required the repetition of the same account, if there
chanced to be some slight variations in the narrative as given by the
different writers, or a difference in chronological arrangement. This
method was unnatural and has been abandoned. Our plan, following
Dr. Robertson, is to place opposite each other the different accounts
of the four Gospel writers whenever they described the same event
or reported substantially the same words of Jesus or of others. Passages which have no parallels will be inserted by themselves in what
seems to be their proper chronological position. We cannot emphasize
too strongly, however, that this process is followed to give order to
the treatment of the life of Christ and the sequence of events is not
beyond question.

The Gospel writers grouped some of their narrative topically, but
they also gave us a broad outline of how things happened. These arrangements are not without their problems because it is necessary,
from lack of distinct evidence, to resort to conjecture in many cases.
In David Smith's book, *Our Lord's Earthly Life,* pages xiii-xv, there
is a very helpful and widely-accepted arrangement:

INTRODUCTION

5 B.C. Birth of John the Baptist.........................March.
        Birth of our Lord ....August.
        Flight to Egypt ....October.
4 B.C. Return to Nazareth ....October.
A.D. 7 His first Passover ....April 9.
A.D. 26 His baptism ....January.
        Wedding at Cana ....Early March.

FIRST YEAR OF HIS MINISTRY

A.D. 26 Passover ....March 21.
        At Bethabara ....April and early May.
        Arrest of the Baptist ....Early in May.
        At Sychar ....Close of May.
        Settlement of Capernaum ....Beginning of June.
        Inland mission ....Close of June till late summer.

A.D. 27 In the cornfield .... March.

SECOND YEAR OF HIS MINISTRY

Passover .... April 9.
Ordination of the twelve.......................... May.
Mission in southern Galilee:........... May till early summer.
    Mary the Magdalene,
    visit to Nazareth,
    commission of the twelve,
    at Nain,
    deputation from the Baptist.

A.D. 28 The Baptist's execution .... January.
Retreat to Bethsaida-Julias .... February.
    feeding the five thousand,
    walking on the water.

THIRD YEAR OF HIS MINISTRY

(Passover .... March 29.)
In Phoenicia .... April–June.
In Decapolis .... June.
Retreat to Caesarea Philippi:.... Close of June to mid-August.
    Peter's confession,
    first announcement of Passion,
    the transfiguration,
    healing of epileptic child,
    second announcement of Passion.
Back in Capernaum................ Till near close of August.
Revisiting inland Galilee................ Till mid-September.
Passage through Samaria................... September 23.
At Jericho .... September 24.
At Bethany .... September 25.
Arrival at Jerusalem .... September 26.
Ministry at Jerusalem .... Till close of December.

A.D. 29 At Bethabara .... Probably till close of February.
Raising of Lazarus .... Close of February.
At Ephraim .... Till April 10.
At Jericho .... Over sabbath, April 11.
Supper at Bethany .... Sunday evening, April 12.

THE PASSION WEEK

Triumphal Entry .... Monday morning, April 13.*
Last Supper .... Evening of Thursday, April 16.
Crucifixion .... Friday, April 17.
Resurrection .... Sunday morning, April 19.
Ascension .... Thursday, May 29.

---

* Editorial note: This date is not undisputed. The discussion in chapter 8 will
refer to this event as having taken place on Sunday.

Jesus' Judean Ministry

Jesus' public ministry began soon after his temptation experiences in the wilderness. According to the Fourth Gospel, he was active in Judea and Jerusalem before John the Baptist was imprisoned (John 1:19 to 4:45). We cannot be sure of the duration of this ministry, but it probably lasted about one year.

THE FIRST DISCIPLES OF JESUS

The story of our Lord's ministry, as told in the Fourth Gospel, begins with John the Baptist recognizing Jesus as the Lamb of God. At this time two of John's disciples left him and followed Jesus. With these two, Andrew and probably John, Jesus commenced his work. Andrew brought his brother Simon Peter to Jesus. The next day Jesus found Philip and called him to join their company. Philip then invited Nathanael to come to Jesus. This band of five disciples, or learners, formed the nucleus for the followers of Jesus. (See John 1:35–51.)

JESUS PERFORMS HIS FIRST SIGN

With his five disciples Jesus left Judea and went to Cana in Galilee. Here, with his mother and his disciples, he helped to celebrate a marriage feast. The number of guests seems to have increased beyond expectation because of the presence of the disciples. When the wine supply failed, Jesus performed his first miracle by turning water into wine. (See John 2:1–11.) This, according to John, was the first of the signs which Jesus did and which manifest his glory.

James Stalker, in the late nineteenth century, said of this miracle:

> It was a manifestation of his glory intended specially for his new disciples, who, we are told, thenceforward believed on him, which means, no doubt, that they were fully convinced that he was the Messiah. It was intended also to strike the keynote of His ministry as altogether different from the Baptist's. John was an ascetic hermit, who fled from the abodes of men and called his hearers out into the wilderness. But Jesus had glad tidings to bring to men's hearth's; He was to mingle in their common life, and produce a happy revolution in their circumstances, which would be like turning the water of their life into wine.[1]

So it is that one of the main lessons which comes from Jesus' first sign is that there is a glory about Christ and it is available in abundant life for all who receive him.

After the miracle of Cana, Jesus, accompanied by his mother, his brothers, and his disciples, went to Capernaum, which became his headquarters during his subsequent labors in Galilee. Capernaum lay on the northwestern shore of the Sea of Galilee. During this brief visit to Capernaum Jesus seems neither to have performed miracles nor to have delivered any public discourses. (See John 2:12.) Since this became his headquarters, it is reasonable to assume that he spent some time arranging to settle there for a time.

JESUS CLEANSED THE TEMPLE

From Capernaum Jesus traveled to Jerusalem to participate in the celebration of the Passover. When he arrived, he found in the vast enclosure of the Temple a market for sacrificial animals and tables

for the exchange of money. Flocks and herds, buyers and sellers, money brokers, and dealers in pigeons and doves were congregated at the Temple. Apparently the demand for sacrifices for the altar had created a very lucrative trade. For convenience, the dealers had established themselves in the court of the Gentiles. Jesus made a scourge of small cords and drove the sheep and oxen out of the Temple. He also overthrew the tables of the money changers and commanded the sellers of doves to depart. This assumption of extraordinary authority was challenged by the Jews. Jesus refused to give any miraculous demonstration of his divine mission. The sign which he gave to them must have seemed evasive and meaningless: " 'Destroy this temple, and in three days I will raise it up' " (John 2:19). (See John 2:13–22.)

There is a problem related to properly dating the cleansing of the Temple. John places it here at the beginning of our Lord's ministry. All of the Synoptics tell of a cleansing at the outset of Passion Week just after the royal entry into Jerusalem. Matthew and Luke place it on the day of the entry, and Mark on the day following. (See Matt. 21:12; Mark 11:15; Luke 19:45.)

In an attempt to solve this problem, we must remember first of all that the writers of the Synoptic Gospels did not attempt to harmonize their accounts chronologically. We must note also that John was even less interested in chronology, for his was primarily a theological Gospel. But we need to take into account also that it is quite possible that there were two Temple cleansings—one at the outset of Jesus' ministry and one at the close. Of this we can be certain: "That Jesus did register such protests against the abuses of the Temple is solidly based on all four Gospels. That he spoke of a true temple, himself and his church, that would replace the 'one made with hands' is featured by John (2:19) and constituted a major charge at his trial (26:61; Mark 14:58; cf. Eph. 2:18ff.)." [2]

The purification of the Temple undoubtedly caused great excitement in Jerusalem. There is reason to believe that Jesus soon became the object of general curiosity. Some persons of the highest rank felt attracted to him. Such a man was the Pharisee Nicodemus, a ruler and a teacher of Israel. He recognized Jesus as a teacher sent from God and came to him at night and addressed him with patronizing courtesy and sincerity. Jesus, knowing what was in the Pharisee's heart (John 2:25), proceeded at once to answer his thoughts rather than his words: " 'Truly, truly, I say to you, unless one is born again [or begotten from above], he cannot see the kingdom of God' " (John 3:3). Jesus made it clear that what is begotten bears the nature of that which begat it. The *flesh* cannot generate a life which is spiritual and immortal. Man cannot originate the spiritual life in himself; it must come from God. This life is a new creation from heaven. (See John 2:23 to 3:21.)

JESUS PRAISED BY JOHN THE BAPTIST

Jesus probably left Jerusalem soon after the close of the Passover week and went to the rural district of Judea, not far from the border of Samaria. It was a place of much water and, therefore, convenient for baptizing. Some of John's disciples learned with some irritation that Jesus was preaching and baptizing in the neighborhood. (The reading in John 4:2 leads us to conclude that the actual baptizing was being done by the disciples in the name of Jesus.) John's disciples came to him with the complaint. John reassured them that no man could go beyond the limits of his commission from God. (See John 3:22–36.)

JESUS' VISIT WITH THE SAMARITAN WOMAN

The growing enthusiasm of the common people who came in large numbers to Jesus' baptism alarmed the Pharisees. Aware that a longer stay in Judea would bring conflict with them, Jesus was determined to return to Galilee. The nearest and most practicable route was through Samaria. If John used Roman time, Jesus arrived at Jacob's Well about 6:00 P.M. But more than likely he reckoned time as it is done elsewhere in the Gospels. This would have placed the encounter at hot midday, a most unusual time for someone to come to draw water.

The well of Sychar is still in existence and is frequently visited by travelers. Here Jesus sat down to rest, while the disciples went into the village to buy food. Soon after their departure, a Samaritan woman approached the place with her waterpot. Jesus engaged her in conversation, drawing a comparison between the water of Jacob's Well and that living water which he alone could give. The Samaritan woman was impressed with Jesus and attempted to engage him in theological debate, but Jesus held her to the point. Then he made clear to her the highest knowledge he had of God and worship. He told her plainly that he was the Messiah, a fact he did not reveal to Nicodemus. Jesus' patience and understanding led to the conversion of the woman and many others. "The soul of Jesus fed on this blessed fruitage. He cared naught for food and water now. The will of God was enough. He was now becoming the Saviour of the World, for even Samaritans can be saved." [3]

The people from the village came out and entreated Jesus to visit
them. According to their request Jesus remained with them two days.
(See John 4:1–42.) We do not know what transpired during those
brief days, but the result was that many more believed. They had
more than the woman's testimony. They encountered the Master himself.

1. James Stalker, *Life of Christ* (New York: Fleming H. Revell Company,
1891), p. 50.
2. Stagg, *The Broadman Bible Commentary, op. cit.,* p. 200.
3. Robertson, *op. cit.,* p. 40.

5

JESUS' PUBLIC MINISTRY
Part 2
Galilee

SOON AFTER John the Baptist was arrested, Jesus came into Galilee preaching the gospel of God, saying: "The time is fulfilled, and the kingdom of God is at hand; repent and believe in the gospel" (Mark 1:15; Matt. 4:17; Luke 4:14–15). To believe in the gospel is here to acknowledge the announcement of the near approach of the kingdom of God and to conduct oneself accordingly. For about eighteen months Jesus engaged in a ministry of preaching, teaching, and healing in Galilee. It was a period of intense activity. It will not be possible for us to follow in detail the events during this phase of his ministry. We will attempt to follow only the main current of the story and to interpret these events.

The Beginning of the Galilean Ministry

HEALING

Probably one of the first events recorded during this period was the healing of a nobleman's son of Capernaum while Jesus was in Cana. This sign demonstrated Jesus' power over both time and space. He was able to heal immediately and at a distance. The performance of this sign showed that Jesus was the Son of God. (See John 4:46–54.)

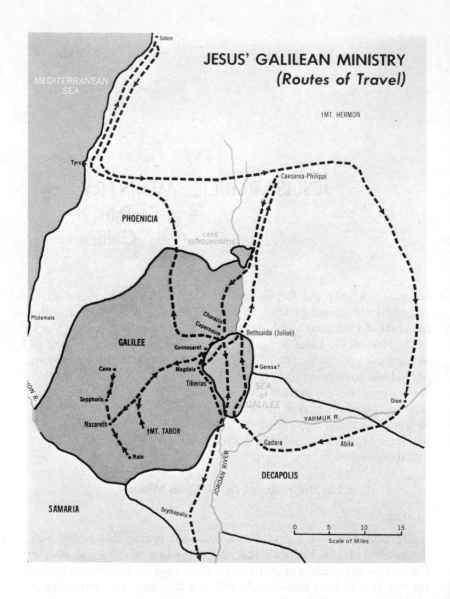

JESUS' GALILEAN MINISTRY
(Routes of Travel)

†MT. HERMON

MEDITERRANEAN SEA

Sidon

Tyre

PHOENICIA

LAKE SEMECHONITIS

Caesarea-Philippi

Ptolemais

Chorazin
Capernaum

Bethsaida (Julius)

GALILEE

Gennesaret

Cana

Magdala

Geresa?

Sepphoris

Tiberias

SEA of GALILEE

Dion

ON R.

Nazareth

†MT. TABOR

YARMUK R.

Nain

Gadara

Abila

JORDAN RIVER

DECAPOLIS

SAMARIA

Scythopolis

0   5   10   15
Scale of Miles

UNWELCOME INTERPRETER

Jesus went to Nazareth, the village where he had been brought up. On the sabbath he attended synagogue worship. An opportunity was given to him to read the lesson from the Prophets. This does not imply that there had not been the usual service, including a reading from the Law. He unrolled the scroll of Isaiah until he came to what we call the sixty-first chapter. He then stood up and read the first verse and part of the second.

THE SPIRIT OF THE LORD IS UPON ME,
BECAUSE HE ANOINTED ME TO PREACH THE GOSPEL TO THE POOR.
HE HAS SENT ME TO PROCLAIM RELEASE TO THE CAPTIVES,
AND RECOVERY OF SIGHT TO THE BLIND,
TO SET FREE THOSE WHO ARE DOWNTRODDEN,
TO PROCLAIM THE FAVORABLE YEAR OF THE LORD.

—Luke 4:18–19

When Jesus finished reading these brief words, he rolled up the volume, gave it to the servant of the synagogue, and sat down in the speaker's seat. Since the reading was almost certainly in Hebrew, it was necessary to give the sense of it in the popular Aramaic speech. Jesus then discussed the passage he had read and told his audience that it had been then and there fulfilled. He announced the near coming of the kingdom of God, the establishment of which would deliver believers from a bondage worse than that of the Babylonian exile.

At first Jesus' hearers were captivated. For the moment their prejudices were overcome, and they listened with delight to their neighbor. But when they began to realize that he claimed to be the divine messenger referred to in the Scripture passage which he had just read, there was a reaction of jealousy and spite. When Jesus perceived the altered tone of feelings in the assembly, he said: " 'No doubt you will quote this proverb to Me, "Physician, heal yourself; whatever we heard was done at Capernaum, do here in your home town as well" ' " (Luke 4:23). The meaning of this proverb was something like this: "Be somebody yourself before assuming to teach us. Make good your lofty claims by doing something." In order to teach that God's helpfulness is available wherever there is faith to receive it, regardless of class or race, Jesus then recalled the stories of Elijah and Elisha. His discourse enraged the people of Nazareth, and they attempted to kill him. There is nothing in the Gospel accounts to indicate how Jesus escaped from the mob which apparently had him completely in its power. (See Luke 4:16–31.)

The thing which most angered the people of Nazareth was Jesus' indication that there had been times in Israel's history when God's goodness had been shown to and through people who had no particular place in orthodoxy. This attitude is not unlike that sometimes displayed in the church today. We often want to avoid the hard demands of our commission. Too often the congregation sees its business as the nurturing of its own life. The people of Nazareth lost their opportunity when they could not accept the all-inclusiveness of our Lord's ministry.

ON TO CAPERNAUM

After Jesus was rejected in Nazareth, he went to Capernaum, a trading city on the northwest shore of the Lake of Galilee, seven hundred feet below sea level. This was to be his residence during the rest of his Galilean ministry. When Matthew spoke of Capernaum as being "in the region of Zebulun and Naphtali," he did not mean that this region was at that time inhabited by these two tribes. The tribes are mentioned because of the reference to them in the quotation from Isaiah 9:1–2. Isaiah wrote about a threatened invasion from Assyria in the first half of the eighth century B.C. When the invasion came, the Assyrians were harsh and cruel. Since the invasion was most difficult for these two provinces, the fact that Jesus first preached there led Matthew to look upon this enlightenment of the people as the real fulfilment of the prophecy. (See Matt. 4:13–16.)

On one occasion, as Jesus was passing along the shore of the lake, the multitude so pressed upon him that it prevented his speaking to them effectively. Seeing Simon's boat, he entered it and asked that the boat be moved out a little from the land. There Jesus sat and taught the multitude. After he had finished his discourse, he directed Simon to go to deeper water and let down the nets. As an experienced fisherman, Peter knew that the conditions did not look promising. However, he obeyed and caught a multitude of fish. Jesus once more called Simon and his brother Andrew and John and his brother James to forsake their fishing business and to follow him. The Gospel writers indicated that Jesus' first disciples were all Galileans. (See Mark 1: 16–20; Matt. 4:18–22; Luke 5:1–11.)

In a synagogue on a sabbath day as Jesus was teaching, he healed a man who was possessed by an evil spirit. This seems to have been the first such cure that he had performed. The healing excited surprise in the beholders not so much because of the remarkable cure effected as because of the novelty and simplicity of the method employed. There were plenty of Jewish exorcists who could cast out evil spirits as Jesus himself recognized (Matt. 12:27). These exorcists did their work with painful effort, making use of magical rites, while Jesus "cast out the spirits with a word" (Matt. 8:16). The people who had witnessed the conflict and victory were filled with amazement. The contrast between the teaching of Jesus and that of the scribes consisted in his speaking out of his own conviction of truth, while they cited the authority of others in support of their statements. Jesus was his own sufficient authority. (See Mark 1:21–28; Luke 4:31–37.)

The importance of this incident seems to have been in Jesus' affirmation that God's kingdom had come. The point of the casting out of demons is to indicate that the kingdom of God was now overcoming the kingdom of Satan. Though final "bringing in" of the kingdom is future, it was already being realized in Jesus.

After the synagogue service, Jesus, accompanied by his other disciples, went to the house of Simon and Andrew who lived in Capernaum. Finding Simon's mother-in-law sick of a fever, he took her by the hand and lifted her up, and the fever left her. The fact that she was able at once to attend to household duties indicated the completeness of her recovery. Soon Simon's home became the center of interest for many sick people, and after sunset they were brought there for Jesus to heal them. This is one of the most beautiful scenes in all of our Lord's ministry. (See Mark 1:29–34; Matt. 8:14–17; Luke 4:38–41.)

Jesus' First Tour of Galilee with the Four Fishermen

Long before dawn Jesus left Simon's house and went to a solitary desert place to pray. While he was thus engaged in prayer, the multitude thronged Simon's house looking for Jesus. Simon led them to him. Fearing that Jesus was about to leave them, the multitude entreated him to remain in Capernaum. However, Jesus declared that his mission required him to preach the good news of the kingdom of God to other cities and villages. So, without returning to Capernaum, he entered upon his first preaching mission in Galilee. This tour appears to have been quite extensive, evidently lasting for several months. Jesus went from village to village of that densely-populated region teaching in the synagogues and performing cures. (See Mark 1:35–39; Matt. 4:23–25; Luke 4:42–44.)

COMPASSIONATE HEALER

While Jesus was passing through one of the cities (probably on this first tour), a leper came to him pleading for help. Leprosy was not only a troublesome disease but, according to the law, disqualified one from fellowship with his fellowmen and especially from joining them in the religious services of the Temple (Lev. 13–14).

Jesus, moved with compassion, put forth his hand and touched the leprous man (in violation of the ceremonial law, Lev. 13:46) and cured him. Instead of receiving defilement, he imparted cleansing. Jesus had no hesitation about disregarding regulations which interfered with his carrying out God's commission. However, he did not encourage laxity in observance of the law. Only a priest could officially declare a leper clean, and a cure was not complete until the leper was removed from Levitical quarantine. The cured man's disobedience about secrecy brought the first phase of Jesus' ministry to an end in an embarrassing popularity. He withdrew to the desert to pray. (See Mark 1:40–45; Matt. 8:2–4; Luke 5:12–16.)

RETURN TO CAPERNAUM

After having completed his first missionary circuit, our Lord returned to Capernaum. His return excited great interest and enthusiasm. Many people gathered around him—scribes, Pharisees, doctors of the law, and the sick. The friends of a certain paralytic resolved to carry him on his bed to Jesus. When they approached the house where Jesus was teaching, they found that it was impossible to enter because of the multitude. Instead of giving up their resolve, they ascended to the flat roof of the house and made an opening in the roof through which to let the sick man down where Jesus was. Jesus addressed the paralytic, "My son, your sins are forgiven" (Mark 2:5). These words do not imply that all illness is caused by sin, but only that this particular ailment had a mental or spiritual cause.

It was one of the fundamental conceptions of Jewish theology that not only bodily suffering and disease but all calamities were the divinely-ordained punishment for sin. The Jews further believed that the removal of the penalty implied the forgiveness of the offense for which it had been imposed. Some of the scribes and Pharisees were scandalized at Jesus' language. They accused him of blasphemy; however, he declared that as Son of man, he had received from God authority to cure bodies and spirits (the whole man). He healed the paralytic and showed that it was as easy for him to do the healing deed as to say the forgiving word. The people were amazed in the presence of what they considered a wonderful manifestation of divine providence, and some of them glorified God. (See Mark 2:1–12; Matt. 9:1–8; Luke 5:17–26.)

This authority to forgive sins which Jesus claimed for himself is the basic issue in this story. This was at the root of the conflict which was shaping up between Jesus and the scribes. The scribes resented his daring to claim the power to forgive which in their minds belonged only to God. But these same scribes taught that sin had to be forgiven before the penalty (in this case, paralysis) could be lifted. That this man was healed should have proven that Jesus' claims were valid.

In this incident Jesus called himself the Son of man, his favorite self-designation. In Mark's use of the term there is a strong relationship to the suffering that Christ would experience. Barclay has written: "He knew himself the divine Son of Man whose triumph was sure; he knew himself the Suffering Servant for whom the cross was the only and the chosen way. As the Servant of the Lord he was to suffer for men; as the Son of Man he must in the end be the King of men. The Son of Man is the title which contains within itself the shame and the glory of Jesus Christ." [1] (See pp. 173–75 in chap. 9 for a fuller discussion of this title.)

Jesus' Early Controversy with the Pharisees

As Jesus' popularity with the common people developed, there also developed a hostility toward him among the religious leadership, especially the Pharisees. They recognized in Jesus a threat to all they held dear. During his early ministry in Galilee, several incidents occurred which brought him into collision with these leaders.

TO FAST OR NOT TO FAST

There were some Jews who accepted employment with the Roman government as tax collectors. These men were banned from the synagogue and were treated by the Jews as the dregs of society. Jesus called one of these tax collectors, Matthew or Levi, to be one of his disciples. Matthew not only accepted Jesus' call but gave a feast for Jesus and invited other tax collectors. Jesus' association with these outcasts exasperated the Pharisees. He replied to their criticism of him for associating with persons of ill-repute with a proverb familiar to Jews and Greeks: "Physicians are accustomed to associate with the sick." Jesus also quoted from Hosea 6:6: "I desired mercy, and not sacrifice" (KJV). As applied by Jesus to the Pharisees, "sacrifice" stood for the legalistic observance of the ceremonial laws, for which they were distinguished. (See Mark 2:13–17; Matt. 9:9–13; Luke 5:27–32.)

The Pharisees observed the regular public fasts and, in addition, fasted twice each week. Because Jesus did not require his disciples to fast, he was indirectly charged with a breach of the law. He defended his disciples on the ground that they were guests at the banquet of the messianic age. The members of a wedding party were exempt from fasting during the celebration; so Jesus claimed this exemption for his disciples. He was celebrating with them the marriage supper of the Lamb!

Jesus seldom said anything at all about fasting. When he did so, it was to condemn its practice in the spirit of religious asceticism. Jesus here laid down the principle that fasting is only appropriate as the natural manifestation of sorrow and grief. By the use of the figures of patching an old garment with new, unshrunk cloth and the unfermented juice in the old wineskins, Jesus brought out more clearly that his teaching was not to be cramped within the narrow limits of the Jewish tradition. (See Mark 2:18–22; Matt. 9:14–17; Luke 5:33–39.)

During his early Galilean ministry, Jesus attended a feast (probably a Passover) in Jerusalem. This story in some ways resembles the story of the paralytic in Mark 2:1–12. Many scholars feel that the events in this chapter of John actually follow those in John 6. If this be the case, then the feast referred to would have been the Passover. If, however, chapter 5 is in its correct position, "the feast of the Jews" would be the Feast of Tabernacles or Pentecost.

WHAT ABOUT THE SABBATH?

While the Lord was in the city, he healed a lame man on a sabbath day, involving himself in an extended controversy with the leaders. They charged him with breaking the Law by healing on a sabbath and

also teaching others to desecrate the sabbath. They were filled with rage and charged Jesus in public with open and flagrant violation of the law. (See John 5:1–47.)

Another incident soon occurred which gave the Pharisees another opportunity to question Jesus' claim to higher religious views. Passing one sabbath day through a wheat field, Jesus' disciples plucked the grain, separated it from the chaff, and ate it. The Pharisees had identified such acts as labors which were prohibited on the sabbath day. It was not the law, but the law as interpreted by tradition, which condemned these acts. When Christ was told of their deed, he knew that the reproof was intended for him rather than the disciples. He defended himself by urging the superiority of a free obedience to the spirit of the law over a slavish conformity to its letter. He did not attempt the practically impossible by trying to show his critics that their traditions had no binding force. Instead, he asserted their fundamental misconception of the very purpose of the sabbath. He referred to the example of David. Only the priests were allowed to eat the bread of the Presence. However, David entered the house of God (the tabernacle) and, by permission of the priest, took for himself and his companions the loaves which had been consecrated to the Lord (1 Sam. 21:1–6). On this occasion necessity was recognized as being above ritual. (See Mark 2:23–28; Matt. 12:1–8; Luke 6:1–5.)

The priests also performed certain labor on the sabbath in discharge of their official duties; the law recognized the necessity and legitimacy of this labor (Num. 28:9–10). Jesus was placing the new life of the spirit above the old worship of the letter of the law. He concluded his declaration of his lordship over the sabbath by affirming that the sabbath was set apart for rest solely for the good of man.

The last illustration which the Gospel writers gave of Jesus' controversy with the leaders during his early Galilean ministry was the healing of a man with a withered hand. In this incident Jesus took the initiative by asking his adversaries a question: " 'Is it lawful on the Sabbath to do good, or to do evil, to save a life, or to destroy it?' " (Luke 6:9). The answer to the question is obvious: It is always right, on any day, to do good and to save life. With Jesus not to do was to undo. Not to cure the man would be to leave him to suffer. When, at the command of Jesus, the man stretched forth his hand, the Pharisees were so incensed with Jesus that they went out and took counsel with the Herodians how they might destroy him. (See Mark 3:1–6; Matt. 12:9–14; Luke 6:6–11.)

> Interest in this story is centered in three points. The first is, of course, the healing of the unfortunate man. The second is more focal: Jesus taught that it is right to do good on the sabbath. The third, however, is the chief emphasis. Opposition to Jesus, so strong as to put his life into jeopardy, came because of men's **hardness of heart.** They were blinded to the good news; they were bound hopelessly captive in the ruts of their own minds and in the hardness and evil of their own hearts.[2]

Jesus Chose the Twelve and Delivered the Sermon on the Mount

Jesus, knowing that the Pharisees and Herodians had conspired to destroy him, withdrew to the sea. Here the multitudes came to him from all regions of Palestine. Again he used a boat as a pulpit to speak to the people on the shore. (See Mark 3:7–12; Matt. 12:15–21.)

It had become apparent that Jesus could no longer personally instruct all who came to him. He could not move about fast enough to heal all the sick or minister to all the needy. After a night of prayer, he selected the twelve disciples who were to be his authorized ministers. He attached them to himself, that he might enjoy their companionship and that they might share with him his labors of teaching and healing. Not only did he select these men to do this special work, but to inaugurate the new Israel. While the selection of just twelve may have been a coincidence, it is much more likely that it was because that was the number of the Jewish tribes. These twelve men were to be witnesses of Jesus' life, death, resurrection, and ascension. Under their care the new Israel (church) would develop. (See Mark 3:13–19; Luke 6: 12–16.)

After a whole night in prayer, the selection of the twelve was completed. They were to teach and work miracles in the name of Christ. They needed special instruction for their work. They needed to be instructed in the fundamental principles of the way of life they were to profess and propagate. This instruction is recorded chiefly in what is called the "Sermon on the Mount." (See Matt. 5–7; Luke 6:17–49.) Jesus was not enunciating a general code of ethics. He was instructing the disciples as to what God would do in them and through them as Christ's servants. Reading Matthew's introduction, one gets the impression that Jesus went up into the mountain for the purpose of freeing himself from the multitudes. He sat down, after the custom of Jewish teachers, and his disciples gathered around him. The presence of more than the twelve is not, however, excluded. Here on a level place on a mountain Jesus addressed his disciples (Matt. 5:1–2; Luke 6:17). This sermon may be outlined as follows:

I. The character of the kingdom man (Matt. 5:1–9; Luke 6:20–21).

II. The influence of the kingdom man (Matt. 5:10–16; Luke 6:22–26).

III. The kingdom man fulfils the design of the Law and the Prophets (Matt. 5:17 to 6:18; Luke 6:27–30,32–36).

   1. Jesus himself fulfilled the Law and the Prophets (Matt. 5:17–19).

   2. Jesus enables kingdom men to abstain from evil deeds (five illustrations—murder, impurity, perjury, retaliation, and hate, Matt. 5:20–48).

   3. Jesus keeps kingdom men from doing good deeds in an evil way (three illustrations—almsgiving, prayer, and fasting, Matt. 6:1–18).

IV. The reign of heaven demands an undivided devotion to God

and a freedom from anxiety born of trust in his providence (Matt. 6:19–34).
V. Judgment of kingdom righteousness in others and in self (Matt. 7:1–12; Luke 6:37–42).
VI. Dangers to the kingdom of man's righteousness (Matt. 7:13–23; Luke 6:43–45).
1. Lack of effort (Matt. 7:13–14).
2. False prophet (Matt. 7:15–23; Luke 6:43–45).
VII. Obedience to the teaching of Jesus is the only true foundation for the life of the kingdom man (Matt. 7:24–27; Luke 6:46–49).

Frank Stagg has said concerning the Sermon on the Mount that the great danger is that less than justice be done to either the awesome demands or the merciful gifts set forth by Jesus in this set of teachings. Dr. Stagg went on to say:

Our proposal is that the Sermon on the Mount is best understood when seen in its setting, seen as God's ultimate and absolute demand addressed to sinners who are also offered acceptance upon the basis of mercy and forgiveness. The demands are not to be toned down or explained away, not even the awesome, "You, therefore, must be perfect, as your heavenly Father is perfect" (5:48). God's claims, i.e., the demands of the kingdom (reign) of God as it confronts us in Christ (anointed to rule), are ultimate and absolute. They are ultimate in that they are final. They are absolute in the sense that God does not divide his authoriy with any other. To enter into the kingdom of God is to acknowledge his right to rule as full and final.

This does not mean that any person, except Jesus, has lived up to this demand. But it does mean that to be a Christian is to live under that claim, however far he falls short of living up to it. God does not ask for 50 percent or 99 percent obedience. His will is that we be perfect.[3]

Jesus Resumed His Ministry

CENTURION'S SERVANT AND A WIDOW'S SON

After finishing his discourse to the disciples, Jesus returned to Capernaum. One of the officers of the garrison in the city, a man esteemed by both Jews and Gentiles, appealed to Jesus for help. His favorite servant was at the point of death.

Two circumstances are especially to be noted. The hesitation of the centurion about asking Jesus to his house indicated a knowledge of and consideration for the Jewish unwillingness to run the risk of ceremonial defilement by closely associating with heathen. Also, the centurion believed that Jesus was able to cure at a distance. The centurion said that if he, a mere soldier acting under the direction of a higher authority, could send subordinates to execute his commands, certainly Jesus had power to cure without himself going into the presence of the sufferer. Not only was the servant healed, but the highest praise of a human being ever uttered by Jesus was addressed to this Gentile. Among other things, this story reflects Jesus' attitude toward the Gentiles and anticipates his mission to them. The incident illustrates for us once again the compassion our Lord had for all persons in need. The attitude of the centurion helps point up the requirements for receiving blessings from Jesus. He had great humility and a wholehearted faith in the Lord Jesus. (See Matt. 8:5–13; Luke 7:1–10.)

Probably the day after healing the centurion's servant, Jesus and many of his disciples walked from Capernaum to Nain. Nain appears to have been a small village in northern Galilee situated on the slope of Little Hermon. (It probably still exists under the name of Nein.) This is the only mention of it in the Bible. As the group approached the village after their eight-hour journey, they met a funeral procession. The dead man was the only son of his widowed mother. Jesus had compassion on her, touched the open coffin, and delivered her son to her. (See Luke 7:11–17.)

> In this story the Saviour's sympathy with the sorrowing and His absolute divine power over the invisible spirit-world are gloriously revealed. We see Him here as the loving Comforter, the Victor over death, and the Reuniter of separated dear ones. What He did here for the widowed mother and son He will one day do for all the faithful in a perfect and final form. He will bring full comfort. He will raise all His people in incorruptibility.[4]

A QUESTION FROM JOHN THE BAPTIST

At this point in Jesus' ministry, John the Baptist was confined to the fortress of Machaerus because he had reproved Herod Antipas for incest and adultery. There is no doubt that John expected the speedy establishment of the kingdom of God. As he lay in his prison, he expected to receive news that Jesus had commenced his reign; but this news did not come. John sent messengers to Jesus and inquired about his identity. (See Matt. 11:2–19; Luke 7:18–35.)

John's inquiry could not be answered by a simple yes or no, since Jesus both was and was not "the coming one." The messianic ideas of Jesus were different from those of John, and Jesus chose to leave it to the Baptist to frame an opinion from the nature of the work in which he was engaged. This work, as John's disciples saw it and as Jesus directed them to report it, was one of human helpfulness in deed and speech. Jesus' message to John indicated that God's promises to him had already come true, though not in the way he had expected.

In an extended discourse Jesus reproached the unrepentant lake cities for their unbelief. The seacoast cities of Tyre and Sidon had an especially bad reputation among the Jews. Yet Jesus declared that in these heathen cities the truth of the gospel would receive a heartier welcome than was given to it in Galilee. When Jesus said that Capernaum, instead of being exalted to heaven, "shall descend to Hades" (Matt. 11:23), he predicted the utter ruin of the city. We are reminded here that the extent of judgment is related to the extent of privilege. One is held accountable only for those opportunities which have come within his grasp—no more, no less. These cities had seen an abundance of Jesus' mighty works, but they had willfully rejected him.

How great was their condemnation in unbelief! (See Matt. 11:20–30.)

The things which had been concealed from the wise men of the world and revealed to those who were but "babes" were the mysteries of the kingdom of heaven. Jesus invited all "who are weary and heavy laden" to accept the relief which he offered. The burdens which his countrymen bore were those placed upon them by the ceremonial and traditional law. The details of these laws were so numerous that even life itself had come to be almost a burden.

Jesus was entirely free from prejudice. He freely mingled with all classes of society, so it was not unusual that the Lord should receive and accept an invitation from Simon the Pharisee. How many others were invited we are not told, but probably several of Jesus' disciples were included. Simon seems to have thought that for this carpenter and his peasant followers, some points of etiquette could be omitted. No servant appeared to wash Jesus' feet or to anoint his head, and he noted the omission. While the feast was in progress, a woman came into the room and stood behind Jesus. She burst into tears and wiped his feet with her hair. She anointed Jesus' feet with expensive ointment. She was a woman of the city, and a "sinner." (There is no reason whatever for supposing that this woman was Mary Magdalene, spoken of in Luke 8:2 as having been cured of demonism by Jesus.) Jesus did not repel her, but Simon watched with a frown. Evidently he knew the history of this woman. Jesus told his host a parable of two debtors and, by it, drew from him the admission that a great love can be the product of a great forgiveness. (See Luke 7:36–50.)

Jesus' Second Tour of Galilee

Jesus and the twelve and certain women which had been healed of infirmities made a tour of Galilee. The route followed or the time involved is not given. (See Luke 8:1–3.)

IN LEAGUE WITH SATAN?

One of the first incidents recorded on this tour was the healing of a blind and dumb demoniac. The cure was so remarkable that the people regarded it as a wonderful miracle. It was so remarkable that Jesus' enemies were unable to deny it; yet, they determined not to admit their wonder at the miracle. They solved the problem not by denying it but by concluding that Jesus was in league with the kingdom of evil and that this miracle was performed with the aid of evil spirits. Jesus addressed them in a discourse of mingled argumentation, reproof, and warning. He showed them the contradictory character of their accusation. It was absurd to suppose that Satan would destroy his own work. Jesus said that if the Holy Spirit convinced a person of truth and that person rejected and opposed it, he had blasphemed against the Spirit. (See Mark 3:19–30; Matt. 12:22–45.)

By blasphemy, Jesus meant that those who had maliciously charged him with being in collusion with the prince of the demons, deliberately calling good evil and evil good, had a hardness of heart not likely to yield to any conviction of the Holy Spirit (Isa. 5:20). Jesus wanted to make still more clear the nature of their guilt, as well as to render it impossible for them to charge his severe language to personal animosity. So he declared that their blasphemy was not in their evil-speaking against him as the Son of man but their insult to the divine Spirit of truth.

> To speak against the Son of man is forgivable, but to speak against the Holy Spirit is not. Possibly Jesus means that the problem is not with himself, *the Son of man;* for he is ever ready to forgive. . . . But to speak against the Holy Spirit, as the Pharisees have done in a wilful act of disbelief and disobedience, is to deny oneself his only hope. It is for one to cut himself off from the one who alone can lead him to repentance.[5]

Certain of the scribes and Pharisees asked Jesus for a sign, but he refused to give it. The sign which was desired must have been something of a more remarkable character than the cures which Jesus had already performed. The scribes and Pharisees did not recognize these cures as furnishing evidence of a divine mission, since almost any rabbi could cure some kinds of disease. Jesus declared that they already had their sign in the story of Jonah; he would give no other.

GROWING OPPOSITION

Jesus had now reached a great crisis in his ministry. He had broken with the powerful sect of the Pharisees whose influence with the people was almost unlimited. It is evident that among those who had been faithful to Jesus there was a strong tendency to doubt or to misunderstand him. His own "friends" or relatives yielded to fear if not to unbelief (Mark 3:21). When his mother and brothers came and called him, he declared that his disciples were his relatives in a truer and deeper sense than those who were such only after the flesh. (See Mark 3:31–35; Matt. 12:46–50; Luke 8:19–21.)

As the opposition to his ministry increased, Jesus began to use parables to carry his teachings. When the disciples asked Jesus his reason for using the storytelling method, he said that the people would not understand his teaching if he spoke to them in any other way. His reply was couched in language not to be understood without reference to certain Hebrew ideas and forms of speech. On the face of it, the Master Teacher seemed to be saying that the purpose of his public teaching was to prevent those who heard from understanding his meaning. Not so, for his limited purpose was to enlighten the minds of his hearers to the extent to which they were capable of comprehending the nature of his mission. If he had made clear to them in the beginning how wrong was their concept of the messianic kingdom, they would not have been willing to listen to him at all. He sought to implant in their minds the fundamental idea that the divine kingdom was to be established by a slow process of growth. To lead his followers to recognize the operation of natural law in the spiritual realm, he used stories from the ordinary workings of nature (the sower and the seed). The people were not yet aware that the kingdom of heaven was primarily a kingdom of the Spirit. This transformation of their thoughts necessitated a process of slow growth. (See Mark 4:1–34; Matt. 13:1–53; Luke 8:4–18.)

CALMING, RESTORING, HEALING

Later, probably to get away from the crowds, Jesus and his disciples got into the boat to cross the lake. Jesus no doubt was weary from the press of the crowds as he taught, so he fell asleep in the boat. While our Lord slept peacefully, a great storm blew up, and the disciples panicked. They immediately awakened Jesus and asked if he cared that they were about to drown. Jesus simply spoke and the storm was stilled. This is the first time that we are told of Jesus' power over inanimate nature. However, faith is the point of this incident. Jesus' ability to sleep calmly while the boat was being swamped stands in contrast to the fear and the lack of faith shown by the disciples.

When Jesus had stilled the waves and shown his disciples that he is Lord of nature also, the group came to the other side of the lake and ran into another type of storm. This storm was raging inside the spirit of one miserable man who ran naked and wild among the tombs. He was a terror to himself and to all who knew him. As our Lord had calmed the waters of the lake, so he stilled the troubled man when he ordered the evil spirits to leave him. (See Mark 4:35 to 5:20; Matt. 8:18,23–34; Luke 8:23–39.)

There are many problems related to the details of this story, but the major teachings are clear. Jesus is not only Lord of the sea but of the spirit of man also. A. T. Robertson, renowned New Testament scholar, has written helpfully about demoniacs:

> The mystery of the demonical possessions never appears darker than in this incident. The destruction of the swine added to the ravings of the man make a dreadful background in the twilight on this heathen shore. The mystery of evil is not relieved by the denial of the devil and demons. The presence of disease here may or may not be in conjunction with the power of the evil one. The assumption that Jesus was merely accommodating himself to custom in speaking of demons cannot solve all the difficulties concerning the demon possession. As previously said, we know too little about psychic matters to say the final word here. But let us at least rejoice that Jesus is master over both sin and disease. He will sometimes bless those who do not appreciate it. The people of the community begged Jesus to leave their shores for good, but the picture of the man, once so wild, sitting clothed, in his right mind, is a comfort to those who battle with sin in country or in city. Here, where no Pharisees are to molest, Jesus tells the man to go to his house and tell what great things God has done for him.[6]

Having met with an unfavorable reception among the Gerasenes, Jesus returned across the lake toward Capernaum. When he reached the western shore, he found the crowd waiting for him. A ruler of the synagogue, Jairus, petitioned Jesus to come to his home and restore his daughter. On the way to the home of Jairus, Jesus performed a cure upon a woman who pressed forward through the crowd to touch his garments. After this delay, he approached Jairus' home. He allowed only Peter, James, and John to enter the house with him. This was the first time these three apostles had been singled out as having the special confidence of Jesus. Jesus put the noisy multitude out of the house and then raised the dead child. As he was returning from the house of Jairus, he healed two blind men and a dumb demoniac. (See Mark 5:21–43; Matt. 9:18–34; Luke 8:40–56.)

BACK TO NAZARETH

Before Jesus began his last tour of Galilee, he went again to Nazareth. Again the results were disappointing. There he experienced afresh the truth of the proverb that "a prophet has no honor in his own country" (John 4:44).

The Gospel writers have given us more information about the family of Jesus in this account of his visit to Nazareth than we find anywhere else in the New Testament. We have learned from Mark that Jesus was a carpenter and from Matthew that he was a son of a carpenter. The names of Jesus' four brothers are given (James, Joses, Simon, and Judas), and sisters are also mentioned. The fact that Jesus still frequented the sabbath assembly and even took an active part in the conduct of its services shows that he was not at that time estranged from the worship of the synagogue and that he continued to reflect the piety of a devout Jew. (See Mark 6:1–6; Matt. 13:54–58.)

Jesus' Third Tour of Galilee

Moving among the people of Galilee, Jesus was impressed as never before with their great spiritual need. There was no evidence that the people were going to receive spiritual guidance from those who were their nominal religious leaders. As Christ viewed the masses in their need, he pictured them as a harvest field waving with ripened grain ready for the harvesting. It is interesting to note that Jesus saw the people as shepherdless when Palestine fairly bristled with Pharisees, Sadducees, and Essenes—all of whom made religion their chief business. Yet in this setting, he urged his disciples to pray so that there would be no lack of laborers for the work. No doubt Jesus spoke of the quality of leadership, not quantity. (See Mark 6:6–13; Matt. 9:35 to 11:1; Luke 9:1–6.)

SENT OUT BY TWOS

The demands of the crowds meant that Jesus alone could not hope to cover all the territory of Israel. Therefore, he enlarged his mission by sending out the twelve by twos to announce the speedy coming of the reign of God. He gave them particular instructions as to their conduct. He gave them power to work miracles. Like Jesus, they were to heal the sick, cleanse the lepers, cast out demons, and even raise the dead. They were directed to conduct their tour in haste, carrying no extra equipment, relying on hospitality, and wasting no time upon the unreceptive and inhospitable.

Our Lord cautioned his emissaries that they should be on their guard lest they get into trouble in the course of their journeys. He knew that they would not be allowed to carry on their mission without interference but would likely be arrested as disturbers of the public peace.

(To carry out the mandates of Christ can sometimes be disturbing to public conscience.) When the disciples would be called upon to make their defense, they were not to think beforehand what was best for them to say. Instead of employing the art of argument, they were to trust the indwelling power of the Spirit of God, through which fitting words would be given to them (Matt. 10:17–20). Frank Stagg has pointed out that this is not a "promise of ready-made sermons" or a "proof-text against an educated ministry." "This," he wrote in *The Broadman Bible Commentary,* "has to do with court trials, not pulpit preaching." There is here comfort and the promise of help from the Spirit of God, but not a crutch for the lazy mind.

After giving them instructions, Jesus probably followed them into many cities where he had sent them. We can be sure that our Lord was busy with his own ministry while the disciples went about the work to which he had assigned them.

The twelve were so successful in their work that they attracted Herod Antipas' attention and excited his curiosity with regard to Jesus. Herod declared that Jesus was John the Baptist risen from the dead. Rumors are said to have varied, some thinking Jesus was Elijah or another prophet. He was the unregenerate ruler who had beheaded John because the prophet had rebuked Herod for his unlawful union with Herodias, the wife of his half-brother. (See Mark 6:14–29; Matt. 14: 1–12; Luke 9:7–9.)

Josephus reasoned that the real reason for the murder of John was Herod Antipas' fear that John would stir up sedition. Since most self-willed people act under the influence of conflicting emotions, the act of the tetrarch is likely to have been prompted by mixed motives with which all the narrators were acquainted.

Jesus' Ministry in Districts Around Galilee

Christ's Galilean ministry came to a close at the death of John the Baptist and its announcement to Jesus. This was a ministry marked by much activity, especially toward the end, at which time Jesus' popularity had reached its height. Everywhere crowds followed him; the fame of his mighty works spread; and no formal opposition had yet developed among the people. His labors were comparatively free and unimpeded. Evidently Jesus saw this as a time for training the twelve, for it was imperative that these men should learn more of the Messiah himself. It was now less than a year until the end.

FEEDING FIVE THOUSAND

The disciples had returned from their mission, reporting great success. Jesus was, as usual, beset and thronged with multitudes. The problem was greater because so many of the people were on their way to Jerusalem to attend the Passover. The apostles were exhausted by their recent labors. Jesus himself may have felt the need for a season of rest and communion with God. Also, the disciples needed instruction if they were to be ready for his death. Therefore, Jesus determined to withdraw with his disciples to some secluded retreat. They took a ship and crossed the lake, probably to the region of Bethsaida Julius in the territory of Herod Philip. Their departure was observed by the crowd who followed them by land around the northern end of the lake. When Jesus and his disciples arrived, they found the vast multitude waiting for them. In order to preach to the people, Jesus abandoned, for the present, his purpose to retire. Late in the afternoon, the disciples became anxious about how the multitude could be fed. Jesus took a lad's lunch, multiplied it, and fed the multitude. This notable miracle is the only one that is recorded by all four of the Gospel writers. Among other things, this miracle gives us another picture of the compassionate Christ.

> The meaning of the feeding of the five thousand goes beyond the **compassion** of Jesus, basic as that is. Clear indication of the symbolism found in the miracle is found in Mark 6:52; 8:17–21; and in Matthew 16:8–11. In the Gospel of John (6:1–71) this is made primary in the discourse on Jesus as the Bread of life. Just as Jesus gave material bread for the body, so he came to impart the higher bread for life eternal.[7]

The people were so filled with wonder and excitement that they sought to take Jesus by force and make him a king. The idea of an earthly king seems to have been shared by the disciples. It was one of the temptations held out to Jesus in the wilderness. But Jesus compelled the disciples to leave. Then he dismissed the multitude and went into the mountain to pray. (See Mark 6:30–46; Matt. 14:13–23; Luke 9:10–17; John 6:1–15.)

COMFORTING MIRACLE

Meanwhile, in crossing the lake, the disciples had encountered a storm. Being infected with the enthusiasm of the multitude, they either had delayed their departure or had made very slow progress across the

lake. It was during the fourth watch of the night, near morning; they
had only covered half the distance across the lake (or about three
miles). Suddenly, they saw through the darkness a human form approaching them over the water. It seemed about to pass by the boat.
They cried out in their fear. Jesus spoke to them, and their terror was
changed to wonder and joy. Peter was allowed the experience of walking on the water. Finally, he was frightened by the wind and needed
the hand of Jesus to stay him. Jesus entered into the boat and, immediately, the wind ceased. Soon they reached the western shore of
the lake. (See Mark 6:47–52; Matt. 14:24–33; John 6:16–21.)

Men have argued about the actuality of this event. They have debated its meaning. We do well to see it as a miracle performed by our
Lord and one that brought especial comfort to the early Christians in
days of martydom and persecution. George A. Buttrick has written
helpfully of this and all of Christ's miracles:

> What is a miracle? Not the arbitrary rending of natural law, but rather
> any event so ordered that it pierces our dullness or despair to convince
> us of the presence and power of God. This miracle blessed the disciples,
> and our world, in Christ. He came in crisis, when the limits of human
> resources had been reached and passed. He came beyond their hope, for
> they did not expect him: they thought he was an "apparition" to fear
> rather than a Savior to bless. He did what men cannot do. . . . He proved
> his lordship. The words **It is I** . . . are those used for the self-disclosure
> of God . . . and their response . . . was properly one of worship.[8]

THE MULTITUDES FOLLOW—FOR BREAD

Jesus' presence on the western shore of the lake was soon known.
Vast multitudes came and brought their sick for him to heal. Christ's
popularity was now at its highest point. The multitude of people who
had been fed followed him across the lake and desired to be fed again.
He refused to feed them and rebuked them for their selfishness. He declared himself to be the living Bread. The multitude was offended and
left him. At this point, Jesus' popularity began to decline. The ill feeling
extended beyond the multitude to his disciples. The disciples were
probably influenced by the widespread popular disaffection and what
they may have felt to be the tendency to fanaticism in the teachings of
Jesus. Even the closest twelve evidently entertained thoughts similar to
those of the other disciples.

After testing the faith and devotion of his disciples, Jesus warned
them that there was a deadly unbelief among them which would yet

work out a dreadful betrayal. The defection and betrayal of Judas did not take Jesus unaware.

While Jesus was busy with his teaching and healing ministry, the Pharisees were untiring in their efforts to prejudice the people against him. They found an occasion for complaint when his disciples ate with unwashed hands (i.e., were ceremonially unclean). To prepare one for fellowship in religious worship, it was necessary to wash in order to remove ceremonial defilement. These ceremonial washings, although especially characteristic of the Pharisees, were diligently practiced by all the Jews (Mark 7:3). Jesus answered that in the sight of God a man stands or falls according to his moral purity or uncleanness, and not according to his ceremonial or bodily condition. Mark summed up Jesus' statements by saying that Jesus made all foods clean; that is, he did away with the distinction between things which might be eaten and those which might not be eaten. (See Mark 6:53 to 7:23; Matt. 14:34 to 15:20; John 6:22 to 7:1.)

Jesus again withdrew from the multitude and sought temporary seclusion near the borders of Tyre and Sidon. His retreat was soon discovered. A Gentile woman with an afflicted daughter kept crying out to Jesus for help.

At first Jesus ignored the pleas of the distressed mother, but she continued to entreat him. The disciples were annoyed and asked Jesus to send her away. Jesus said, in effect, that he had no commission from God to begin a ministry among the Gentiles. The woman sensed that Jesus' word was not final, and she was quick to show him that he could help her without giving up his concentrated mission to the Jews. Jesus praised her faith and assured her that her daughter would be healed. This is a difficult passage to understand, but from it we can know that though Jesus may have rebuked the Jews for their preoccupation with tradition, he did not turn his back on them. He offered himself to them, but only in terms which understood the acceptance of the Gentile also. (See Mark 7:24–30; Matt. 15:21–28.)

After Jesus healed the daughter of the Syro-Phoenician woman, he continued his journey. His route probably took him through the territory of Sidon, then along the southern slope of Lebanon to the upper Jordan. After crossing the Jordan, he journeyed southward through the Decapolis to the eastern shore of the Lake of Galilee. The region known as the Decapolis (combination of Greek words "ten" and "city") lay southeast of the Lake of Galilee. This area received its name from the fact that it was comprised of a group of ten cities.

The length of this journey is not recorded. During this time outside the territory of Herod Antipas, Jesus was seeking rest. Yet Matthew recorded that great multitudes came to him bringing their sick for healing (Matt. 15:30–31). Only one cure of a stammering deaf man was reported by Mark (Mark 7:32–37).

Jesus seems to have fed another multitude numbering about four thousand people. Although the company was smaller, they had been together longer. Jesus' compassion for the people furnished the starting-point of the account. The loaves and fishes were somewhat more numerous than before but were still very few. The fragments left over from the meal filled seven large baskets instead of the twelve small ones as on the former occasion. (See Matt. 15:29–39.)

This journey also took Jesus into the territory of Magadan, where the Pharisees and Sadducees assailed him with ensnaring questions. Among other things, they wanted him to show them a sign from heaven which would establish authority for his claims. Jesus told them that if they were blind to all the overpowering proofs which he had given of his divine mission, they would be left to their own unbelief. He told them, also, that since they were so shrewd in interpreting the signs of the weather, they might be expected to have some skill in reading the signs of the times. He had attempted, in vain, to call their attention to these signs of the times which pointed to an impending crisis in the history of the nation. With a hint about his resurrection, he departed. (See Mark 7:31 to 8:12; Matt. 15:29 to 16:4.)

WHO AM I?

Jesus again retired to Bethsaida-Julius on the northeastern shore of the Lake of Galilee where he healed a blind man. He seems to have journeyed next to Caesarea Philippi, situated on a limestone terrace at the foot of Mount Hermon, some twenty-five miles north of the lake and near the sources of the Jordan. It was near this city that an important conversation between Christ and his disciples occurred.

> The day at Caesarea Philippi marks the watershed of the Gospels. From this point onward the streams begin to flow in another direction. The current of popularity which seemed likely in the earlier days of Jesus' ministry to carry him to a throne has now been left behind. The tide sets toward the Cross. The Galilean sunshine is suddenly clouded over, and the air grows sultry and heavy with the gathering storm. The

voices shouting applause die away, and another more ominous note is heard. At Caesarea, Jesus stood, as it were, on a dividing line. It was like a hilltop from which he could see behind him all the road he had traveled and in front of him the dark, forbidding way awaiting him. One look he cast back to where the afterflow of happy days still lingered and then faced round and marched forward toward the shadows. His course was now set to Calvary.[9]

In reply to Jesus' question about his identity, the disciples reported the various opinions they had heard expressed about him. These opinions indicated the kind of impression Jesus had made on the popular mind. He was thought to be John the Baptist, Elijah, Jeremiah, or one of the prophets. All four views expressed identified Jesus only as a fearless spokesman for God. Jesus knew how little he was understood by the multitudes, but the time had come for him to draw from the disciples a confession of their faith.

In response to Jesus' question, Simon Peter said, "Thou art the Christ, the Son of the living God" (Matt. 16:16). No sooner had Peter made this confession than Jesus told his disciples to tell no man of him. Jesus pronounced Peter blessed because he had received so great a revelation. He had received a revelation; it was not a conclusion of mere human reason. Our Lord continued by talking about the rock on which the church is built, the keys of the kingdom, and the power of binding and loosing. The rabbis had assumed the right to determine what the law allowed and what it did not allow, or, as they expressed it, the power to bind and to loose. In this sense, Peter and the other apostles were at this point constituted authoritative interpreters of the teaching of Jesus. However, Jesus saw that Peter's declaration also needed correction and not just praise. Although Peter had made a marvelous affirmation, it was inherently weak for he had a faulty concept of the Messiah.

A SUFFERING MESSIAH?

Jesus at once began to teach a new and startling conception of messiahship—suffering. He told the disciples that, instead of being a conquering Messiah, he was to suffer persecution and death. Peter began to rebuke Jesus. It was difficult to believe that the Messiah should suffer. The temptation which Peter uttered and that which the devil proposed in the wilderness were really the same temptation—namely, to take the crown without the cross. Jesus then declared that his disciples must also share in his suffering. Disciples today must pay a price for following their Lord.

> But does the confession of Jesus as Messiah have any relevance today? What did the messianic idea mean but just this—that someone was coming who would be the hope of the world, the fulfillment of every promise, and the answer to every prayer; one who would straighten out all human tangles and right all earthly wrongs and bring in a better day of God? That was the idea. And we can see that, so far from having lost its meaning by the passing of the years, it has now more meaning than ever. For we are being driven by the very stress of our difficulties to realize that the one hope of the world is the recognition and the acceptance of Jesus as God's guiding word to our generation. Everything depends upon whether we are ready to say with Peter, "Thou art the Christ." [10]

Employing a phrase found nowhere else in the New Testament, Jesus declared that one who wished to be his follower must "deny himself"; that is, he must place the service of God above the gratification of personal desire. That this involves the constant readiness to sacrifice self to duty is more clearly brought out in Luke by the addition of the adverb "daily." (See Mark 8:13 to 9:1; Matt. 16:5–28; Luke 9:18–27.)

THE TRANSFIGURATION

Six days after the conversation with the disciples at Caesarea Philippi, Jesus selected three of his disciples—Peter, James, and John—and led them up into a high mountain, presumably in the region of Caesarea. The name of the mountain is not given in the Gospels. Jesus had just told the disciples that he must suffer. The disciples would now see that glory and suffering were joined together. The character and mission of Jesus as the God-man were to be at least partially recognized by the disciples.

As Jesus prayed, he underwent a striking change of appearance. And in the midst of the glory, Moses and Elijah appeared on the scene and entered into conversation with Jesus concerning his impending death in Jerusalem. Peter, dazed by the glory but never without words, proposed to build booths for Jesus and the two visitors. In the midst of Peter's speaking a heavenly voice out of a cloud announced, as at his baptism, the divine sonship of Jesus. Then, suddenly, the three disciples found themselves alone with Jesus. As they were coming down from the mountain, Jesus commanded that the men be silent as to the "vision" until after the resurrection. Jesus also told the disciples that Elijah's expected function of preparing for the coming Messiah had already been fulfilled by John the Baptist, and that they were to look for no personal appearing of the old prophet. (See Mark 9:2–13; Matt. 17:1–13; Luke 9:28–36.)

There is no doubt but that this experience strengthened Jesus for what lay ahead. Only a short while after this, Luke reported, "He set his face to go to Jerusalem." The voice must have been for him a sort of seal of approval. But the event also met a need for the disciples. They were told once again that Jesus was God's Son and that they were to listen to him. Such an experience must have strengthened the disciples during the days just before and after the crucifixion.

IN-SERVICE TRAINING

When Jesus and the three disciples returned to the valley, the other disciples were in a controversy with some of the scribes. The disciples had failed in their efforts to cure a demoniac. They turned to Jesus and he cured the youth. Then he lectured his followers about the need for faith if they were to grapple successfully with difficulties of such magnitude. The power of faith is here set forth in the language of hyperbole (the method of overstatement to make a point graphic). The figure used was familiar to those addressed. To have faith as a grain of mustard seed was to have it in small measure. To remove mountains was simply to do that which, at first, seemed impossible.

Returning from the north Jesus came again into Galilee, but not to resume his public ministry. He sought to be alone with his disciples, for he wished to teach them about his death and its meaning for them. Again and again he forewarned them of the fearful events which were approaching, but they failed to understand his words. The inhibiting power of accepted and inherited ideas was great. (See Mark 9:14–32; Matt. 17:14–23; Luke 9:37–45.)

Jesus' retreat had been discovered. It was no longer possible for him to be alone with his disciples. As he traveled through Galilee, he instructed them on the way. At length they arrived in Capernaum, where the collectors of the annual tax for the maintenance of the Temple sought payment. Every male Israelite twenty years old and older was required to pay annually a half shekel (Ex. 30:13). Jesus felt that the mission in which he and his disciples were engaged should exempt them from the tax. Yet, rather than have any difficulty with the Temple authorities, he instructed Peter to pay the tax for both of them. Possibly our Lord would also have us see in this an example of how one can relinquish a right in the interest of others. The fact that no provision was made for the other disciples may imply that they were all under twenty years of age. (See Matt. 17:24–27.)

Jesus had been trying in a variety of ways to teach his followers the principle of self-denial even to the point of death. How his disciples must have saddened him as they disputed among themselves as to who should be the greatest under the Messiah's reign. They came to him with the problem of who would be the greatest in the kingdom. He condemned the selfish spirit which led each of them to desire for himself the highest place of honor. Jesus' eye fell on a little child whom he used as an object lesson. Taking the child in his arms, Jesus declared him to be a type of the true disciple. He said that entrance into God's kingdom requires the trusting humility of a child. Growth in the kingdom involves childlike obedience, faith, selflessness, and love—the essence of Christian discipleship. He assured the disciples that service to others, as opposed to self-seeking, gives the highest claim to honor. Since one enters the kingdom of God by becoming like a child, it follows that greatness in such a kingdom could only come through becoming still more like a child. The disciples' preoccupation with greatness indicated they did not understand the nature of the king or his kingdom. (See Mark 9:33–37; Matt. 18:1–5; Luke 9:46–48.)

Even after the incident about greatness, the disciples had not learned their lesson. Shortly thereafter, John earned a rebuke from Jesus when he reported that he had seen a man casting out demon's in the Master's name and had stopped him. Even though the man was successfully casting out demons, John thought he should be stopped because he did "not follow us." "John expected to be promoted for extra zeal in orthodoxy! Here we have a needed lesson in tolerance about methods of work for Christ. How little John here understood the spirit of Jesus. But Christ was patient with the narrowness of John as he is today with ours. What poor earthen vessels we are after all, with our bickerings, jealousies, and prejudices. . . . We preach the spirit of service for other people and practice too often self-aggrandizement and self-seeking. It was pitiable then and it is lamentable now." [11] (See Mark 9:38–41; Luke 9:49–50.)

Jesus went on to speak about those who receive the disciples of Jesus in a spirit of helpfulness, and assured his hearers that such treatment is worthy of reward. On the other hand, there are those who put temptation in the way of his "little ones" and so hinder their spiritual progress. Jesus stated that it would be better for such a person to lose his life than to be the cause of spiritual harm to others. Jesus always was concerned for the "little people." These may have been children, women, "people of the land," his own followers—"little ones" could have referred to any of these, for Jesus was concerned for all persons.

The statement in Mark 9:50 about salt losing its saltiness may be indicative of that loss of fraternal spirit which led the twelve to quarrel about precedence. The injunction to have salt in themselves would then be an injunction to preserve the true spirit of brotherhood.

From offenses against his "little ones," Jesus passed to a consideration of the way his followers should treat each other. Jesus said that when one of his followers was injured by a brother, he should consider carefully his own conduct and regulate it according to the principles of Christlike love. If the offender stubbornly refused to be reconciled and even disregarded the authority of the church, then he was to be treated as an unbeliever. It is not that the church was so much to withhold fellowship from such a person as it was to simply acknowledge that the person had removed himself out of fellowship range.

After Jesus had assured his disciples of their authority to act in his name and in his Spirit, he gave a parable of an unforgiving servant to illustrate the principle of forgiveness. He stated that he who does not show forgiveness toward his fellowman cannot expect divine forgiveness for his own shortcomings. (See Matt. 18:15–35.) The unforgiving remain unforgiven because they are in a condition which will not permit forgiveness. It is not that God is unwilling to forgive but that such persons are unable to receive God's pardon.

As the time drew near for the Feast of Tabernacles (the fifteenth of Tishri, about October), the most joyous of all the festivals observed among the Jews, Jesus' brothers urged him to go to Jerusalem. These brothers evidently did not believe him to be the Messiah. Jesus replied that he was acting under divine dictation and that he would follow the schedule appointed by God.

About the same time, three followers were warned by Jesus to reckon with the conflict of loyalties which discipleship brings. After his brothers left for the feast, Jesus, knowing perfectly what would befall him, purposed to go to Jerusalem. He sent messengers to make arrangements for his hospitality. He resolved to go to Jerusalem by the direct route through Samaria; however, the inhospitality of the Samaritans caused him to change his plans. On the way, Jesus rebuked James and John for their violent language and for their spirit of hatred and prejudice. Luke 9:56 states that "they went on to another village." This "other village" may have been in Samaria; however, it is more likely that he left the country and went to Perea, where he resumed his work of teaching and healing. Strict Jews from Galilee who were afraid of being defiled by coming into contact with the Samaritans were accustomed to journeying to Jerusalem by this longer route. (See Matt. 8:19–22; Luke 9:51–62; John 7:2–10.)

---

1. William Barclay, *Jesus As They Saw Him* (New York: Harper & Row, 1962), p. 92.
2. Turlington, *The Broadman Bible Commentary,* Vol. 8, p. 286.
3. Stagg, *The Broadman Bible Commentary, op. cit.,* p. 103.
4. Geldenhuys, *op. cit.,* p. 223.
5. Stagg, *The Broadman Bible Commentary, op. cit.,* p. 149.
6. Robertson, *op. cit.,* p. 85.
7. Stagg, *The Broadman Bible Commentary, op. cit.,* p. 163.
8. *The Interpreter's Bible* (Nashville: Abingdon Press, 1951), VII, 443.
9. Stewart, *op. cit.,* p. 106.
10. *Ibid.,* p. 112.
11. Robertson, *op. cit.,* pp. 115–16.

6

JESUS' PUBLIC MINISTRY
Part 3
Judea (Later)

JESUS left Galilee because his ministry was rejected there. He had already been turned away in Jerusalem. With his enemies in the Holy City, Christ had been on the defensive. He had kept aloof from his enemies in Galilee. But now, at the Feast of Tabernacles, which began about October, Jesus boldly appeared in Jerusalem. A. T. Robertson suggests that his appearance then was in the nature of an attack upon the enemy's country. In any case, six months before Passover and the crucifixion, Jesus left Galilee for Jerusalem.

The Feast of Tabernacles

WILL HE COME?

The report had been circulated that Jesus would attend the feast, but in its opening days he had not been seen. People had come from Galilee and were no doubt recounting the amazing teachings and miracles of the man from Nazareth. All at once Jesus was the chief topic of conversation: Will he come to the feast? What do you think of him now? Is he a blasphemer? Is he really come from God? It was probably in the middle of such conversations that on the fourth day Jesus made his appearance in the Temple and began to teach. Many of the people were wonder-struck at this teaching, but his enemies kept interrupting him with bitter and insulting remarks. Yet even the hostile Jews were astonished that he could speak so well since he had not been to their rabbinical school in Jerusalem. Jesus proclaimed himself publicly as a teacher sent from God and declared that if anyone did not believe his teaching, it was because he was not obedient to the will of God. His words were favorably received by the multitude. His enemies, however, were irritated by the popular good will evidenced toward Jesus and sought to seize him. But even the soldiers sent to arrest him were so in awe of him and his teaching that they failed to take him prisoner.

WATER AND LIGHT

On the last day of the feast, in a grand and thrilling moment, Jesus divided the multitude by claiming to be the fulfilment of their expectations about water flowing from the altar. Two ceremonies related to the feast were particularly meaningful to the Jews—the outpouring of water by the priests at the Pool of Siloam and the lighting of the candelabra in the Court of the Women. As the water was poured from a golden vessel, trumpets blew and the priests spoke: "With joy shall ye draw water out of the wells of salvation" (Isa. 12:3, KJV). The lighting ceremony took place earlier in the festival. These lights were atop two lofty stands and they threw light not only into the courts of the Temple but far and wide over the city. They were intended to represent the glory cloud of the wilderness wanderings. Against the background of these two vivid and symbolic ceremonies, Jesus said: "If any one thirst, let him come to me and drink" and "I am the light of the world; he who follows me will not walk in darkness" (John 7:37; 8:12, RSV).

SIN NO MORE

Possibly during this time as Jesus was teaching, the scribes and the Pharisees brought an adulterous woman to Jesus for judgment. The account is not found in the oldest manuscripts. However, it is found in several places in some Greek manuscripts: after John 7:52; at the end of the Gospel of John; after John 7:15; after John 7:36; and after Luke 21:38. (See John 7:53 to 8:11.)

Whether the story was originally Johannine, the incident is undoubtedly authentic. Whenever it happened, the woman's accusers determined to take advantage of the incident to elicit from Jesus a judgment opposed to the law of Moses (Lev. 20:10; Deut. 22:22–24). When the case was presented to Jesus, he stooped down and began writing with his fingers in the sand. The accusers continued to press the question. He gave them a judgment, but it was not what they expected. The words of Jesus caused them to forget the woman's crime and examine their own sins. The accusers began to slink away, until all had departed. Our Lord forgave the woman and dismissed her with the admonition to sin no more.

SUPERIORITY COMPLEX

Evidently Jesus remained in Jerusalem after the Feast of Tabernacles, which placed him in the midst of his enemies without the protection of the multitude of pilgrims from Galilee. The people of Jerusalem were different from the Galileans. Their city was the center of Jewish religion and life, and they prided themselves upon their superiority. They looked with contempt upon Jesus because he was a Galilean. For several days Christ taught in the vicinity of the Temple and entered into dialogue with the people and the rulers. He described their spiritual crisis and set forth the momentous issues of faith and unbelief. Many of the people in Jerusalem believed on him. He addressed his new converts and carefully distinguished the essential differences between the men who gave permanence to the Old Dispensation and himself who fulfilled it. In their fury at Christ's teaching, the Pharisees attempted to stone him; but he hid himself from them. (See John 8:21–59.)

WHO HAS SINNED?

Later, as the sabbath was drawing to a close, Jesus and his disciples were walking from the Temple, perhaps near one of its gates. Beggars were accustomed to sit at the Temple gates, and it was probably among these beggars that Jesus spotted a blind man. The disciples asked if the man's congenital blindness was caused by his own sin or by the sin of his parents. Jesus replied, "It was neither that this man sinned, nor his parents" (John 9:3). In effect, he said that the man's blindness was not a subject for speculation but an opportunity for the manifestation of the works of God. (Bear in mind that Jesus had just declared that he is the Light of the world.)

When the disciples asked whose sin caused the victim's blindness, they assumed, as did most Jews, that illness is inevitably caused by sin. The only question was, Whose sin was to blame? The simple aspect of Jesus' reply is that suffering is not always the result of individual sin. "There is a chain connecting the sin of humanity and its woe, but the links are not traceable by the human eye" (Ellicott).

Therefore, it was that God might be glorified that Jesus made clay of saliva and anointed the eyes of the blind man, telling him to go wash in the Pool of Siloam. When he obeyed Jesus, the man received his sight. Then his neighbors were disturbed because the miracle had been performed on the sabbath. They brought him to the synagogue and there he and his parents were questioned. Because of the healed man's candidness in his replies, he was cast out of the synagogue. When Jesus found the outcast, he received him into the "New Society." And those who followed Jesus had another illustration of his mission to the world.

Time Running Out

Probably soon after the Feast of Tabernacles, Jesus left Jerusalem. There were still many Jewish towns and villages that he wanted to visit and time was running out. He appointed seventy men to go before him to preach the gospel of the kingdom and to announce his coming in every place which he intended to visit. He gave his task force many of the same instructions which he had given to the twelve disciples when he sent them earlier on a similar mission. It is possible that as they went out in twos, they frequently returned to report progress. They reported that even the demons were subject to them through the name of Christ. This foreshadowing of Satan's doom brought joy to Jesus' heart and a prayer of thanksgiving to God. In our Lord's Prayer, we get another insight into the intimate relationship that existed between Jesus and the Father. (See Luke 10:1–24.)

The events and teachings of this last portion of Jesus' ministry are recorded only by Luke. He made a distinct contribution to our understanding of the life of Christ by giving us largely the last six months of Jesus' life. Some of the sayings of Jesus recorded in Luke are much like portions of the Sermon on the Mount. It is, of course, possible that Luke recorded what Jesus said in Galilee, but it is also quite possible that Jesus repeated his teachings.

On one occasion, a lawyer asked Jesus a question about eternal life. But then his interest seemed to center more on whom he should consider to be his neighbor. Perhaps the man realized that he appeared to have asked a question to which he already knew the answer. And, maybe he was trying to save himself embarrassment when he pretended that the real point of difficulty was to determine who is one's neighbor. Jesus replied with the parable of the good Samaritan. With this story he taught that the relation of neighborliness is established by the giving and receiving of needed help and is not dependent either upon "nearness" or race. (The noun "neighbor" and the adverb "near" are the same word in Greek.) Jesus gave to the word "neighbor" a new application, since heretofore a Jew's neighbor could only have been another Jew. Jesus wanted his questioner to know and he would have us to understand that one is *to be a neighbor,* not look for limits to his responsibility, including some and excluding others. (See Luke 10:25–37.)

It was probably soon after the discussion with the lawyer that Jesus went to the home of Martha and Mary in Bethany. When Martha wanted to call Mary from her conversation with the Master to assist in the preparation of the meal, Jesus chided Martha for her unnecessary anxiety. He declared that only a little ("one thing" or "one dish") was needed and that what Mary was doing was even more important than the preparation of food. Jesus probably did not mean that the contemplative form of religion is right and Christian action is wrong. No doubt he did mean that we are not to busy ourselves with outward things and neglect quiet worship and learning more of the Master. (See Luke 10:38–42.)

After Jesus had been praying, one of his disciples requested that he teach them to pray. In answer, Jesus gave a Model Prayer. This prayer includes all that a son needs to say to his Father. To encourage persistence in prayer, he told a parable about a friend coming at midnight to borrow bread. If a selfish man can be persuaded by such insistence to give, even against his will, how much more certainly will the heavenly Father grant the requests of his children. We must not suppose that Jesus intended to intimate that there is any reluctance on God's part to bless his children. He simply said that if in human relations, parental love could be trusted to help and not harm the children, how much more should we have confidence in the love of God.

At another time Jesus was accused of performing his cures by the most powerful demon of them all, Beelzebub. He replied that it was absurd to think that Satan would destroy his own work. By refuting the charge that he cast out demons by Satan's power, he established the counterposition that he did it by power derived from God. He declared that it is impossible for anyone to remain neutral in the struggle between good and evil. The life of a man is like a house which must have an occupant. He said that the only way to be sure it is not taken over by the spirit of evil is to see that it is inhabited by the Spirit of God. (See Luke 11:1-36.)

Later Jesus accepted the invitation of a Pharisee who probably was not yet hostile to him. The host was shocked when his guest disregarded the usual Pharisaic custom of washing his hands ceremonially before eating. Thus the opportunity was there for Jesus to comment on the folly of outward shows of religion which have no basis in the spiritual life of a man. He found no fault with the character of the instruction given by the authorized teachers of the people, but blamed them for the inconsistency of their lives. He also condemned their desire for prominent positions in the synagogues and at feasts. In Oriental countries, in the course of the daily routine, men and women frequently staggered under immense loads. Jesus used this fact to picture the heavy demands placed upon the people by the many unnecessary laws. These criticisms caused the Pharisees to seek all the more diligently to find something in his words with which to accuse him. (See Luke 11:37-54.)

Making Every Minute Count

In a long discourse to the disciples (Luke 12:1-12), to the multitude (vv. 13-21), again to the disciples (vv. 22-40), to Peter (vv. 41-53), and again to the multitude (vv. 54-59), Jesus taught about hypocrisy, covetousness, anxiety, watchfulness, his crucifixion, and the necessity of repentance.

He warned his disciples about the mushrooming power of hypocrisy and told them that whatever they taught would become known everywhere. He told them that a timid and hesitating proclamation of truth would not insure their safety; therefore, they should speak out boldly, fearing nothing. They were not to be afraid of those who merely threaten the life of the body; but they were to fear only God, whose power over both body and soul is absolute. Jesus assured the disciples that although he was sending them out into the midst of dangers, they could nowhere be beyond God's care. He gave them no assurance that they would not suffer, but only that their sacrifice would be observed by God.

Jesus encouraged his disciples to be patient, faithful, and prayerful as they waited for the coming of the Son of man. He likened the suddenness of the appearing of the Son of man to the unexpected coming of a thief when the master of the house is not watching. He gave the general lesson that obligation is in proportion to knowledge and that the divine chastisements are heaviest where the consciousness of neglect of duty is greatest. He also taught that no man is entitled to a reward simply for doing his duty. A debtor is not deserving of praise for paying his debts, but only of blame for neglecting to pay them. (See Luke 12:1–59.)

Jesus warned the people that the entire unrepentant population of Jerusalem would be destroyed. He rejected the idea that the worshipers who were violently suppressed by Pilate's soldiers or the men who suffered in an accident at Siloam were unusual sinners who had to have especially harsh punishment. They served to provide a reminder that the whole unrepentant nation was headed for disaster.

A fig tree which did not bear fruit for three consecutive years was looked upon as worthless. Therefore, like an unfruitful fig tree which was given one last chance to produce, the Jewish nation had been given its last opportunity to produce fruits of righteousness. It could no longer expect a continuance of divine favor. Jesus was the vineyard keeper who pled for a little longer time in which to nurture the tree. It was he who had undertaken to help his countrymen. He knew that unless there was a speedy change in the lives of the Jews the divine judgment upon them would no longer be delayed. Once again Jesus emphasized the urgent need for true repentance that brings forth fruit. (See Luke 13:1–9.)

On a sabbath, Jesus healed a woman in a synagogue who had been afflicted for eighteen years. Instead of directly criticizing Jesus for healing on the sabbath, the ruler of the synagogue found fault with the people for bringing the sick on that day. Jesus understood that the criticism was really aimed at him. He addressed not only the ruler but all those who were present and accused them of using sabbath observances to advance their personal interests. Jesus was fulfilling the purpose of the sabbath by freeing men and women from the reign of Satan and bringing them under the gracious reign of God. This is the last account in Luke of Jesus' appearance in the synagogue. The hostility of the religious leaders was reaching a fevered pitch. (See Luke 13:10–21.)

The Feast of Dedication took place in the month Kislev (December). It was instituted in 165 B.C. by Judas Maccabeus in commemoration of the cleansing and rededication of the Temple after its defilement by the Syrians. It was also known as the "Feast of Lights" and was a festival of patriotism and religion which could be celebrated anywhere. Jesus came to Jerusalem for this feast in order to dedicate himself to death. As he walked on Solomon's Porch, he was encircled by the religious leaders and asked if he were the Christ. They probably wanted to ensnare him and accuse him before Pilate. Jesus reminded them that he had previously told them who he was, and they did not believe him. He then proceeded to tell them the relation which existed between himself and God. Because he claimed deity, his enemies took up stones again to stone him. The conflict between Jesus and the Jewish leaders had reached its climax. Christ challenged them to judge his words. They did not stone him, but they tried to seize him. Jesus walked away and later withdrew from Jerusalem. (See John 10:22–39.)

7

JESUS' PUBLIC MINISTRY
Part 4
Perea

JESUS did not remain long in Jerusalem. His encounter with the religious leaders there was sharp and brief. When he left Jerusalem, he went first to Bethany beyond the Jordan. It was there that John the Baptist first identified him and where he won his first disciples. This is the period which A. T. Robertson designates as the later Perean ministry.

(The reader is reminded once again that chronology in the life of Christ is difficult to establish and can be quite confusing. This is especially true of Luke's account of the later Perean ministry. See A. T. Robertson, *A Harmony of the Gospels,* pp. 276–79 for a thorough and helpful discussion of this problem.)

"Set His Face"

The public ministry of Jesus was about to come to a close. As far back in Luke's account as 9:51, Jesus had "set his face" to go to Jerusalem. Every moment since that time he had been moving steadily and with complete dedication toward the completion of his mission. He had taught; he had healed; he had interpreted his kingdom. And now the time had come for him to enter Jerusalem for the last time.

After Jesus was rejected by the Jews he left Jerusalem and went to Perea for a brief sojourn. This is the land east ("beyond") of the Jor-

118

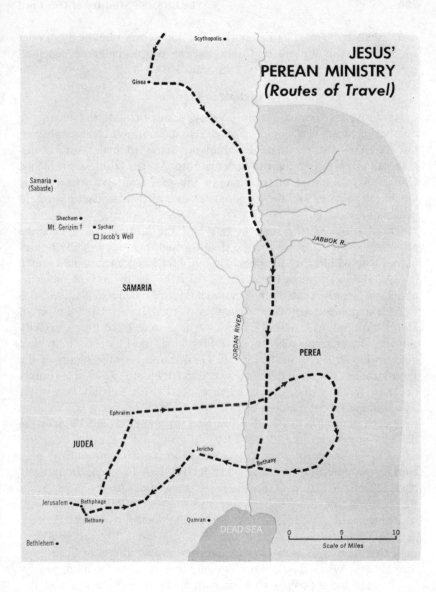

JESUS'
PEREAN MINISTRY
(Routes of Travel)

Scythopolis •

Ginea •

Samaria •
(Sabaste)

Shechem •
Mt. Gerizim †   • Sychar
□ Jacob's Well

JABBOK R.

SAMARIA

JORDAN RIVER

PEREA

Ephraim •

JUDEA

Jericho •

Bethany •

Jerusalem • Bethphage

Bethany •

Qumran •

DEAD SEA

Bethlehem •

0   5   10

Scale of Miles

dan, paralleling Judea and Samaria. How long Jesus remained in Perea we are not told. We are told only that the people in Perea benefited from his presence and ministry. (See John 10:40–42.)

Teaching in Transit

As Jesus progressed in his journey, someone inquired as to the number of those who would be saved. He did not give a direct answer, but told the inquirer that he would do better to make sure of his own salvation rather than to speculate upon such fruitless problems. Christ also said that in the time of the messianic judgment, many would fail to enter into the kingdom because of their neglect of present opportunities.

Christ spoke of the narrow gate and the straight way. Then he emphasized the shortness of the time through the story of the householder who would shut the door. He told how latecomers would knock in vain. The picture in Luke 13:28–30 is of the dismay of the Jews at finding Gentiles seated at the banquet table of the messianic feast.

At this point some of the Pharisees warned Jesus of the danger of Herod Antipas (13:31–35). This warning may have been perfectly sincere. Or, as some scholars have suggested, the Pharisees may have been trying to drive him back into Galilee and into the hands of the Jewish rulers. The men did not succeed in frightening Jesus. He frankly declared that he would take the time needed for finishing his work. The thought of completing his task caused him to utter a lamentation over Jerusalem. Soon, divine protection no longer would be over the beloved city. (See Luke 13:22–35.)

Jesus again accepted an invitation to eat with a prominent man among the Pharisees. (It was customary to feast more bountifully on the sabbath than any other day of the week.) At the meal, Jesus was being watched by the lawyers and Pharisees. Perhaps they were watching especially because there was a man present who had a disease. The common opinion of the Pharisees on the subject of sabbath healing caused Jesus to question them about the lawfulness of healing on the sabbath. When they did not answer, Jesus healed the man, justifying the act by appealing to their own ideas of helpfulness and humanity.

At the same feast, Jesus gave a parable teaching humility in all circumstances (14:7–14). He also gave his host a lesson in unselfishness and benevolence. In another parable he taught that those who disregard the gospel invitation will not be included in the resurrection of the just (14:15–24).

Jesus continued to teach the multitude that followed him. He told them that even their families must not be allowed to dominate their convictions. "Hate" here refers to relative preference of one thing over another. It expresses a disregard for the claims of one person or thing relative to those of another. Jesus did not mean that we are to *hate* our parents; we are not to place parents or anyone above the claims of Christian discipleship.

Jesus used a striking figure of speech, declaring that he who would be a true disciple must take up his cross and follow him. By law, anyone who was sentenced to death by crucifixion was compelled to carry his cross to the place of execution. Jesus meant that his followers must be ready to suffer anything in his cause.

Teaching by Parable

The two parables of the unfinished tower and the king going to war illustrate inadequate protection. An unfinished military tower or a very small defensive army could not protect a country. Jesus warned the crowds to examine their ground of confidence. If it were not sufficient to protect them, they should renounce it and become his disciples. In this parable, Jesus was not saying that it is better not to begin if one does not complete, though such inconsistency should be discouraged. Rather, he was saying that one should count the cost before beginning. (See Luke 14:25–35.)

Jesus was charged with associating with "sinners." He justified his attitude by claiming that it was also God's attitude. The stories of the lost sheep, the lost coin, and the lost sons illustrate the truth that God takes the initiative to bring about restoration of the sinner. Jesus told these three stories to entreat the respectable Jews to rejoice with him over the restoration of sinners. He warned them that, until they did, they were not acting in harmony with God's character. (See Luke 15:1–32.)

Jesus told the parable of the unjust steward to commend to the disciples the shrewdness and worldly wisdom practiced by the steward. He had the wit to salvage from the vocation he was about to lose the means of providing for the future. Jesus said that the sons of light would do well to imitate "the sons of this age" in using their wealth to promote the interests of their life. Jesus set forth in concrete terms the impossibility of having two ruling masters. We must choose between serving God and not serving him.

The story of the rich man and Lazarus depicts the consequences of the selfish and, therefore, unrighteous use of wealth. The scene is laid partly upon earth and partly in hades. (In the New Testament, hades is the realm of the dead—both good and bad.) On earth the rich man lived in selfish luxury; he did nothing to alleviate the suffering of Lazarus who lay at his gate. In hades their lots were reversed. Lazarus was received into paradise and the rich man suffered torment. It was not because the rich man had wealth that he suffered, but because he did not make good use of his wealth. His efforts to obtain even the slightest relief was fruitless, because the consequences of his course of life were inevitable.

Jesus dealt with offenses against his "little ones" and then gave consideration to the way his followers should treat each other. He declared that it is better for one to lose his life than to be the cause of spiritual harm to others. He concluded this discourse by showing once again that no man is entitled to a reward for doing his duty. (See Luke 16:1 to 17:10.)

Jesus Wept

While our Lord was in Perea, his friend Lazarus of Bethany became dangerously ill. Lazarus' sisters, Martha and Mary, sent a messenger to inform Jesus of the illness, but he remained in Perea two more days. In the meanwhile, Lazarus died and was buried. The disciples and their teacher returned to Bethany. When they reached the edge of the village, Martha and then Mary came out to meet the group. After a discussion about the manifesting of God's power, Jesus directed someone to take away the stone from the door of the sepulcher; and Lazarus was called from the tomb after four days. This miracle created a profound sensation not only among the eyewitnesses, but also in Jerusalem and throughout the whole country. It was a decisive test between faith and unbelief. The Council decided to execute Jesus. Again he retired to the wilderness, "into a city called Ephraim." (See John 11:1–54.)

Journeying with the Pilgrims

It appears that Jesus remained in Ephraim until the Passover season was near. Then he traveled northward near the border of Galilee and Samaria. Here he joined the multitudes of pilgrims who were on their way to the Passover feast. When he came to a certain village, he was met by ten lepers. They did not approach Jesus (Lev. 13:45–46), but prostrated themselves before him and called to him for help. He cleansed them, not immediately, but soon after they left him.

In reply to a question by the Pharisees about the manner of the coming of the kingdom, Jesus said that the foundations of the kingdom had already been laid in his own acts and teachings. The kingdom of God is a spiritual and, hence, an invisible kingdom. He wanted to correct the false belief that there was to be a restoration of the throne of David. He also corrected an erroneous idea of the disciples that the coming of the "Son of man" would be "with signs to be observed" (Luke 17:20, RSV). The Pharisees were expecting the messianic exaltation; but, because of their misconceptions, they would not see it when it occurred. Yet, strange paradox, his "coming" would be so evident to his disciples that not one of them could fail to see it. Suffering and defeat would precede spiritual victory. In vivid language, Jesus pictured the woes about to befall Jerusalem. To those who refused to heed his warnings, the threatened crisis would come as suddenly and unexpectedly as the flood came in the days of Noah and the destruction of the cities of the plain in the time of Lot. Jesus predicted that men would be pursuing their ordinary occupations and conducting themselves as though no danger were at hand. His puzzling answer to his disciples as to the location of these events points to Jerusalem as the carcass about which the Roman vultures would hover. (See Luke 17:11–37.)

Apparently on the same occasion, Jesus told the parables of the importunate widow and the Pharisee and the tax-gatherer. If an unethical judge could be influenced by the persistence of a helpless widow, how much more would a wise, just, and merciful God be moved by persistent prayer. It is the persistence of the one making the request that was cited as a lesson to the disciples. The character of the judge has no relation whatever to the moral of the story.

In the parable of the Pharisee and the tax-gatherer, the Pharisee stands for those who have such lofty opinions of their own virtues that they regard others with disdain. The tax-gatherer represents those who recognize and humbly confess their sins. (See Luke 18:1–14.)

Somewhere on the journey, the Pharisees, with some ulterior design, questioned Jesus concerning divorce. Jesus removed the case from the jurisdiction of the Mosaic law, to which they had appealed, and carried it to a higher tribunal. Moses, he said, allowed divorce as a concession to human weakness.

Jesus found the principle for marriage in the history of the original couple (Gen. 1:27; 2:24). Citing Genesis, he placed marriage upon the immovable foundation of the primary purpose of creation. The union of husband and wife was intended to be indissoluble. Christ's statement seemed hard to the disciples, but he told them that the heart must be devoted to the interests of the kingdom and these interests, therefore, modify all the relations of life. (See Mark 10:1–12; Matt. 19:1–12. For especially helpful discussions of Jesus' teachings on marriage, see *The Broadman Bible Commentary,* Vol. 8, pp. 186–89, Stagg; pp. 345–47, Turlington.)

The experiences with the little children and the rich young ruler gave Jesus an opportunity to describe the conditions of entry into the kingdom. Some little children were brought to him, probably by their parents, so that he could touch them and pray for them. The apostles, annoyed at what probably struck them as superstition, rebuked the persons who interrupted the discourse. Our Lord rebuked the apostles for their interference. He said that the traits of childhood (teachable-ness, simplicity, receptivity, and so on) are necessary for citizenship in the kingdom. Jesus' personal interest in little children plainly ap-peared in his kindly treatment of them as he took them into his arms.

The rich young ruler was told to devote his wealth to the service of the poor and to join those who were proclaiming the gospel. Jesus encouraged him to put his trust in God and not in his own achieve-ments and wealth. The test proved too severe. Christ demanded com-plete self-surrender to the cause of the kingdom. In this incident, he employed hyperbole to emphasize the truth that no one, not even the rich, can *enter* the kingdom. It requires divine power to accomplish this remarkable feat. On the surface, Jesus seemed to have completely shut the door to the kingdom. However, he reassured his disciples that what is humanly impossible can be accomplished by divine power.

The disciples continued to lack spiritual understanding. Peter asked what they were to receive as their compensation for sacrificing every-thing to follow him. Jesus replied that the new spiritual rewards would more than make up for their sacrifice. With the parable of the laborers in the vineyard, he showed the disciples that the rewards of the king-dom were not of debt but of grace. (See Mark 10:13–31; Matt. 19: 13 to 20:16; Luke 18:15–30.)

Talking Straight to Disciples

As Jesus advanced toward Jerusalem, his disciples were expecting him to be recognized there as the Messiah. Surely, now his kingdom would be established. Jesus took the twelve aside and plainly declared to them his approaching sufferings and death, but they did not under-stand.

About the same time, James and John asked to be assigned to the chief posts of honor in Jesus' coming kingdom. This request reveals that they still had not understood the spiritual nature of his mission nor his prediction about his approaching death. Jesus did not reprove them for their self-seeking, but he told them that they did not realize what they were asking. He inquired whether they were prepared to share with him, not his triumphs, but his sufferings. He declared that James and John would share his fate, but their places in the kingdom would depend upon their degree of acceptance by the heavenly Father. This request of James and John also reveals that there was more selfish greed than spirit of brotherhood among the twelve. Jesus tried to impress upon the minds of all the disciples that they were to seek service and not position. He emphasized this truth by calling attention to the fact that his life had been one of self-sacrifice for the good of the world. This was the fourth time the Savior had announced that he would be delivered to suffer and die. Still the disciples could not believe it; for they did not believe there could be a Suffering Servant (Messiah). (See Mark 10:32–45; Matt. 20:17–28; Luke 18:31–34.)

Probably, Jesus and his disciples then passed from old Jericho to the new city built by Herod the Great. The Savior was now on his last trip to Jerusalem. On the way he healed two blind men who appealed to him as "son of David" for help. Mark indicated that one of these was named Bartimaeus, that is, "son of Timaeus."

Approaching Jerusalem

In Jericho the chief officer of the revenue was a Jew named Zacchaeus. Through his lucrative employment, he had accumulated a large fortune. He had heard of Jesus and wished to see him. As Christ and the disciples were passing through Jericho, Zacchaeus, a man of small stature, climbed up into a sycamore tree to get a better view. When Jesus came to the tree, he called for Zacchaeus to come down. Hurriedly, the tax collector descended and conducted his unexpected but welcomed guest to his home.

Because of Zacchaeus' occupation, he was scorned by the patriotic Jews. The people murmured. Jesus had made himself a guest in the home of a "sinner." Jesus declared that Zacchaeus had not forfeited his birthright but was a son of Abraham. This sonship now was because it could be said, "This day is salvation come to this house." Sonship in the kingdom of God is now based squarely on one's relationship to the Father through his Son (Luke 19:1–10).

There was wild enthusiasm among the multitude of those who believed that the kingdom of God was on the very point of appearing. Would not a short day's journey bring them to Jerusalem where the Messiah was to take possession of his own? Jesus told a parable of the pounds (*minas,* worth about $20 each). In the parable, certain servants were given a trust to administer. When the master returned, he rewarded each servant in proportion to the faithfulness of his service. One has to be careful in understanding Jesus' parables allegorically. However, in this story it seems clear that the nobleman was Jesus.

The citizens who were not willing to be under his rule were the majority of the Jewish people. The enemies who were to be slain were those Jews who would perish in the destruction of Jerusalem. The fundamental thought in the parable, however, is that the disciples were to labor as well as wait. (See Luke 19:11–28.)

8

JESUS' ULTIMATE SACRIFICE AND MESSIANIC VICTORY

AT LEAST from the time of his baptism, Jesus had known that he was called to fulfil the role of the Suffering Servant of the Lord. This role anticipated that he would be put to death in the fulfilment of his mission. In Isaiah, the Servant songs indicate that the Servant would be anointed, labor in vain, endure bitter persecution, and suffer ignominious death. (See Isa. 42:1–9; 49:1–13; 50:4–11; 52:13 to 53: 12.) In the study of the life and ministry of our Lord, we come now to that period to which each of the Gospel writers devoted much detail. In our study we have come to Passover time, the time for him to die.

In his experience in the wilderness, Jesus was tempted to take the easy road to success and safety. He rejected these suggestions of Satan. At least on three occasions during Jesus' ministry, he had forewarned his disciples concerning his Passion.

Mark 8:31	9:31	10:32–34
Matthew 16:21	17:22–23	20:17–19
Luke 9:22	9:44	18:31–33

On several other occasions during his ministry, Jesus made veiled reference to his death. Death seemed to be inherent in his vocation as the Servant-Messiah. His victory would be achieved by shedding his blood (that is, his life would be sacrificially released by death).

128

The necessity for his death was based in the character and will of God. God is love, and because of his love, he was compelled to come in the flesh and rescue man from sin. Because he loved, Jesus came into conflict with man's sin of rejection. God's love for man and man's sin of rejecting God made Jesus' death inevitable. In his death, Jesus gave us a clear demonstration of the love of God (1 John 4:9–10).

The Gospel writers agreed that Jesus not only anticipated his death, but that he attached to it a saving significance. It was part of the work which he came into the world to accomplish (John 4:34).

Last Public Appeal to Jerusalem

Jesus came to Jerusalem with a determination to make a final appeal to the unrepentant city. He knew full well what fate awaited him there. For several weeks he had been in the land east of the Jordan (Perea). He was now convinced that his hour had come. He knew that he would die by violence, and he wished his death to be on the Passover.

The sinister forces opposing Jesus had been growing since the beginning of his ministry. He came to Jerusalem determined to declare himself the Messiah of the Jewish nation. Jesus was always in command of every situation, and this last week of his life was filled with activity of his choosing. During the days, he taught large multitudes in the Temple area and was frequently involved in controversies with the scribes and Pharisees. In these controversies Jesus directly attacked the orthodox religious hierarchy with great severity. Several plots to destroy him were prevented by his popularity with the multitudes. Each night he apparently left the city.

Jesus' Daily Ministry in Jerusalem

We will attempt to trace the events of his last week, day by day. We will reckon the hours of each day by Roman time (from midnight to midnight).

FRIDAY

Jesus arrived in Bethany, the village of Martha, Mary, and Lazarus, on Friday afternoon. On his last visit to Bethany he had raised Lazarus from the dead. The multitude of people who had come up with him from Jericho went on to Jerusalem, which was only about two miles away. They carried the news to the city that Jesus had come up to attend the Passover. This news created intense excitement in the city. The disciples were filled with hope and joy, for they expected the immediate coming of the kingdom of God. The miracle of the raising of Lazarus had convinced many people of Jesus' divine mission and had kindled a great enthusiasm among the multitude. The chief priests feared a popular uprising in his favor. They considered the advisability of killing Lazarus, as well as Jesus. (See John 11:55 to 12:1,9–11.)

SATURDAY

Jesus probably spent most of the sabbath in seclusion with his friends in Bethany. In Jerusalem the anxious conspirators likely spent the day in consultation. The pilgrims in the city heard with startled interest of the works and words of Jesus.

SUNDAY

The time had come for Jesus to manifest himself to his people as the King of the kingdom of God. The dramatic event which took place on Sunday seems to indicate a determination on the part of Jesus to place no further check upon the enthusiasm of his followers. He would allow them to proclaim him as the coming Messiah. This would hasten the fate which he had almost courted by coming to Jerusalem. The narratives hint that previous arrangements had been made, probably by Jesus, for the royal march into the city.

Jesus planned the demonstration, even though he knew it would hasten his death. He sent two of his disciples to get a colt on which he would ride. His entry into Jerusalem would thereby dramatize the rabbinical interpretation of Zechariah 9:9–13. The colt symbolized the King of peace who was to proclaim the way of humility and suffering. A horse was symbolic of a conquering king, but the ass was used to symbolize the king's visit to his subjects in peace (1 Kings 1:5–45). The young colt upon which Jesus was to ride had never been ridden before. In order to emphasize the fact that this was the first use of the animal, Jesus sent for the foal and its mother. The owner or whoever was in charge of the animals was someone who needed only the password to deliver them for Jesus' use.

When all the arrangements were complete, the disciples spread their garments on the animal and helped Jesus to mount. The road from Bethany to Jerusalem on which he traveled was on the Mount of Olives. Along the way he was met with tumultuous rejoicing. The

enthusiastic crowd hailed him as the initiator of the messianic kingdom. Jesus was proclaiming that God was asserting his sovereignty over Jerusalem, but he wanted to make clear the nature of this long-promised reign. It was not to be a political takeover.

Some Pharisees protested this outburst of enthusiasm. Jesus replied that his reign was the event for which the whole history of Israel had been a preparation. The lamentation over Jerusalem showed how little Jesus counted on the immediate success of his final appeal. He made a clear prediction of the approaching destruction of the city. This catastrophe was brought upon the Jews of that day by their own refusal to accept their King of peace.

Later, Jesus entered the Temple and performed some cures. (See p. 75 for a discussion of an earlier cleansing of the Temple.) The chief priests, scribes, and principal men of the people were offended because Jesus performed cures in the Temple and allowed the children to continue to shout that he was the Messiah. The question "Do You hear what these are saying?" (Matt. 21:16) was an appeal to him to check these demonstrations. Jesus made no reply except to refer his questioners to an appropriate passage of Scripture (Ps. 8:2). He then withdrew to Bethany. (See Mark 11:1–11; Matt. 21:1–11,14–17; Luke 19:29–44; John 12:12–19.)

MONDAY

On Monday morning Jesus returned to the city from Bethany. He was hungry. Seeing a fig tree standing close to the road, he looked for fruit among its abundant foliage. It was not the time for the full crop, but the mature leaves on this particular tree indicated that it belonged to an early variety. Since fruit and leaves appear together, there should have been fruit; when he found nothing but leaves, Jesus pronounced the doom of utter barrenness upon the tree.

This action was another dramatic demonstration of Jesus' warning to Israel. This is Jesus' only recorded miracle dealing with judgment, unless we count the destruction of the swine in the healing of the Gadarene demoniac (Mark 5:13; Matt. 8:32; Luke 8:33). It was both an acted parable and a prophecy. The tree was not only fruitless but false. It gave signs of vigorous life and promised fruit, but delivered nothing.

After Jesus' pronouncement of doom on the barren fig tree, he entered the city and made his way to the Temple. The same practices which he had found in the Temple near the beginning of his ministry seem to have been resumed (John 2:13–22). These practices were taking place in that part of the Temple called the Court of the Gentiles where animals for sacrifices were offered for sale and where money could be changed. This exchange of money was necessary to provide Jewish money to those from abroad who had to pay the Temple tax. No Gentile coin was allowed to go into the treasury of the Temple.

These practices were sanctioned by the rulers of the Temple. Jesus expelled the traders from the Temple and quoted passages of Scripture which declare that the house of God is a house of prayer and that traffickers had turned it into a robber's cave (Isa. 56:7; Jer. 7:11). The chief priests, scribes, and principal men, though inwardly enraged, were restrained from opposition by their fear of him and by the enthusiasm with which he was regarded by the people. These leaders had already decided to put Jesus to death, but they did not know how to accomplish it under the circumstances. The next few days disclosed their subtle policy as well as their hatred. It was an essential part of their scheme to discredit Jesus with the multitude. To do this they resolved to ask him questions which, they hoped, he would not be able to answer without alienating the people. (See Mark 11:12–18; Matt. 21:18–21; Luke 19:45–48.)

There were some Greeks among the multitude who filled the courts of the Temple during this Passover week. Whether they had heard of Jesus prior to their coming we do not know. These Greeks, desiring to see Jesus, asked Philip to arrange an interview. Philip consulted Andrew, and the two men brought the request to Jesus.

This request must have excited and inspired Jesus. He recognized those Greeks as forerunners of a great multitude who would accept him. Should he obey their call, leave impenitent Jerusalem, and go away with the Greek seekers to establish his kingdom in their midst? There once again was the old temptation which had assailed him in the wilderness and had reappeared on previous occasions. This was a moment not only of solemn joy but of mental distress and anguish. The life of the world would spring out of his death, even as the wheat springs forth from the seed that is planted. He prayed. When he had finished his prayer, a reassuring voice came from heaven. Jesus explained that the voice came not for his benefit but for the benefit of the multitude in the Temple. Jesus spoke to the crowd with deep emotion and gave them counsel and warning. He returned to Bethany for the night.[1] (See John 12:20–50.)

TUESDAY

The next morning Jesus and his disciples returned to Jerusalem by the same path they had traveled on Monday. The disciples observed with wonder that the fig tree had withered away.

When Peter called attention to the tree, Jesus took the occasion to teach his disciples the nature and power of faith. He spoke of faith and prayer as inseparable. The removal of a mountain is, in effect, impossible. The rabbis were sometimes called "uprooters of mountains" as a figure to describe their power in removing difficulties. Jesus used this figure to emphasize the wonderful power which comes through the possession of faith. He was assuring his disciples that all obstacles would disappear if they had faith in God. (See Mark 11:19–25; Matt. 21:20–22.)

Callers from the Sanhedrin.—As Jesus was teaching in the Temple, he was interrupted by a deputation from the Sanhedrin. They had resolved to discredit him, if possible, with the people. By virtue of their

position as the recognized religious leaders of the people, they presumed to call him to account for infringing upon their privileges. It did not occur to them that he might have within himself an authority higher than any of which they had knowledge. Jesus countered by asking them the source of John the Baptist's authority. They could not deny, without risking the loss of their reputation and influence with the people, that John the Baptist's had been a divine mission. Yet, they could not affirm it because John had given public and emphatic testimony to Jesus. When they declined to answer his question, Jesus refused to answer theirs about his authority. The rulers lingered to hear what he would say.

Parables that expose.—Christ then spoke to the multitude, giving the most transparent of all his parables. In the parable the son who repented of his refusal to obey his father represented the reformed evildoer (or the "tax collectors and harlots"). The son who promised to obey, but broke his promise, represented those who pretend to a righteousness which they do not possess (or the religious leaders to whom he spoke). Jesus plainly told his hearers that the most immoral and infamous classes of people had shown more spiritual discernment than those who sat in Moses' seat. He declared that the self-righteousness of the religious leaders was a greater hindrance to their entrance into the kingdom than the vices of those whom they scorned. Such were slaves only of passion, which they might learn to control. The scribes and Pharisees were guilty of an overmastering selfishness. The main point of this parable is that one shows his respect for authority through obedience. (See Matt. 21:28–32.)

Jesus continued his exposure of their character by giving the parable of the faithless vinedresser.

> Authority is the continuing theme in the parable of the wicked tenants. This is a story of rebellion against authority and its consequences. The parable is in the form of an allegory, largely patterned on Isaiah 5:1-7. The **vineyard** is a familiar figure for Israel, and that is its symbolism here. God is the owner of the **vineyard,** and the **tenants** are the rulers of Israel or Israel itself. The **servants** are the prophets, and the **son** is Jesus. The **other tenants,** to whom the **vineyard** is given, are the Christian leaders or the church itself.[2]

The religious leaders to whom Jesus spoke were like vinedressers who hold back from their master his share of the fruit of the vineyard which has been entrusted to their care. The leaders had so perverted the truth as to make their ministry to God's people fruitless. As a consequence of their conduct, their office would be given to teachers who would render faithful service. (See Mark 12:1–9; Matt. 21:33–41; Luke 20:1–16.)

Jesus concluded this discourse by giving another parable. In this parable he represented the kingdom of God as a marriage feast given by a king (God) to his son (Jesus Christ). The guests first invited were the Jewish people. The gathering in of chance guests, not included in the first invitation, signified the calling of the Gentiles. The wedding garment was the righteousness of faith. Here, Jesus again declared that the kingdom would be taken from the Jews and given to the Gentiles. (See Matt. 22:1–14.)

The chief priests, elders, scribes, and Pharisees retired temporarily from the contest with Jesus for some private conferences. They resolved not to change their policy. They would continue to try to draw from Jesus some statement which would compromise him with the people or with the Roman authorities.

Tribute to Caesar?—The Pharisees selected a group of their students to go with the Herodians to present Jesus with a dilemma about paying tribute to Caesar. The Herodians seem to have been partisans of the family of Herod the Great (Mark 3:6; 12:13). They were probably Jews who were convinced that the Herodian rule was the main pillar of Jewish nationality. It was decided that the group would ask Jesus a question having a double thrust, both religious and political: "Is it lawful for us to pay taxes to Caesar, or not?" (Luke 20:22).

It was a perilous question that his enemies put to Jesus. Recent events seemed to indicate that he had messianic pretensions. If he should say yes, he would lose the support of the common people who longed to throw off the Roman yoke. On the other hand, should he say no, he would lay himself open to the charge of encouraging sedition. Jesus asked for a coin of the tribute money. He then explained that the use of Roman money by the Jews was a recognition of Roman authority. It was as the great legal authority of the Jews, Moses ben Maimonides, expressed it later: "Wherever the money of any king circulates, there the inhabitants recognize that king as their master." Jesus, in effect, said: "You have already answered your own question by using this money and thus placing yourselves under obligation to Caesar. What you have forgotten is that you also have obligations to God." The plot was skillfully contrived, but it failed utterly because the plotters did not understand Jesus' real thought and purpose. They were baffled and withdrew without saying a word. (See Mark 12:13–17; Matt. 22:15–22; Luke 20:20–26.)

Questions from the Sadducees.—Presently, the Sadducees approached Jesus. These men were members of the aristocratic order and stood in direct and bitter opposition to the Pharisees. They rejected the oral tradition which had been built upon Old Testament law and recognized only the written law. They denied the doctrines of resurrection, angels, spirits, and a future judgment. The design of the Sadducees was to confound Jesus by exposing the absurdity of the idea of the resurrection. They brought forward a striking case under the law of Deuteronomy 25:5–6, to show the confusion which would result in the next world if such plural marriages were practiced in this life. They evidently used this passage to prove that death ended all.

Jesus answered their question by charging them with two errors. He said that they did not know the teaching of the Scriptures about life after death, neither did they know the power of God. God's power can accomplish a resurrection, for the Scriptures teach that God is the God of living persons, not dead ones (John 11:25–26). Jesus also said that in the world to come there will be no marriage. As a further point, Jesus mentioned the relation between a living personal God and the patriarchs. There is a statement in Exodus 3:6 which emphasized that God *is* the God of the patriarchs; therefore, they must still be alive, since he cannot be the God of dead men. "Belief in continuing life for man is bound up with belief in a living God" (Stagg). The Sadducees had nothing to say in reply to the Teacher's argument, but some of the scribes forgot for the moment their hostility and exclaimed: "Teacher, You have spoken well." (See Mark 12:18–27; Matt. 22:23–33; Luke 20:27–40.)

Jesus' answer to the Sadducees had contained such a new and profound exposition of a difficult passage of Scripture that even the scribes had been surprised and delighted. However, they must have had mixed emotions. Jesus had overcome all of his assailants and had put them to shame in the presence of the multitude. No one had been able to elicit from Jesus a single statement that would bring him into discredit with the people or furnish ground for judicial procedure against him.

Questions and counterquestions.—To test Jesus' insight and knowledge, the Pharisees next put forward a certain scribe, distinguished for his knowledge of the law. The rabbis had concluded that the law contained 613 "light" and "heavy" precepts. They could not agree upon which precepts should be in the two divisions. The lawyer, hoping to entangle Jesus in the controversy, asked: "What commandment is the foremost of all?" (Mark 12:28). This question was often discussed by the rabbis.

Jesus replied by combining the commandments in Deuteronomy 6:4–5 and Leviticus 19:18. The rabbinical schools had already combined these two precepts as summarizing religion in its two aspects—Godward and manward. The lawyer agreed that Jesus had answered correctly. Jesus had now gained a reputation for skilful reasoning. After this, no one tried to puzzle him with difficult problems. (See Mark 12:28–34; Matt. 22:34–40.)

Having been questioned at length himself, Jesus now seized the opportunity to propose a question to the Pharisees. He did not wish to embarrass them but to suggest to the people a higher view of the Messiah than they had held. He asked whose descendant the Messiah was to be and received the only reply which any Jew would give—David. Every intelligent Jew knew that the Messiah was to be born of the lineage of David. But the most enlightened of the nation had yet to understand the divine and eternal generation of God's Messiah.

Jesus then posed a searching question. In effect, he asked: "How could David [Ps. 110:1] speak of one of his own descendants as Lord?" No Jew would speak of his son as "lord." This title was often used by a son when referring to his father, but never by a father when referring to his son. David did speak of the Messiah as his Lord; therefore, he could not have been thinking of Messiah as his son. Jesus did not mean that he was not the son of David in any sense. He was, as a part of the mystery of the incarnation, both son of David and Lord of David. His purpose in this question was to confront the people with the necessity to examine their concept of the Messiah. He knew that if he could remove their false conception of the Messiah as a political Davidic king, there was a possibility that his true spiritual messiahship might be recognized. (See Mark 12:35–37; Matt. 22:41–46; Luke 20:41–44.)

Scathing denunciations.—Jesus then publicly denounced the scribes and Pharisees in the most scathing indictment that he ever delivered. In this extended discourse he denounced their hypocrisy and pronounced upon them sevenfold woe. He declared in plain, direct, and severe language their sins of pride, ambition, covetousness, and love of applause. He pronounced judgment on the scribes and Pharisees, the priests and rulers, the city and nation, and even on the Temple itself. He closed his discourse with a lament over the city. He repeated the word "Jerusalem" to indicate his deep pity and great love for the city. He wanted to help, but his help was refused. He declared to the inhabitants of Jerusalem that divine protection would no longer be over them. It should be remembered that these words were cries of woe, not curses. They were warnings to privileged leaders, not threats to little people. (See Mark 12:38–40; Matt. 23:1–39; Luke 20:45–47.)

Jesus was sitting in the forecourt of the women where the trumpet-shaped receptacles for offerings for the Temple treasury were located. He watched the worshipers as they dropped their contributions into the trumpets. The rich made large oblations. In contrast, a poor widow cast in two *lepta* (two copper coins, worth less than a half cent). This was the least that anyone was allowed to contribute. Jesus commended the widow because she had given more than the others in proportion to her ability. (See Mark 12:41–44; Luke 21:1–4.)

When Jesus was leaving the Temple, his disciples called his attention to the immense stones of which the structures were built. Jesus had previously intimated some dire calamity which would fall upon the city; but to the disciples, the Temple seemed built for eternity. Its total destruction was inconceivable. They knew that such a destruction of the Temple would involve the ruin of the city, the nation, the theocracy, and the whole existing order of things under the old covenant.

Discourse on last things.—When the disciples mentioned the magnificent edifice, Jesus predicted the total destruction of the Temple. Shortly after the prediction, Jesus and his disciples left the Temple and went out to the Mount of Olives. The Temple could be seen clearly from where Jesus was sitting. He was asked by some of the disciples when the destruction would occur; what would be the sign of his presence (*parousia;* i.e., presence after return); and what would mark the end of the age (Matt. 24:3). Jesus answered these questions in an extended discourse. The development of this discourse on things to come in relation to Christ and the kingdom can probably be seen better in outline form:

- The prediction of the destruction of the Temple (Mark 13:1–2; Matt. 24:1–2; Luke 21:5–6)
- The questions of the disciples (Mark 13:3–5; Matt. 24:3–4; Luke 21:7)
- Warning as to misinterpretation of events and conditions (Mark 13:5–13; Matt. 24:4–13; Luke 21:8–19)
- The corrective for false signs (Matt. 24:14)
- The destruction of Jerusalem (Mark 13:13–31; Matt. 24:15–35; Luke 21:20–33)
- The coming of Christ (Mark 13:32–37; Matt. 24:36 to 25:30; Luke 21:34–36)
- Admonitions in view of the consummation of the age (Matt. 25:31–46)

What to do now?—After Jesus left the Temple, his enemies felt the need for immediate action. During the past few weeks, a series of events had occurred which left them no alternative but to put him out of the way. The raising of Lazarus had been followed by the public proclamation of Jesus as the Christ on his royal march into the city. He had entered the Temple and had driven out the buyers and sellers. He had publicly denounced the religious leaders. The power of the hierarchy, if not its very existence, was menaced. (See Mark 14: 1–2; Matt. 26:1–5; Luke 22:1–2.)

The members of the Sanhedrin, of which Joseph Caiaphas was president, were summoned to a meeting at the palace of Caiaphas. It was decided that Jesus should die. How to accomplish the execution without creating a riot among the people was their problem. Jerusalem was full of people who had come up to attend the Passover. Many of these were Jesus' own disciples from Galilee. It was decided that it would be best to wait until after the feast. The Passover proper was celebrated in the evening of the fourteenth day of the first month (Abib or Nisan) and the following seven days were set apart for the eating of unleavened bread. (See Lev. 23:4–8; Num. 28:16–17.)

The anointing of an honored guest was not a rare occurrence in oriental homes. Jesus likely received such a token of respect on more than one occasion. While the Sanhedrin was in session, Jesus, his disciples, and Lazarus were guests at a feast in the home of Simon the leper. Martha was among those who served, and Jesus was reclining at the table (couches were commonly used as tables). During the feast Mary took an alabaster vase of precious ointment and anointed Jesus' feet and head, wiping his feet with her hair. (See Mark 14: 3–9; Matt. 26:6–13; John 12:2–8.)

WEDNESDAY

We have followed the life of our Lord to the close of the third day (Tuesday) of the Passion Week. After the feast in the house of Simon the leper, Jesus probably retired to the home of a friend in Bethany. The next day, Wednesday, seems to have been spent in seclusion. The Gospel writers have drawn a veil over that day which we shall not attempt to raise through mere supposition.

THURSDAY

On Thursday the disciples asked Jesus where they should prepare the Passover feast. He directed Peter and John to go into Jerusalem. Upon entering the city, they would meet a man bearing a pitcher of water. They were instructed to follow him to his house. It seems probable that Jesus had previously made arrangements with one of his disciples in Jerusalem to celebrate the feast at his house.

Peter and John found everything as was predicted, and they made ready the Passover. The institution of the Passover is recorded in

Exodus 12. While the substance of the festival was perpetuated, the mode of celebrating it in the first century had been considerably modified. The use of hyssop, the sprinkling of the doorposts with blood, the standing posture, the girdling of the loins, the staves, and so on were omitted.

How Passover is celebrated.—A brief explanation of the mode of the celebration of the Passover feast will help us to understand the events of the evening. On the fourteenth day of the month Nisan (or Abib), every house was purged of all leaven. Every male, not ceremonially unclean, appeared before the Lord at the Temple and presented an offering of money in proportion to his ability. When the sun was setting, a lamb was slain and the blood and fat were given to a priest. The lamb was then roasted whole, and all of it was eaten with unleavened bread and bitter herbs. The same night, the fat was burned by the priest and the blood of the animal was sprinkled on the altar. The next day there was a holy convocation with special sacrifices and more joyous festivities. This was the day that the harvest was consecrated by the waving of the first sheaf before the Lord. This was the beginning of the Feast of Unleavened Bread, which lasted seven days (Ex. 34:18–21). In the first century the entire week had become one great Passover feast. (See Mark 14:12–16; Matt. 26: 17–19; Luke 22:7–13.)

When was the last meal?—The question as to whether the date of the last meal which Jesus ate with his disciples was the thirteenth or fourteenth of the month is much debated. According to Mark, Matthew, and Luke, Jesus ate the Passover feast with his disciples. The Gospel of John seems to indicate that Jesus ate a meal twenty-four hours earlier than the time it was eaten by the rest of the Jews. (See A. T. Robertson, *A Harmony of the Gospels,* pp. 279–84.)

Although we cannot be certain, the view taken in this discussion is that the last meal which Jesus ate with his disciples was a Passover feast. In the evening after sunset, Jesus and his disciples assembled in the dining room, which had been prepared according to ritual. When the hour came, all reclined at the table. Jesus took his place as the master of the household. In his introductory statement, Jesus declared that he would not again eat of the Passover meal with his disciples until it (the Passover) had been fulfilled (Luke 22:15–17).

Jesus serves the Supper.—The Gospel accounts themselves do not detail all that took place; but because we are familiar with how the

Passover was observed, we can assume that something like the following took place: On the table before Jesus and his disciples were the
whole roasted lamb, the unleavened bread, a paste of crushed fruit
moistened with vinegar, bitter herbs, and a pitcher of wine. All things
being in readiness, Jesus filled the first cup of wine and asked a bless-
ing on the feast. The cup was passed, and each drank. The bitter herbs
were passed, and each person dipped one in the paste and ate. Jesus
then broke the bread and passed it, after which the second cup was
filled and passed.

In response to a prescribed question (Ex. 12:26), Jesus explained
the meaning of the feast and gave an account of the sufferings of the
Hebrews in Egypt and of their deliverance, with a particular explanation of Deuteronomy 26:5. Having led them in singing the first part
of the Hallel (Pss. 113 and 114), Jesus then carved the lamb and
passed it and it was all eaten. He then passed the third cup of wine
and each drank. Soon he passed the fourth cup and each drank. The
feast was concluded by Jesus leading the group in singing the second
part of the Hallel (Pss. 115 and 118). (*Hallel* is a term similar to
"hallelujah" but here it refers to a particular psalm or psalms.)

A lesson in humility.—The prescribed order of observance was
interrupted several times during the feast. It seems that as the disciples
were taking their places at the table, strife broke out among them.
The old contention about priority arose again. There may have been
another cause for the strife. It was the custom when guests arrived at
the home of their hosts to have slaves to receive them and wash their
feet. If it was a poor home without slaves, the wife performed this
courtesy. This assignment was given to the lowliest slave in the household. This ceremony also had religious significance. On this occasion
no servant was present. Jesus and his disciples were not guests, and
none of the disciples were willing to render the service. Jesus was
grieved at their selfish pride and used the occasion to set forth the
spirit of the kingdom in contrast with the spirit of the world. To
exemplify the spirit of the kingdom, he arose from the table, laid aside
his outer garments, and girded himself with a towel. Pouring water
into a basin, he began to wash the disciples' feet.

Peter was overwhelmed with shame that Jesus would perform this
menial task for him and his fellow disciples. When Jesus approached
him, he drew back in horror and exclaimed: "Never shall You wash
my feet!" (John 13:8). Jesus rebuked this outburst of false humility

with severe words that carried an appeal to the bottom of Peter's heart. If washing were necessary to continue fellowship with Christ, then Peter was willing to offer his hands and his head for Jesus to wash. Jesus explained that the foot washing presupposed a total cleansing. It was the partial cleansing of one who, after bathing, had walked in the dust. The disciples had been cleansed by regeneration, but they needed to be cleansed from such defilement as saved persons contact day to day. Thus Jesus passed, in his explanation, from natural pollution to spiritual defilement.

> This exchange between Jesus and Peter brilliantly illumines the dynamics of a growing faith. At first Peter refused to learn the hard lesson of the cross on the assumption that his commitment was already complete, only to be told that deeper discoveries were essential to a relationship with Jesus. Overreacting to this rebuke he then embraced the opposite error of supposing that all of his earlier commitments were now invalid. But Jesus assured him that one does not have to start over again in order to outgrow previous limitations. . . . Jesus both honors our beginnings in the past (v. 10a) and demands openness to the future (v. 8b).[3]

After Jesus had finished washing the disciples' feet, he again reclined at the table and explained the real meaning of what he had just done. He had been overcoming the effects of Judas' disaffection, selfishness, and pride upon the disciple group. After his death each disciple must overcome these characteristics among themselves.

Serious conversation.—Jesus then gave expression to a great sorrow which was weighing upon his heart. He announced that he was about to be betrayed by one of the twelve, who was present and sharing with them in the Passover meal. This announcement excited great surprise and deep sorrow among the disciples. Jesus did not identify the traitor with an open declaration, but no doubt Judas understood that his crime was known by Jesus. Judas was then sent out into the night to complete his fearful task. The real meaning of Jesus' words was not understood by the other disciples; they thought that Jesus had sent Judas on some special mission connected with his office as treasurer.

After Judas left, Jesus gave expression to the mingled joy and sorrow which was in his heart. He expressed his love for the disciples and warned them of the danger to which they would be exposed after he went away. He was interrupted by Peter with the question, "Lord, where are You going?" (John 13:36). Jesus answered in a veiled reference to his death and entrance into the realm of *hadēs* (the Greek word which designates the place of the dead, literally "the unseen").

Peter asserted that, though everyone else should be offended and desert the Master, he would not. Jesus predicted that Peter would deny him many times before morning. In fact, he announced the defection of all the disciples. However, he added a promise of hope and told them he would meet them again in Galilee. He enjoined them to be on their guard against their enemies. When the disciples took him to mean literally that they must arm themselves, he did not try to explain. He merely said, "It is enough." This was a gentle way of ending the conversation. It is plain that he was not speaking of the defense of that night. Jesus sadly dismissed the subject (see 1 Kings 19:4; Mark 14:41).

The Passover feast had been interrupted by the disciples' contention about priority, the washing of the feet, Judas' departure, and Jesus' warning about desertion. The feast was now well advanced. Probably, the first and second cups of wine had been drunk, the unleavened bread and bitter herbs had been eaten, and the farewell morsel of the lamb had been received. The time had almost come for the third cup and the singing of the Hallel. It seems that at this stage of the meal, its character was suddenly changed. The old covenant (or testament) Passover became, by an act of Jesus, a new covenant (or testament) supper. He told his disciples that the bread was his body "given" for them, and the cup was the new covenant or testament in his blood. Then, he told them that, whenever they should meet together for a meal after his departure, they should remember how he had given his whole life for them. (See Mark 14:17–31; Matt. 26:20–35; Luke 22:14–38; John 13:1–38.)

It was customary for the company to remain together at the table for several hours after the conclusion of a Passover feast and talk about the Passover miracles of the past and the future. On this occasion Jesus and the disciples continued long in conversation about things past and things to come.

It is clear that Jesus was not surprised by the tragic end of his mission. He had expected and foretold it. In the midst of his disciples he discussed his departure in language that was almost joyous. If he seemed troubled at all, it was because his disciples were unable to understand the relation between his sufferings and God's presence with them. He assured them that his going from them in death would mean his coming to them in the energy of the Holy Spirit. He promised them that they would not be left as lonely orphans, but that he and the Father would make their abode with them.

To the Mount of Olives.—It was now late on Thursday night. A hymn, probably the Hallel, was sung. Jesus and the disciples left the dining room and went toward the Mount of Olives. It is probable that Christ expected Judas and the Sanhedrin's emissaries to come to the dining room in search of him. It was necessary for him to change his retreat in order to finish his discourse. (See John 14:1–31.)

After Jesus and the disciples had left the dining room and were on their way to the orchard, Jesus resumed his discourse. It is quite possible that they passed near the Temple, over the gates of which was a golden vine. The clusters of grapes on this vine were six feet in length. This may have been used by Jesus as the occasion for his parable of the vine. The lesson of this parable is the spiritual unity between Christ and his people. Under the old covenant the Jewish people were God's vine (Ps. 80:8–19; Isa. 5:1–7); now Christ declared that he was the "true vine" and his disciples were the branches.

Jesus assured the disciples of his love. He commanded them to love one another and to bring forth much fruit to the glory of God. He warned them of persecutions which would befall them and fortified their minds with the thought that they would suffer for his name's sake. Four times he told them he would send another Paraclete (i.e., Holy Spirit). His departure was an indispensable prerequisite to the presence of the Paraclete.

Jesus told the disciples that the Holy Spirit is the Spirit of truth, without whom even his work would not be complete (John 16:7–13a). He assured them that the Holy Spirit would reveal the truth in its fulness as he had taught it (14:26). He further declared that the Holy Spirit would not give a new revelation to supersede that which he had given them. Instead, the Spirit would unfold to their hearts and minds the whole meaning of Christ's life and death (15:26; 16:14–15). Jesus repeatedly spoke of his own coming as connected with that of the Paraclete.

> Because everything to be done by the Paraclete was also said to have been done by Jesus, the former functions as the continuing reality of the latter in the world after his ascension.

The primary mission of the Paraclete is described as twofold: (1) to indwell the disciples as that source of strength which formerly was theirs in Jesus; (2) to judge the world by the victory which Jesus won in his earthly trials with Satan.[4]

Jesus assured his followers that their prayers made in his name would be answered. Having reassured his disciples, he lifted up his eyes and uttered a high-priestly prayer of self-consecration, thanks-giving, and intercession. (See John 15:1 to 17:26.)

The place to which Jesus withdrew was across the brook Kidron, on the slope of the Mount of Olives. It was an olive orchard, a spot to which Jesus had often gone with his disciples. It probably derived its name "Gethsemane" or "oil press" from the fact that formerly an oil press had been located there. The group probably arrived between the hours of eleven and twelve o'clock at night.

Before entering the orchard, Jesus divided the disciples into two groups. The three who had been with him on the Mount of Trans-figuration accompanied him into the garden. He then withdrew a little even from these and engaged in prayer. He had reached the crisis of his redeeming work. He had freely offered himself, and now the sacrifice was to be required of him. The pain and anguish which he felt were so intense that he seems to have experienced death. When he said that his soul was "deeply grieved to the point of death" (Mark 14:34), he used the strongest possible language to give expression to the intensity of his mental agony.

Three times Jesus prayed. Three times he returned to find Peter, James, and John sleeping. In that dread and lonely hour he craved sympathy. When the traitor suddenly appeared, he told the sleeping disciples to arouse themselves: "Rise, let us be going; see, my betrayer is at hand" (Matt. 26:46, RSV). (See Mark 14:26,32–42; Matt. 26:30,36–46; Luke 22:39–46; John 18:1.)

FRIDAY (Probably soon after midnight.)

After Judas left the dining room, he hurried to the rulers and told them that he would, that night, implement his bargain. The Sanhedrin gathered a multitude armed with swords and clubs, officers of the Temple police, and a detachment of Roman soldiers. Jesus had been denounced to the Romans as a political messiah with a large, dan-gerous, and unpredictable following. The Romans were anticipating armed resistance. In spite of all the precautions they had taken, they expected a general riot.

These elaborate preparations, then, were prompted both by fear and policy. The search party was provided with lanterns and torches, not only because this was usual in all night military expeditions, but because they thought that it might be necessary to search for Jesus among the caves or trees of the orchard.

Doubtless, many of the search party, especially the Romans, did not know Jesus by sight. In order to identify Jesus in a crowd and thus prevent a mistake, it was agreed by Judas and the search party that he would kiss Jesus when they found him. A kiss on the hand was the customary greeting of a rabbi by his disciple. The betrayal took the form of a kiss which was a sign of honor.

It is probable that the search party first went to the dining room where the Passover had been observed. When Judas did not find Jesus and the disciples there, he led the search party to Gethsemane. He knew that Jesus often went there (John 18:2). Jesus seems to have heard the sound and seen the glare of the torches while he was deep in the orchard. Hastily rousing his sleeping disciples, he advanced to the entrance, probably where the other eight disciples were waiting. He arrived just as Judas, walking in front of the search party, was entering the orchard.

The traitor's kiss.—When Judas saw Jesus, he advanced, greeted him with a show of honor: " 'Hail, Rabbi' " (Matt. 26:49), and kissed his hand effusively. His betrayal was motivated by secret malice under the veil of friendliness. Jesus responded to Judas' greeting with a question which contained both sorrowful gentleness and bitter reproach. " 'Judas, are you betraying the Son of Man with a kiss?' " (Luke 22: 48). Having thus rebuked Judas, Jesus proceeded toward the search party and inquired whom they sought. He had reason for ascertaining just how far their warrants extended. When the spokesman answered " 'Jesus the Nazarene.' He said to them, 'I am He' " (John 18:5). The use of the unutterable name for God ("I am"), the tone and bearing which he expressed, or the majesty of his person overawed them. They stepped back in consternation and fell to the ground.

Jesus repeated his question: "Whom do you seek?" and again they answered: "Jesus the Nazarene" (John 18:7). Probably members of the search party had been seizing the disciples. Jesus now declared that if he were the object of their search, the disciples should be released. It appears that Jesus had hastened to the entrance of the orchard in order to protect his disciples, whom he had left there when he had

gone into the orchard to pray.

Jesus had recognized the authority of the officers, had identified himself as the one whom they were seeking, and had surrendered himself. Peter, seeing that they were about to bind Jesus, drew his sword, and aimed a deadly blow at Malchus, the high priest's servant. The Master reproved his rashness and healed the servant, intimating that if it had been the will of God that he should escape from his enemies, a providential way of deliverance would have been provided. Having declared to the search party that he yielded himself up to suffering and death, Jesus was bound and led toward the city.

Disciples flee.—The disciples, seeing Jesus bound and inferring from his words and actions that he would not defend himself, forsook him and fled. Two or three of them, including Peter and John, lingered near the place, and finally followed the mob into the city. A young man, clad only in linen cloth or wrapper, had probably risen from his bed in haste when he learned what was going on. He was roughly seized by one of the search party, but eluded his grasp by leaving the linen cloth in the soldier's hands. Tradition says that this young man was John Mark, the author of the first written Gospel, in which alone the incident is recorded. (See Mark 14:43–52; Matt. 26:47–56; Luke 22:47–53; John 18:2–11.)

To Annas.—For the preliminary and comparatively private examination, Jesus was led first to Annas, the ex-high priest and father-in-law of Caiaphas. He was taken to Annas, perhaps at Annas' own request or in deference to his age and acknowledged preeminence. Caiaphas was the legal high priest, but Annas wielded the real power behind the office and was revered by the people as the high priest.

Annas questioned Jesus about his teaching and the number of his disciples. He assumed that Jesus had a secret doctrine and that he was the head of a secret society. Jesus denied that he taught a secret doctrine by referring his inquirer to his hearers. One of the officers who had Jesus in custody struck him, charging him with lack of respect for the high priest. When Annas decided that he could elicit nothing of importance from the prisoner, he sent him to Caiaphas. (See John 18:12–14,19–24.)

To Caiaphas.—The members of the Sanhedrin had been assembling in the house of Caiaphas. This court was composed of seventy, some say seventy-one, members among whom were the chief priests, elders, and scribes. The Sanhedrin usually met in a stone chamber, called Gapith, in the Temple enclosure, though on extraordinary occasions it met at the palace of the high priest. The proceedings of this court were ordinarily conducted in accordance with established rules and precedents.

It was an essential rule that no capital case should be tried at a night session, and that no sentence should be pronounced until after at least one adjournment. Both of these rules were violated in the trial of Jesus. The members regarded this case as extraordinary, and they hurried through it. They were afraid their purpose would be frustrated by a sudden rising of the multitudes. They prejudged the case. It had been determined that Jesus should die; the judicial process was only intended to throw a decent veil over the murder.

On several occasions some of the Jews had tried to kill Jesus because he made "Himself equal with God" (John 5:18). Therefore, it seems that the officers of the Sanhedrin had decided that the indictment of blasphemy would be the easiest charge to establish against him.

During the trial many witnesses were brought forward, but their testimony was so contradictory that they were speedily dismissed. Jesus made no answer to any of the charges. Finally Caiaphas, perplexed and alarmed, availed himself of a prerogative of his office and put Jesus under oath. Then he asked, "Are you the Christ?" Jesus could no longer remain silent. To refuse to answer when he was under oath by the theocratic head of the nation would be to deny that he was the Christ. Jesus had to make his statement. It was his moment of revelation, and he replied, "I am; and you shall see the Son of Man sitting at the right hand of Power, and coming with the clouds of heaven" (Mark 14:62). Hearing these words, Caiaphas tore off his clothes. Not waiting for the formal verdict of the Sanhedrin, he pronounced Jesus guilty of blasphemy. By a unanimous vote our Lord was sentenced to death. This judgment made him a criminal to whom no respect was supposed to be given, so that even some connected with the high court disgraced themselves by treating Jesus shamefully. (See Mark 14:53,55–65; Matt. 26:57,59–68; Luke 22:54,63–65.)

Jesus' trial before the Sanhedrin was in the house of Caiaphas (Matt. 26:57; Luke 22:54). The plan of construction of this house was probably like that of others of the time. They were usually built around a quadrangular court, the entrance to which was protected by a heavy gate. After Jesus had been led through the passage, the gate was closed.

Disciple's denial.—Peter and another disciple (probably John) had been following at a distance. The unnamed disciple, who was known by the high priest, entered into the court with Jesus. Peter was excluded but was later admitted because of a word by the unnamed disciple. A fire had been kindled in the courtyard. While Jesus was being tried in the palace, those not entitled to enter the house remained in the courtyard.

As Peter warmed himself at the fire, three times he was charged with being a follower of Jesus. He firmly denied all knowledge of his Lord. When Peter was making his third denial with oaths, the cock crowed. At that same moment, Jesus looked into the courtyard at Peter. It was a look of grief and pity. Peter's repentance was deep and bitter. (See Mark 14:54,66–72; Matt. 26:58,69–75; Luke 22: 54–62; John 18:15–18,25–27.)

Early morning trial.—To give legal effect to the proceedings during the night, the high priest deemed it necessary to hold a formal session in the morning. Jesus therefore was led, apparently in a large and formal procession, from the high priest's palace into the council chamber on the Temple mount.

At this session Jesus was questioned, but no witnesses were examined. The sentence of death followed as a matter of course. This morning consultation was simply for the purpose of considering how best to secure from the Roman procurator a decision conformable to their wishes. They devised a plan of procedure which could scarcely fail. The plan was for them to go to Pilate in a body and inform him of Jesus' guilt, requesting his approval of the sentence. They hoped that Pilate would grant their request without any investigation of the charges. Should this fail, they resolved to accuse him of crimes against civil order and the authority of the emperor. Meanwhile, their emissaries were instructed to stir up the mob of Jerusalem (not Galileans) to clamor for the death of Jesus. All the emissaries needed to do was to announce that Jesus had been convicted of blasphemy by the Sanhedrin. (See Mark 15:1; Matt. 27:1; Luke 22:66–71.)

When Judas learned that Jesus had been condemned, he was seized with remorse and despair. He went to the Temple and confessed his crime to the priests and elders. He cast down the thirty pieces of silver and went and hanged himself. (See Matt. 27:3–10; Acts 1: 18–19.)

The Roman trial.—Jesus was led to the palace of the Roman procurator by the members of the Sanhedrin. As they would have contracted defilement by entering the house of a Gentile, and thus disqualified themselves from the Passover, they remained outside and notified Pilate. When Pilate was told that the Sanhedrin in a body, with the high priest, were waiting for him at the gate, he went forth to hear their complaint. Pilate must have been informed about the career of Jesus. He also must have known something of the feeling of the Jewish rulers toward Jesus. He probably had sent the soldiers to assist in arresting Jesus, but with a certain secret sympathy for him as the leader of a party opposed to the Pharisees and rulers. (These groups were certainly not favorites of Pilate.)

When Pilate arrived at the gate, he demanded to know what crime Jesus had committed against the Roman law. The chief priest replied that they had investigated the whole matter and the fact that they had condemned him to death was in itself sufficient proof that he was guilty. Pilate took them at their word and told them to take Jesus and judge him according to their law. When the leaders were compelled to present definite charges, they did not mention blasphemy, but accused him of plotting sedition (Luke 23:2). The charge was so serious that Pilate was forced to go through the form of an investigation.

Pilate retired to the judgment hall and directed Jesus to follow him. When they were alone, Pilate questioned Jesus about his kingship. Pilate then took Jesus back to the gate and said to the waiting Sanhedrin and the multitude: "I find no guilt in this man" (Luke 23:4). He apparently understood the real motives of Jesus' prosecutors as well as the essential falseness of their charges and declared that no case had been made against him. The chief priests and elders at once broke forth in a storm of accusations. Jesus stood silent. The infuriated multitude continued to pour forth a torrent of accusations in which Pilate caught the word "Galilee." The discovery that Jesus was a Galilean opened the door of escape for the procurator. He determined to send Jesus immediately to Herod Antipas, who was then in Jerusalem attending the Passover. (See Mark 15:1–5; Matt. 27:2,11–14; Luke 23:1–5; John 18:28–38.)

To Herod briefly.—Herod Antipas was overjoyed when Jesus was brought before him. The fact that Pilate sent Jesus to Antipas, although on the surface an act of courtesy, may have been dictated either by policy or by a desire to get rid of an unpleasant duty. The act in any case was pleasing to Antipas, for his pride was flattered by such attention from the Roman procurator. He hoped to prevail on Jesus to perform some miracle in his presence. He had no thought of trying him, much less of condemning him to death. Though Herod asked Jesus many questions, Jesus answered him not a word. Annoyed by his silence, Herod and his men mocked him for a time, and then arraying him in a robe, sent him back to Pilate. This interchange of civilities produced a reconciliation between the tetrarch and the procurator, who, for some cause, had before this time been estranged. (See Luke 23:6–12.)

Back to Pilate.—Pilate again had the case on his hands. He now must face the responsibility. He called together the Sanhedrin and the multitude with the purpose of giving a judgment in the case. His judgment seat had been set up on the pavement in front of the palace. He determined on a compromise which he hoped would satisfy all parties. Pilate offered to release Jesus Christ or Jesus Barabbas, a notorious criminal awaiting execution. It was customary to release political prisoners at Passover to cause national unrest. Evidently, this Barabbas was an insurrectionist who had taken arms against Rome. There seems to be strong evidence that the Barabbas' first name was Jesus. "If the name Jesus is original for Barabbas, Pilate's question

is pointed, Which Jesus did they want released? Jesus means savior
[Matt. 1:1], Jesus the Christ as the Saviour from sins and Jesus Barabbas as a savior from Rome." [5]

Pilate hoped that the verdict of the crowd would coincide with his
own inclination and make it possible for him to do justice under cover
of granting a favor. While he was awaiting the decision of the people,
he received a warning message from his wife. Tradition says that she
was named Claudia Procla and was a proselyte to Judaism.

The people made their decision and asked for Jesus Barabbas to
be released. Pilate then asked: "'What then shall I do with Jesus
who is called Christ?'" (Matt. 27:22). The answer came back
emphatically, "'Let Him be crucified!'" (v. 22). Pilate resolved to
appeal to the mob in another way. He tried to free himself from all
responsibility of the evil deed about to be performed. Washing his
hands before them, he said: "'I am innocent of this Man's blood'"
(Matt. 27:24).

The procurator desired to release Jesus, but he was unable to resist
the popular clamor for the execution of the sentence passed by the
Sanhedrin. He then released Jesus Barabbas and gave sentence that
Jesus Christ should be crucified. Jesus was led away into the Praeto-
rium to be scourged. A crown of thorns was pressed upon his brow
and a reed, a mock scepter, was thrust into his right hand. The soldiers
made sport of him by clothing him in a garment of scarlet or purple,
suggestive of the rich robes of royalty.

After this attempt to humiliate Jesus, Pilate again tried to save him.
He tried to satisfy the clamor of the Jews for Jesus' punishment by
inflicting upon him, though innocent, a slight chastisement. But the
Jews, seeing his purpose, appealed to his fear. They made it clear to
him that he must either crucify Jesus Christ or defend himself before
Tiberius. Pilate finally sat down on the judgment seat and formally
delivered Jesus up to be crucified. (See Mark 15:6–19; Matt. 27:
15–30; Luke 23:13–25; John 18:39 to 19:16.)

Delivered up for crucifixion.—The execution was entrusted by
Pilate to a band of soldiers, commanded by a centurion. Roman custom and Jewish law (Num. 15:35) required that the crucifixion be
outside the city walls. We do not here enter into the controversy about
the place of the crucifixion and burial. It is possible that all the guesses
are wrong.

The preparations for the execution were completed. A white tablet

with an inscription or title in Hebrew, Greek, and Latin was carried before Jesus or suspended from his neck. This title, overlooked by the Jews until it was fastened on the cross, was framed by Pilate in a spirit of revenge and mockery. In essence, he put on the tablet: "Jesus the Nazarene, the King of the Jews."

The soldiers laid the cross on Jesus, according to custom, and the procession moved forward. On the way Jesus, already weak from scourging and fasting, sank under the load. A certain Simon of Cyrene, in Africa, was compelled to bear the cross on to Golgotha. Jesus addressed some weeping women who followed him. He told them that a worse fate than his awaited those whose sins would bring down upon their city the divine retribution.

Having reached Golgotha (a Hebrew word which means "skull"), the soldiers offered him a cup of some sort of artificially-flavored wine. He took the cup, tasted the wine, and then gave it back to the soldiers. The cross having been fixed in the earth, the soldiers stripped Jesus of his garments, and raising him up to the cross, bound his arms and his feet to the wood. Then nails were driven through his hands and his feet to secure him to the cross. He was placed on the cross about nine o'clock in the morning. The deed was done; Jesus was crucified. (See Mark 15:20–23; Matt. 27:31–34; Luke 23:26–33; John 19: 16–17.)

Two notorious robbers were crucified with Jesus, one on his right hand and the other on his left. The tablet with Jesus' title was now fastened over his head. The chief priests hastened to Pilate and requested him to change the title, but he refused. Pilate had deliberately put a terrible meaning into the title: "The end of Jewish nationality."

According to Luke 23:34, Jesus prayed for his executioners after he had been raised on the cross. Though many of the oldest and best Greek manuscripts do not contain this verse, it no doubt is a genuine utterance of Jesus. Scholars suggest that if a scribe inserted the words he did so with a deep understanding of Jesus, for it is most typical of the forgiving spirit of our Lord. Its omission from the manuscripts may be accounted for by the disinclination of Jesus' disciples to excuse the deed of his murderers, a disinclination even at the present time.

The executioners took Jesus' clothes and divided them among themselves. His tunic was seamless, woven all in one piece. Instead of tearing it into four pieces, they cast lots for it. The chief priests, scribes, and the crowd derided his agonies with insulting remarks. The robbers also reviled him. Presently, however, one of them ceased his reviling and reproved the other thief for his brutality. In a prayer combining ignorance and faith, he asked Jesus to remember him when he came into his kingdom. Jesus promised the thief that he would that day be with Jesus in paradise, that portion of hades which is the dwelling-place of the blest.

Some of the disciples had by this time gathered close to the cross. Among them were the Marys, an unnamed disciple (probably John), and the mother of Jesus. Jesus spoke to his mother and to John, committing his mother to John and John to his mother. (See Mark 15: 24–32; Matt. 27:35–44; Luke 23:33–43; John 19:18–27.)

At the sixth hour, the hour of noon, a strange darkness gradually spread through the sky and enshrouded the earth. For three hours this darkness spread over the land. In the midst of the darkness Jesus became thirsty and gave expression to it in words. A soldier took a sponge and, filling it with vinegar, raised it to Jesus' lips. The darkness had continued for about three hours when, suddenly, Christ cried out: " 'Eloi, Eloi, lama sabachthani?' which is translated, 'My God, My God, why hast Thou forsaken Me?' " (Mark 15:34). He was forsaken, that is, given over to the suffering of death. In his complete abandonment of himself in his identification with sinful man, he felt cut off from God. However, he knew that God was his God and could never absolutely forsake him. It was indeed obedience to the Father which had brought him to that hour. Some of those who heard Jesus, not understanding the dialect in which he spoke, thought he called for Elijah. Some, interpreting his cry simply as one of pain, offered him some sour wine.

It was probably about this time that the darkness broke. Jesus cried again with a loud voice, " 'It is finished!' " (John 19:30). " 'Father, into Thy hands I commit My spirit' " (Luke 23:46). It was about three o'clock in the afternoon when he bowed his head and died.

The possible order of Jesus' sayings from the cross is as follows:

• The prayer for his executioners (Luke 23:34)
• The promise to the repentant robber (Luke 23:43)
• The charge to his mother and John (John 19:26–27)
• His cry of astonishment (Mark 15:34; Matt. 27:46)
• His cry of thirst (John 19:28)
• His cry of victory (John 19:30)
• His cry of resignation (Luke 23:46)

(See Mark 15:33–37; Matt. 27:45–50; Luke 23:44–46; John 19:28–30.)

Death and burial.—The death of Jesus was accompanied by several phenomena. There was a great earthquake. The curtain which separated the "holy of holies" from the "holy place" was torn from the top to the bottom (Ex. 26:31; Lev. 21:23; Heb. 6:19; 10:20). These incidents made a deep impression, not only on the centurion and his soldiers who had been stationed to watch the crosses, but on the multitudes. (See Mark 15:38–41; Matt. 27:51–56; Luke 23: 45,47–49.)

Jewish law forbade a crucified body to be left hanging overnight (Deut. 21:23). Pilate, therefore, at the request of the Jewish rulers, ordered that the legs of the victims be broken in order to hasten their deaths, so that their bodies could be removed. With a heavy mallet the soldiers broke the legs of the two robbers. When they came to Jesus, they found that he was dead already and so did not break his legs. To make sure that Jesus was really dead, one of these soldiers drove a spear into his side.

The next day was a sabbath of unusual solemnity. For this reason it was necessary for the bodies to be taken down from the crosses before the close of the day. Joseph of Arimathea, a rich member of the Sanhedrin and a secret disciple of Jesus, went boldly to Pilate and requested the body of Jesus. Pilate granted his petition after he ascertained from the centurion in charge of the execution that Jesus was already dead. Joseph was joined by Nicodemus. Together they took the corpse down from the cross and prepared it for burial (John 3: 1–5; 7:50–52; 19:39–42). With lovingly extravagant care, they anointed the body with myrrh and aloes and wrapped it in linen cloths. Joseph owned a new tomb which had been hewn out of a rock in his garden. The body of Jesus was laid in the tomb, and a large stone was rolled against the door. The women of Galilee, including Mary Magdalene and the other Mary, followed Joseph and Nicodemus to see where Jesus was buried. (See Mark 15:42–47; Matt. 27:57–61; Luke 23:50–56; John 19:31–42.)

SATURDAY

The sabbath began at sunset on Friday. This was the great sabbath of the Passover and therefore a day of special sacredness. The chief priests and the Pharisees, always ready to find fault with Jesus for any act which he did on a sabbath, were now busy with their plans to make their work secure.

They had somehow come to the knowledge that Jesus had said that he would rise from the dead the third day. They possibly had heard him make the direct assertion. They knew that if the body were missing, the belief would prevail that Jesus was really risen. The chief priests felt the importance of keeping watch over the tomb until the third day had passed. They applied to Pilate for a watch, which he contemptuously granted. Having placed the guards at the door of the sepulcher, they sealed the stone to ensure discovery if anyone were to break in. Late Saturday afternoon, after sunset, the two Marys visited the sepulcher where Jesus had been buried, bringing spices and ointments for his permanent entombment. (See Mark 16:1; Matt. 27: 62 to 28:1.)

SUNDAY

It is not easy to determine the order of the events which transpired on Sunday. The writers of the Gospels were not attempting to give full accounts of the resurrection of Jesus. We must keep this fact in mind in attempting any general view of the incidents which took place on that day. The events recorded may have happened in the following order.

The women see him.—Early Sunday morning, while it was yet dark, Mary Magdalene, Mary the mother of James, Salome, Joanna, and other women went to the tomb with the spices and ointments which they had prepared. When they reached the sepulcher, they found that the stone had been rolled away. When Mary Magdalene saw that the stone had been removed, she feared that the body had been stolen by Jesus' enemies. Running to Peter and John, she announced what she thought had happened. Peter and John then hastened to the tomb.

Meanwhile, the other women entered the sepulcher, where they saw two divine messengers in human form. One of the angels announced to the women that Jesus had risen and was going into Galilee. Leaving the sepulcher, agitated with fear rather than with hope, the women hastened with their message to the disciples. While they were on their way, Jesus himself met them with words of love and victorious joy. The women communicated the events to the disciples, but they did not believe the message.

Peter and John arrive.—Scarcely had the women departed from the tomb when John arrived. He did not enter the tomb at once. Stooping down, he saw the linen grave clothes. When Peter arrived, he went immediately into the sepulcher with John following. The tomb was indeed empty. The linen clothes were lying in one place. The napkin which had been about Christ's head was carefully folded and was lying in another place. The two disciples returned to the city, filled with unutterable emotions.

Mary Magdalene's joy.—Mary Magdalene returned to the sepulcher. When she looked into the tomb, she saw two angelic forms sitting where the body of Jesus had lain. The angels entered into conversation with her. Standing nearby was a man whom Mary Magdalene thought was the gardener. She did not recognize Jesus until he had twice spoken to her. She struggled to embrace his feet, but he restrained her. He implied that after his ascension he would be present with her and the other believers in a higher sense than during the period of his earthly life. Mary Magdalene seems to have been the first person to see the resurrected Lord. Jesus then commissioned her to go and tell the disciples that he was about to ascend to the Father. (See Mark 16:2–11; Matt. 28:2–10; Luke 24:1–12; John 20:1–18.)

On Sunday morning when the Roman guards discovered that the tomb was empty, they went into the city and reported to the chief priests. A meeting of the Sanhedrin was immediately convened. It was resolved that they must conceal the disappearance of Jesus' body to avoid an uprising. Therefore, the guards were bribed to circulate the report that while they were asleep, the body of Jesus had been stolen by some of his disciples. This action was in keeping with the whole course of their procedure from the time they bargained with Judas to betray Jesus for thirty pieces of silver. (See Matt. 28:11–15.)

On the road to Emmaus.—On the evening of the resurrection day two disciples, Cleopas and an unnamed disciple, were joined by Jesus as they were on their way to Emmaus. Emmaus was about seven miles west or northwest of Jerusalem. The sudden close of Jesus' career had convinced these disciples that their conception of "the coming one" was erroneous. It was evident that they regarded the ministry of Jesus as ended. Their hopes for the coming of the kingdom were buried in the sepulcher. The unknown traveler joined them and showed them that the Scriptures spoke of a suffering as well as a conquering messiah. They did not recognize him until he was breaking bread with them; then he mysteriously vanished from their sight. From this experience they learned that Jesus was liberated from the conditions of his former life in the flesh. (See Mark 16:12–13; Luke 24:13–32.)

To Peter and then to the group.—These two disciples hurried back to Jerusalem, found the apostles and others gathered together, and learned from the group that Jesus had appeared to Simon Peter. They also told their own story of Jesus' appearance on the road to Emmaus, and how they had recognized him in the breaking of bread. (See Luke 24:33–35; 1 Cor. 15:5.)

While the company of disciples were listening to the stories of those who had so recently been with Jesus, he suddenly appeared in their midst. They were struck with superstitious dread. In order to reassure them, he asked them to observe his hands and his feet lacerated by the crucifixion and to satisfy themselves that he had a substantial body by touching him. Since they still disbelieved, he asked for food and ate in their presence. Thus he demonstrated to them that, whatever change had passed upon him, he was still in connection with the natural world. He only intended to teach them the reality of his resurrection.

Having calmed their fears, Jesus reminded his followers that all which had happened to him was in fulfilment of his own words as well as the ancient prophecies. Then he commissioned the disciples to witness to what had taken place, and he bestowed power for the fulfilment of the commission he had given them.

Thomas was not present at this meeting. When he was informed by the others of the appearance of Jesus, he utterly refused to believe it. He demanded to see and touch Jesus for himself.

In eight days Jesus had marched into Jerusalem, confronted the Jewish leaders, been arrested, tried, crucified, and resurrected. His resurrection was the first decisive step that he took on the way to his final glory, after his incarnation and descent into the darkness of night. (See Mark 16:14; Luke 24:36–43; John 20:19–25.)

SUBSEQUENT APPEARANCES

The following Sunday night the disciples met again behind closed doors. This time, Thomas was present. Suddenly Jesus was seen stand-

ing in the midst of the group. He offered Thomas the proof which
he had said would be necessary to satisfy him. It appears that Thomas
did not avail himself of Jesus' permission to touch his scars.

> Confronted with one who was tangible enough to bear the marks of
> his passion, yet intangible enough to appear and disappear at will,
> Thomas realized that he was dealing not just with an earthly man who
> had been his **Lord** and Master, nor only with a spiritual being who had
> been his **God,** but rather with one who united both the temporal and the
> eternal, the seen and the unseen, the human and the divine, in his own
> person. In confessing Jesus to be **"my Lord and my God,"** Thomas
> brought the Gospel story full circle to the point at which it had begun
> (1 : 1).[6]

Thomas forgot his doubts and his required proof, and made his simple
but moving declaration of faith: "My Lord and my God!" (See John
20:26–31.)

Jesus had commanded the disciples to go into Galilee, but they
remained in Jerusalem for at least one week after the resurrection
before going to Galilee. Some of them went on a fishing expedition
led by Simon Peter. The expedition was unsuccessful at first, and they
fished all night without catching anything. When dawn came, following the suggestion of a stranger on the beach, the fisherman made a
large catch. Then John recognized the presence of the Lord. The
disciples joined him on the beach, and he gave them bread and fish to
eat. Jesus then restored and commissioned Peter for his future work.
He also predicted the manner of Peter's death. (See John 21.)

It is almost certain that at this same appearance, the five hundred
brethren mentioned by Paul were assembled with the apostles, who
are mentioned in the Gospels only by Matthew. The circumstances
of this meeting are not given us. When the disciples saw the Lord,
they prostrated themselves in adoration.

Jesus accepted their worship, and said to them: "All authority has
been given to Me in heaven and earth. Go therefore and make disciples
of all the nations, baptizing them in the name of the Father and the
Son and the Holy Spirit, teaching them to observe all that I commanded you; and lo, I am with you always, even to the end of the
age" (Matt. 28:18–20). (See Mark 16:15–18; Matt. 28:16–20;
1 Cor. 15:6.)

At another appearance Jesus led some of his disciples to the true
method of interpreting the prophecies about the Christ. They became

conscious of a new spiritual power of insight and knowledge which they had not possessed before. Again, he commissioned his disciples to preach the gospel. (See Luke 24:44–49; Acts 1:3–8.)

During the forty days subsequent to Jesus' resurrection, he had manifested himself at intervals to his disciples. His body had been mysteriously changed and glorified. In his resurrected body, matter was transmuted into a "spiritual body." It was no longer bound by the laws of the natural body. He no longer belonged to the natural world, though the natural world still belonged to him, and was more than ever subject to his will.

After his resurrection, our Lord was no longer mortal. He had entered into a mode of existence which transcends that of finite man. However, he was able to appear personally to the disciples. It is probable that he showed himself to them daily (Acts 1:3). They needed these frequent reassurances from him. The recorded appearances may have been in the following order:

- To Mary Magdalene (John 20:11–18)
- To a group of women (Matt. 28:9–10)
- To the two disciples on the way to Emmaus (Mark 16:12–13; Luke 24:13–32)
- To Simon Peter (Luke 24:34; 1 Cor. 15:5)
- To the ten apostles and others (Luke 24:33–43; John 20:19–25)
- To the eleven apostles (John 20:26–31)
- To the fishermen disciples beside the Lake of Galilee (John 20)
- To about five hundred in Galilee (Matt. 28:16–20; 1 Cor. 15:6)
- To James (1 Cor. 15:7)
- To the disciples (Luke 24:44–49; Acts 1:3–8)
- To the disciples before the ascension (Luke 24:50–53; Acts 1:9–12)

The significance of the ascension depends on Jesus' mode of existence after his resurrection. If he was glorified in his resurrection, then the ascension was the last of his appearances to his disciples. Though he remained on earth for a time, after the resurrection he was an inhabitant of the heavenly realm. When the resurrection ministry had been completed, Jesus ascended into heaven. Our Lord's earthly life and ministry had been completed.

But he will return in person, "not in order to suffer once again, but to bring the sovereign dominion of God to complete and everlasting realization, and to establish his kingdom in perfection. By reason of all this, the disciples . . . returned to Jerusalem with jubilant hearts. And there, while awaiting the fulfilment of the promise of the Holy Ghost, they continued together in prayer . . . and went to the Temple regularly, praising and thanking God that He had accomplished such a mighty work of redemption in Jesus and that in it all He had wonderfully blessed and privileged them." [7]

1. For a fuller discussion of this idea, see David Smith, *The Days of His Flesh* (New York: Harper & Row), pp. 417–21.

2. Stagg, *The Broadman Bible Commentary, op. cit.,* p. 203.

3. William Hull, *The Broadman Bible Commentary,* Vol. 9.

4. *Ibid.*

5. Stagg, *op. cit.,* pp. 242–43.

6. Hull, *op. cit.*

7. Geldenhuys, *op. cit.,* p. 646.

9

INTERPRETING
OUR LORD

THE EVENTS of our Lord's earthly life were finished. The incarnation was complete. The child had been born. He had grown up in Nazareth. He had preached, taught, and healed. He had been arrested, tried, executed, buried, and raised. In this study, we have attempted to follow the historical Jesus through his earthly life. But who was this extraordinary person?

The mystery of Christ's identity was the topic of discussion of his contemporaries even during his ministry. The impressions he made on the minds of men were varied. He was regarded with the deepest interest and the most intensive curiosity. He was passionately hated and deeply loved. He excited jealousy and opposition from many and faith and devotion on the part of others. He could not be ignored by anyone. His life forced itself upon public attention. People were much perplexed. They were impressed with his greatness, yet they failed to recognize his high purpose. Was there anyone who understood him? Was there anyone who recognized him for who and what he was?

Throughout his ministry, Jesus purposed to reveal the mystery of his person to the disciples. For months, they had gained impressions of him as they lived with him day by day. The one essential element in their relationship to him was personal devotion, and that is what he sought to secure from them.

After Christ's resurrection and ascension, his disciples reached a

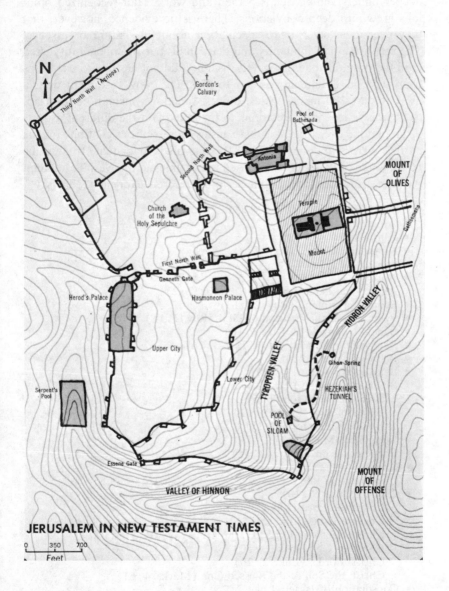

JERUSALEM IN NEW TESTAMENT TIMES

0   350   700
Feet

(Map labels:)

N

Third North Wall (Agrippa)

Gordon's Calvary

Pool of Bethesada

Second North Wall

Antonia

MOUNT OF OLIVES

Church of the Holy Sepulchre

Temple Mount

Gethsemane

First North Wall

Genneth Gate

Hasmoneon Palace

Herod's Palace

Upper City

KIDRON VALLEY

TYROPOEN VALLEY

Gihon Spring

HEZEKIAH'S TUNNEL

Lower City

Serpent's Pool

POOL OF SILOAM

Essene Gate

MOUNT OF OFFENSE

VALLEY OF HINNON

deeper understanding of his person and work. Half-recognized opinions grew into deep convictions. There is no evidence, however, that they ever engaged in deep speculation about his nature or essence. The relationship of humanity and deity in his person was not discussed until the postapostolic times. His disciples did not hesitate to use terms from the Old Testament to refer to him. The New Testament writers used at least 173 names, titles, offices, functions, metaphors, descriptive phrases, and interpretations to try to explain the different aspects of his unique life. Many of these terms were self-designations on the part of Jesus. Any one, or all, of these terms is inadequate to describe Jesus. Some of these terms are used many times in the New Testament. An alphabetical listing with one Scripture reference for each follows:

- The last Adam (1 Cor. 15:45)
- Advocate (1 John 2:1)
- Almighty (Rev. 1:8)
- Alpha and Omega (Rev. 1:8)
- Amen (Rev. 3:14)
- Apostle (Heb. 3:1)
- Author and Perfecter of faith (Heb. 12:2)
- Beginning and end (Rev. 22:13)
- Beginning of the creation of God (Rev. 3:14)
- Beheld by angels (1 Tim. 3:16)
- Believed on in the world (1 Tim. 3:16)
- Beloved (Matt. 12:18)
- Beloved Son (Matt. 3:17)
- Bread (John 6:41)
    Bread, Living (John 6:51)
    Bread of God (John 6:33)
    Bread of life (John 6:35)
- Carpenter (Mark 6:3)
- Carpenter's son (Matt. 13:55)
- Child (Matt. 2:8)
- Child Jesus (Luke 2:27)
- Christ (Matt. 16:16)
    Christ the Lord (Luke 2:11)
    Christ a King (Luke 23:2)
    Christ Jesus our Lord (1 Tim. 1:12)
    Christ of God (Luke 9:20)
    Christ, Lord's (Luke 2:26)
    Christ, the Son of the Blessed One (Mark 14:61)
- Consolation of Israel (Luke 2:25)
- Cornerstone (Eph. 2:20)
- Cornerstone, chief (Matt. 21:42)

- David, Son of (Matt. 9 : 27)
- Deliverer (Rom. 11 : 26)
- Descendant of David (2 Tim. 2 : 8)
- Door (John 10 : 9)
- Door of the sheep (John 10 : 7)
- Exact Representation of God's nature (Heb. 1 : 3)
- Faithful and True (Rev. 19 : 11)
- First and last (Rev. 1 : 17)
- Firstborn (Heb. 1 : 6)
    Firstborn of the dead (Rev. 1 : 5)
    Firstborn among many brethren (Rom. 8 : 29)
    Firstborn of all creation (Col. 1 : 15)
- Firstfruits of those who are asleep (1 Cor. 15 : 20)
- Forerunner (Heb. 6 : 20)
- Foundation (1 Cor. 3 : 11)
- Friend of tax-gatherers and sinners (Matt. 11:19)
- Gentle (Matt. 21 : 5)
- Gift of God (John 4 : 10)
- Glory of Israel (Luke 2 : 32)
- God, the true (1 John 5 : 20)
- God, blessed forever (Rom. 9 : 5)
- God with us (Matt. 1 : 23)
- God's well-beloved Son (Col. 1 : 13)
- Guarantee of a better covenant (Heb. 7 : 22)
- Guardian of souls (1 Pet. 2 : 25)
- Head of every man (1 Cor. 11 : 3)
- Head of the body (church) (Col. 1 : 18)
- Heir of all things (Heb. 1 : 2)
- High Priest (Heb. 3 : 1)
- High Priest of good things to come (Heb. 9 : 11)
- Holy (Rev. 3 : 7)
    Holy and Righteous One (Acts 3 : 14)
    Holy One of God (Mark 1 : 24)
    Holy Servant (Acts 4 : 30)
    Holy offspring (Luke 1 : 35)
- Hope, Our (1 Tim. 1 : 1)
- Horn of Salvation (Luke 1 : 69)
- I AM (John 8 : 58)
- Image of God (2 Cor. 4 : 4)
- Immanuel (Matt. 1 : 23)
- Jesus (Matt. 1 : 21)
    Jesus Christ our Savior (Titus 3 : 6)
    Jesus the Nazarene (John 19 : 19)
    Jesus the King of the Jews (Matt. 27 : 37)
    Jesus the Son of God (Heb. 4 : 14)
- Judge of the living and the dead (Acts 10 : 42)

- Judge, righteous (2 Tim. 4 : 8)
- King (Matt. 21 : 5)
    King of Israel (John 1 : 49)
    King of the Jews (Matt. 2 : 2)
    King of kings (1 Tim. 6 : 15)
- Lamb (Rev. 5 : 6)
    Lamb of God (John 1 : 29)
    Lamb that was slain (Rev. 5 : 12)
- Leader (Matt. 23 : 10)
- Life (John 14 : 6)
- Life, our (Col. 3 : 4)
- Light (John 12 : 35)
    Light of the world (John 8 : 12)
    Light, true (John 1 : 9)
- Lion, from the tribe of Judah (Rev. 5 : 5)
- Lord (Matt. 3 : 3)
    Lord and Savior Jesus Christ (2 Pet. 2 : 20)
    Lord Christ (Col. 3 : 24)
    Lord Jesus (Acts 1 : 21)
    Lord Jesus Christ (Rom. 1 : 7)
    Lord of all (Acts 10 : 36)
    Lord of glory (1 Cor. 2 : 8)
    Lord of lords (1 Tim. 6 : 15)
    Lord of heaven and earth (Acts 17 : 24)
    Lord of the dead and living (Rom. 14 : 9)
    Lord of the sabbath (Mark 2 : 28)
- Man (John 19 : 5)
- Man, second (1 Cor. 15 : 47)
- Master (2 Tim. 2 : 21)
- Mediator (1 Tim. 2 : 5)
- Mediator of the new covenant (Heb. 12 : 24)
- Messiah (John 1 : 41)
- Morning star (Rev. 22 : 16)
- Nazarene (Matt. 2 : 23)
- Offspring of David (Rev. 22 : 16)
- Only Sovereign (1 Tim. 6 : 15)
- Only begotten God (John 1 : 18)
- Our Passover (1 Cor. 5 : 7)
- Power of God (1 Cor. 1 : 24)
- Priest forever (Heb. 5 : 6)
- Prince (Acts 5 : 31)
- Prince of life (Acts 3 : 15)
- Proclaimed among the nations (1 Tim. 3 : 16)
- Prophet (Luke 24 : 19)
- Propitiation (expiation) (Rom. 3 : 25)
- Rabbi (John 1 : 38)

- Rabboni (John 20:16)
- Radiance of his (God's) glory (Heb. 1:3)
- Redemption (1 Cor. 1:30)
- Resurrection (John 11:25)
- Revealed in the flesh (1 Tim. 3:16)
- Righteous (1 John 2:1)
- Righteous One (Acts 3:14)
- Righteousness (1 Cor. 1:30)
- Rock (1 Cor. 10:4)
- Rock of offense (1 Pet. 2:8)
- Root of David (Rev. 5:5)
- Root of Jesse (Rom. 15:12)
- Ruler (Matt. 2:6)
- Ruler of the kings of the earth (Rev. 1:5)
- Same yesterday, and today, and forever (Heb. 13:8)
- Sanctification (1 Cor. 1:30)
- Savior (Luke 2:11)
    Savior of the body (church) (Eph. 5:23)
    Savior of the world (1 John 4:14)
- Servant (Matt. 12:18)
- Servant-Jesus (Acts 4:27)
- Shepherd and Guardian of souls (1 Pet. 2:25)
    Shepherd, Chief (1 Pet. 5:4)
    Shepherd, Good (John 10:11)
    Shepherd, Great, of the sheep (Heb. 13:20)
- Son, Chosen (Luke 9:35)
- Son of God (Luke 4:41)
- Son of man (Matt. 16:28)
- Son of Mary (Mark 6:3)
- Son of the Blessed (Mark 14:61)
- Son of the Father (1 John 1:3)
- Son of the Most High God (Mark 5:7)
- Son of the living God (Matt. 16:16)
- Source of eternal salvation (Heb. 5:9)
- Sovereign (1 Tim. 6:15)
- Star, bright morning (Rev. 22:16)
- Stone (Matt. 21:42)
- Stone of stumbling (1 Pet. 2:8)
- Sunrise from on high (Luke 1:78)
- Taken up in glory (1 Tim. 3:16)
- Teacher (John 3:2)
- The One who baptizes in the Holy Spirit (John 1:33)
- Truth (John 14:6)
- Vindicated in the Spirit (1 Tim. 3:16)
- Vine, true (John 15:1)
- Way (John 14:6)

- Wisdom (1 Cor. 1 : 30)
- Wisdom of God (1 Cor. 1 : 24)
- Witness, faithful and true (Rev. 3 : 14)
- Word (Logos) (John 1 : 1)
    Word (Logos) of God, The (Rev. 19 : 13)
    Word (Logos) of life (1 John 1 : 1)

Some of these terms will be considered briefly in an effort to understand how they were used by Jesus himself and by the New Testament writers. The question **Who is Jesus?** is answered best by considering how men named him. It is in this manner that a deeper understanding of the person of Christ can be obtained. **Salvation, however, does not consist in knowing the names and titles of Jesus, but in knowing Jesus.**

Jesus

The name "Jesus" (Greek: *Iēsous*) is a transliteration of the Hebrew "Jehoshua" (shortened to Joshua). It means, "Jehovah is salvation," or "Jehovah is Savior." In obedience to the command of an angel to Joseph, this name "Jesus" was given to the son of Mary (Matt. 1:21). It was the name he bore as a human being, suggesting his humanity. However, the name itself implied that he was the salvation, the help, of God. The name "Jesus" was very common among the Jews. Josephus mentioned ten persons by this name who were contemporaries of Jesus Christ. This name is used for our Lord five or six hundred times in the four Gospels.

The fact that Christianity centered around a real man, a human being, a historical person is reflected in the personal name Jesus. The gospel was permanently anchored to historical events and to a historical person. In addition to all else that he was, Jesus was a real man. The earliest Christians could not forget that the grace of God had been manifested to them in his human personality.

In the first recorded sermon delivered by an apostle, Peter spoke of the risen Lord as "Jesus the Nazarene, a man attested to you by God with miracles and wonders and signs" (Acts 2:22). The word used here for man is *anēr* which describes a man as an individual of worth. Many years later Paul wrote to Timothy and said: "There is one God, and one mediator also between God and men, the man Christ Jesus" (1 Tim. 2:5). The word used here for man is *anthropōs* which describes a man as a human being. The early Christians did not hesitate to refer to Jesus by the two words for man in Greek. Jesus was a man.[1]

The docetists (Gnostics) of the first and second centuries claimed that Christ could only *appear* to be in human form. He just *seemed* (*doceo*) to be a man. They eliminated the historical element almost entirely. The first heresies of the Christian religion denied the humanity of Christ. One is as unsound in his Christology when he denies the humanity of Jesus as when he denies his divinity. In the incarnation God did not masquerade as a man, but the humanity of Jesus was completely united with God; and everything he did and said as a man was at the same time the word and the activity of God.

Our Lord was most often called Jesus. That name summed up the things he came into the world to do. In the well-known words attributed to St. Bernard of Clairvaux:

> The name of Jesus . . . can restrain the impulse of anger, repress the swelling of pride, cure the wound of envy, bridle the onslaught of luxury, extinguish the flame of carnal desire—can temper avarice, and put to flight impure and ignoble thoughts. For when I name the name of Jesus, I call to mind at once a Man meek and lowly of heart, benign, pure, temperate, merciful; a Man conspicuous for every honourable and saintly quality; and also in the same Person the Almighty God—so that He both restores me to health by His example and renders me by His assistance. No less than this is brought to my mind by the name of Jesus whenever I hear it.[2]

Christ (Messiah)

In the New Testament the title "Christ" is the exact Greek equivalent of the Hebrew for "Messiah" (*mashiah*). The root meaning of the words is "Anointed One."

In the Old Testament the term *mashiah* was used to refer to the appointing of kings, priests, and prophets (1 Kings 19:16; Ex. 28: 41; 1 Sam. 10:1). Ultimately the title was developed to designate a person connected with last things (eschatology).[3] This use may have grown out of hopes which were kindled in the anointing of each king. The reign of each new king was regarded as offering the opportunity for the fulfilment of these hopes.

The root of the messianic idea is to be found in the relations which God sustained with his chosen people throughout the Old Testament. The promise which he made to the Israelites while they were still in the land of Egypt, "I will take you to me for a people, and I will be to you a God" (Ex. 6:7, KJV), had been conditioned upon their faithfulness to the divine commands. Their repeated unfaithfulness did not alienate them forever from the good will of God. He declared, through his prophets, that he would "make a new covenant with the house of Israel, and with the house of Judah" in place of that which they had violated (Jer. 31:31).

The prophets often stressed the blessedness of the coming time, when the national prosperity would be restored and even multiplied a hundred fold. This coming time included increased fertility of lands and flocks and herds, as well as freedom from the hand of the oppressor. Sometimes all of this was represented as coming to pass under the leadership of an anointed king, a *messiah*. Since most of the prophets who envisioned the "good time coming" belonged to the Southern Kingdom, it was natural that the king whom they expected was to be a "son of David."

Not only would the messiah rule over the people of Israel freed from servitude in foreign lands, but heathen nations would come to know God, worship in his Temple, and bring their tribute to Jerusalem (Isa. 19:25; 66:20,22). To these features of the national hope, the later prophets and the intertestamental writers added predictions of a coming judgment. In the literature of the period between the Testaments, we trace many fluctuations of thought and feeling. However, the fundamental concept of a future golden age for the saints of God is ever present. Usually, it was thought that this world kingdom would be brought into reality through the use of military means by the messiah. In Jesus' day the term "messiah" was popularly understood as primarily military and political in its implications.

No doubt Jesus thought of himself as the divinely-designated deliverer. In this sense, he clearly understood that he was the Messiah. However, the fact that he rarely used the term indicates that he was unwilling to accept the contemporary interpretation of the title (Mark 8:27–37; 14:60–65; 15:1–5). "It is an irony that a term which Jesus accepted but did not encourage has become the major title for him." [4] This title occurs in every book of the New Testament except 3 John.

The very fact that early Christians gave prominence to the title "Christ" indicates that Jesus did not disapprove of the use of it provided it was properly understood. However, Jesus had proved to be far more than the Christ of Jewish expectations, a name suggestive of the misery of war and not of the blessings of peace. In the early church there was a change of the term's meaning from a title to a personal designation, charged with deep religious significance.

There was a special appropriateness of this title in view of its specifically national character. As Jesus was the Christ, he realized the purpose of God which was manifested to Israel in the Old Testament. The persistence of the messianic significance of the term is seen in the fact that the Gospels retain this meaning although they were written at a time when the title had become little more than a personal name. Jesus Christ appears in the Gospels as a double proper name.

Son of Man

The title "Son of man" was the chosen self-designation of Jesus. He seems habitually and purposefully to have substituted this title for Messiah. The term "Son of man" appears fourteen times in Mark, thirty times in Matthew, twenty-six times in Luke, and twelve times in John. There is no evidence that the term was ever widely used in the early church. In the Gospels the term was used by Jesus for self-designation. Stephen is the only other person who used this title of Jesus in the New Testament (Acts 7:56).

"Son of man" is used more than one hundred times in the Old Testament as a synonym for "man." The outstanding exception to this general usage is Daniel 7:13, in which some of the later Jews found a prophecy of the Messiah. It is also used in the intertestamental writings, especially the books of Enoch. In Daniel, the Son of man is said to bring a rule which would not pass away, an eternal and universal kingdom. This is exactly what Jesus came to do. His rule was not to be over a nation, but over peoples of all nations.

Perhaps the principal reason Jesus used this title was because of its inclusiveness. It encompassed more of his total ministry than did Messiah in its popular usage. However, the meaning of the term is not explained anywhere in the New Testament. Its meaning is elusive, and any conclusion about it must be a matter of conjecture and inference. When Jesus called himself the "Son of man," he probably designated himself as the following:

MAN

Probably Jesus spoke Aramaic, as well as Greek. In Aramaic no distinction would be made between "man" and "Son of man." Nine tenths of all the Old Testament passages containing the term "Son of man" (90) are found in the book of Ezekiel. From the beginning to the end of this book God constantly addresses the prophet as "Son of man." This fact leads to the conclusion that Jesus, in speaking of himself as the "Son of man," intended to announce himself as a prophet. He was sent to warn his people of the danger which threatened them if they did not turn from their evil ways.

Nothing is clearer in the Gospel records than that Jesus believed himself to be entrusted with a divine message. When he stood up to read in the synagogue at Nazareth, he proclaimed himself at once, both by his selection from the Scriptures and his comment, to be a preacher of good tidings to the poor and a messenger of freedom to those who were in the bondage of sin (Luke 4:16–21). In his sympathy with human suffering and his earnest longing to be a true Savior of men, it was not "Messiah" which he wished to be called, but simply "man," a member of the human family, a brother to all mankind.

SUFFERING SERVANT

Immediately after the confession of Simon Peter at Caesarea Philippi, Jesus began to teach his disciples "that the Son of Man must suffer many things" (Mark 8:31). This was a new element which Jesus introduced into the concept of this title. The disciples did not understand this teaching. Evidently, to them the idea of Messiah and Son of man left no room for suffering and death.

In Matthew's account, Jesus accepted Peter's equation of the Son of man with the Messiah, but Peter did not accept Jesus' teaching that the Son of man must suffer. For Peter's first statement, he was praised; for his second, he was sharply rebuked. Mark recorded eight sayings which incorporate into the concept of "Son of man" the idea of suffering and rejection (Mark 8:31; 9:12,31; 10:33–34,45; 14:21,41). Most of the essential elements of these sayings are found in Mark 8:31—suffering, rejection, death, and resurrection. Jesus thus fused two figures which seemed to be contradictory when he joined the Suffering Servant and the Son of man.

> So then Jesus took this title Son of Man and reminted it, in such a way that his use of it shocked those who heard it. He intended all who heard him use it to listen, to be startled and to think. He knew himself the divine Son of Man whose triumph was sure; he knew himself the Suffering Servant for whom the Cross was the only and the chosen way. As the Servant of the Lord he was to suffer for men; as the Son of Man he must in the end be the King of men. The Son of Man is the title which contains within itself the shame and the glory of Jesus Christ.[5]

IDEAL MAN (Community)

In Daniel 7:13–14 the writer described a figure like a man coming with the clouds. He was moving toward the Ancient of Days who gave him the kingdom. The term "the Son of man" denotes a figure in human form. In apocalyptic writings, heavenly beings are symbolized by human form; but men are symbolized by beasts. The figure represents both a king and a kingdom. In Daniel 7:22, the saints were to possess the kingdom. Therefore, this "Son of man" symbolizes the kingdom of the saints. He is thus described as an individual person and as a community. Jesus alone proved to be the true Son of man. Humanity failed. Israel failed. The remnant failed. Jesus stood alone to show the perfect response to God's claim of kingship. He was the representative Man, the Man in whom humanity found its peak, example, and end. It was in him alone that the true destiny of man was achieved. Jesus not only was Son of man; he created "Son of man."

ESCHATOLOGICAL FIGURE BELONGING TO THE END OF TIME

The portrayal of the Son of man in Jewish literature outside the New Testament is that of a figure who is exalted and who will be a judge. In many of the New Testament passages a glorious figure is presented as the eternal, preexistent Man in whom human nature found its highest and most complete expression. He was in beginning with God and was divine (John 1:1). He conquered death (Mark 9:9; Matt. 17:9). He will come in glory (Mark 8:38). He will come in the clouds in power and great glory (Mark 13:26; 14:62; Matt. 24:30; 26:64; Luke 21:27).

It is with these apocalyptic and *Parousia*-sayings that the Son of man is revealed in such a way that the people would recognize him. In a way foreign to Jewish thought, Jesus was the Son of man while he was on the earth. But they were able to understand when he spoke of himself as a glorious Son of man of the future. In a way, he did not become the Son of man in his fulness until after the resurrection. In a larger sense, he will fulfil the concept of the Son of man in its completeness only when he appears as the judge of all men.

Son of God

The background of this title is both Jewish and Greek. Because it is found in both Greek and Hebrew thought, it is possible that the

New Testament conception may be closely related to either or both of these backgrounds. The Greek view was dominated by the ideas of physical conception and the reception of supernatural power to work miracles. In the Greek view the rulers of Egypt, Assyria, Babylonia, Greece, and Rome were thought to be sons of God, in a most literal sense. The Greek son of God was a gifted hero or king, with unusual power.

In the Old Testament, angels (Job 2:1), the Hebrew nation (Ex. 4:22), and kings (2 Sam. 7:14) were called sons of God. In contrast to the Greek view, the Jews never used the term Son of God in a procreative sense. Nor did they use it as a special title. The Jewish view was dominated by the ideas of likeness, election, and obedience.[6]

LIKENESS

The Hebrew language has few adjectives. When a Jew wished to describe something, he often used the prepositional phrase "son of" instead of an adjective. In the early church a man named Joseph was given a new name by his fellow members because of his generosity. They named him "Barnabas" (Acts 4:36). This name is composed of two words: "son" and "prophecy." The church gave Joseph the name Barnabas because of his talent for speaking or exhorting the people to dedication to God. He preached and he practiced dedication; therefore, he was named Barnabas. He was *like* this in his teaching and practice. These Christian Jews used the phrase "son of prophecy" to describe Joseph because this was the kind of man he was. So the Jews would not have said, "There is one who is like God." They would have used the term "*Son of* God."

ELECTION

In the Jewish view, a son was the peculiar possession of the father. In Deuteronomy 7:6–7 the choice of Israel, God's Son, is grounded in God's initiative and love (see Ex. 4:22). In John 8:29 Jesus based his message and mission on the fact that God had commissioned and sent him to do God's work. He was the Son of God because he was God's peculiar possession.

OBEDIENCE

The idea of sonship in the Jewish view implied absolute obedience. The relation which a *real* son had to his father was such that he would not disobey him. Jesus never referred to procreation as the evidence that he was God's Son, but he often used obedience to God as the evidence that he was God's Son (John 4:34; 8:29).

The Old Testament concept of sonship seems to dominate the New Testament idea. There is only one passage in the New Testament where Jesus is apparently designated Son of God due to a miracle (Matt. 14:33). Jesus seems to have repudiated the idea of basing proof of his sonship upon miraculous powers when he withstood his temptations.

Although Jesus' use of the term "Son of God" was based on the Old Testament, the New Testament meaning goes far beyond Hebrew understanding of the term. Because of the enlarged meaning of the term, it seems reasonable to suppose that the source of the title was Jesus himself. Jesus then was the Son of God in a unique sense. This is the emphasis of the only begotten Son of the Johannine writings. Jesus is Son of God in a sense in which no other can be. He made it clear that he was not merely *a* son, but *the* Son of God.

The dominant emphasis of the New Testament concerns the functional aspects of Jesus' sonship. Jesus was *the* Son of God because he revealed God. Jesus is what God is like. If you want to know what God says, listen to Jesus. If you want to know how God acts, watch Jesus. If you want to know how God loves, feel the love of Jesus. The one who has seen Jesus (Son) has seen God (Father). Jesus is also *the* Son of God because he was elected by God for his work. At Jesus' baptism, God anointed him with the Holy Spirit for his mission (Matt. 3:16). Jesus is also *the* Son of God because he completely conformed to the will of God.

The question which still remains to be answered is why Jesus alone was able to achieve perfect, ethical union with God when all other human beings have not done so. Jesus' sinlessness is not accounted for unless a fundamental and permanent distinction between himself and others is recognized. This demands the metaphysical. And this explanation can be found in the doctrine of the virgin birth. Although this doctrine does not explain all there is to know about the nature of Jesus, it does help to point up the uniqueness of his person and seems essential to a clearer understanding of Jesus as *the* Son of God.

Lord

When one turns to the study of the title "Lord" as related to Jesus, three problems immediately become evident.[7] The first of these is the problem of translation. The second of these problems is the matter of the origin of the title. Closely related to this is the question of the relation between the title and the concept of the deity of Jesus. These problems are very vitally related to the question of the early church's estimate of Jesus.

TRANSLATION OF THE WORDS

Two words in the Greek New Testament are translated Lord in English. One of these words is *despotes*. This was the term used to refer to a master, particularly the owner of slaves. It was the word used to refer to one who possessed supreme authority. It is used to refer to God in Luke 2:29; Acts 4:24; Revelation 6:10. It is used of Christ in 2 Timothy 2:21, 2 Peter 2:1, and Jude 4. This title had both a secular and religious significance in the first century.

Kurios (Lord) is an adjective used as a noun, variously translated in the New Testament as "Lord," "Master," "master," "owner," and "Sir." It occurs in every book of the New Testament except Titus and the Epistles of John. It was used in the Septuagint (Old Testament in Greek) to translate YHWH (Jehovah or Yahweh), one of the names for God. In the New Testament it is used to refer to one to whom service is due on any ground (Matt. 6:24). It is used of one who owns another (Gal. 4:1). It is also used as a title of respect or address to a father, husband, master, ruler, or an angel (Matt. 13:27; 21:29; 27:63; 1 Pet. 3:6).

ORIGIN OF THE TITLES

The term *kurios* was frequently used in the Oriental-Hellenistic religions of the Roman empire. It first occurred in the early part of the first century B.C. in Egypt. In time the Roman emperors felt that it would be to the advantage of the unity of the empire for them to use this title. The title as applied to the emperors had political significance and probably because of the close relationship of emperor worship had this element also in it.

It is probable that this title *kurios* as a designation for Jesus goes back to Jesus himself. It is almost certain that it was used in the primitive Palestinian church. Paul used this title more than 220 times. In 1 Corinthians 16:22 he used an Aramaic expression *Marana tha* ("Our Lord, come!") in a benediction. This Aramaic original must have had some special significance for the Corinthians. It is almost conclusive evidence that Jesus was called Lord in the worship services in the early church.

The New Testament affirms that Jesus became Lord in the truest sense through the resurrection (Acts 2:32–36), for it was therein that his lordship was manifest. The resurrection revealed him as the vanquisher of death and the living Lord who rightly claimed the absolute obedience of the believers.

Although the title *kurios* was especially applicable after the resurrection, it was used to refer to Jesus during his ministry. Jesus indirectly referred to himself as Lord in Mark 12:36 when he quoted Psalm 110:1. In a real sense, however, the lordship of Jesus was seen to be vitally connected with his death, and the term was especially filled with meaning when it was used after his resurrection.

RELATION OF THE CONCEPT TO THE DEITY OF JESUS

Jesus very clearly asserted that his kingdom was not of this world. However, the disciples were slow to comprehend the "otherness" of his kingdom. When they were confronted by his death, they were filled with despair. It was only in the encounter with the risen Lord that they realized the significance of his death. His lordship was realized in its fulness only when he overcame the world (John 18:36). This victory over the world came through his death. It was in the resurrection that his lordship, made possible through his death, was made evident.

Jesus, by his death and resurrection, became Lord of the whole universe (Rom. 10:12). All authority had been given to him (Matt. 28:10). All creatures in heaven and earth must acknowledge him as Lord (Phil. 2:9–10). God was pleased through Christ to reconcile all things to himself (Col. 1:20).

Kurios was the word which brought early Christians into a to-the-death struggle with Rome. Not even with tongue in cheek would they say "Caesar is Lord." They were willing to die rather than own any other master than Jesus the Lord. *Kurios* was the creed of the early church. And it must be the activated creed of every contemporary Christian. We too must deny all lordship over our lives except Christ's.

Only at Christ's return will the lordship of death and flesh be destroyed and his lordship be complete (1 Cor. 15:24). Death and the flesh were conquered in the death and resurrection of our Lord, and their destruction at the consummation will only be a fulfilment of what has already taken place.

The lordship of Jesus is theocratic—subject to the lordship of God. The purpose of the lordship of Jesus is that God may be "all in all" (1 Cor. 15:28). Thus at the consummation, the lordship of Christ is taken up into the lordship of God.

The lordship of Christ has a more specific expression than the authority over the created order. He is the Lord of the church. The main distinction between the two lordships is that the church is aware of Christ's lordship over it. This is expressed in the Aramaic prayer formula *Marana tha* (1 Cor. 16:22). For the early church it was always a personal relationship. It was always "my Lord," or "our Lord." Christians today also recognize Jesus Christ as "our Lord."

Prophet

The Hebrew word for prophet means literally one who speaks forth or one who speaks for another. The Old Testament prophets were men who were sent from God. In the customary language of the New Testament, men were "apostled" on a special mission from God.

The New Testament record treats Jesus as such a "sent" one. It thus designates him as "prophet." [8] In Nain when he brought the widow's son back to life, the multitude promptly spoke of a great prophet having arisen among them (Luke 7:16). On another occasion, his enemies would have arrested him but for fear of the multitude who "held him to be a prophet" (Matt. 21:46, RSV). Furthermore, the statements given by the disciples in answer to his question of his identity reveal that some of the common people thought Jesus was a prophet (Mark 8:28). Again, when Jesus made his royal march into Jerusalem on the Sunday before his crucifixion on Friday, the people along the way designated him as "the prophet" (Matt. 21:11).

Jesus must have thought of himself as a prophet. When he preached in Nazareth and was rejected by his own townspeople, he said: "No prophet is welcome in his home town" (Luke 4:24). On another occasion, when leaving Samaria to go to Galilee, he said that a prophet has no honor in his own country. Later in his ministry when he was warned about going to Jerusalem, he said: "It cannot be that a prophet should perish outside of Jerusalem" (Luke 13:33). On more than one occasion Jesus described Jerusalem as the killer of prophets (Matt. 23:37; Luke 13:34). In each of these references Jesus was referring to himself. Therefore, it is reasonable to conclude that Jesus acknowledged that he was a prophet.

The chief point of interest, however, centers around the question of whether or not Jesus fulfilled the role of the final, ultimate, eschatological prophet about whom Moses prophesied and for whom Jewish expectation was aroused (Deut. 18:15; John 1:45). There can be little doubt that the early community of believers equated *the* prophet with Jesus. This is revealed in Simon Peter's discourse in Acts 3:12–26. Stephen, in the same book, implied that the prophecy of Moses was fulfilled in Jesus (Acts 7).

When he was recognized by his followers as the prophet of whom Moses spoke, Jesus did not deny the title. The account of the feeding of the multitude bears this out (John 6:14).

Jesus also thought of himself as completing and fulfilling the work of Moses. The authoritative way in which he handled the law of Moses is rather clear evidence of this fact. He spoke with authority, not like the scribal interpreters of the old law: "You have heard that the ancients were told . . . but I say to you" (Matt. 5:21–22).

In contrast to the scribes who sought for a consensus in interpreting the law, Jesus spoke with independence of judgment. He taught with an understanding not limited to the learning of the schools, but with the authority of his own God-given insight. This authority which he claimed for himself was his because he was *the* prophet from God. This was apparently the impression he made on his hearers. It is highly probable that this impression was due to his own understanding of his prophetic role. God was speaking to his people in the old and accredited way. The long-expected prophet who would be like Moses had now appeared. Thus, the writers of the New Testament regarded Jesus as the prophet par excellence. He was, therefore, the fulfilment of the prophecy of Deuteronomy 18:15—the prophet like Moses.

Son of David

The title "Son of David" is the most Jewish of all the titles applied to Jesus.[9] It identified Jesus as a human figure, the descendant of David who was to be a national deliverer. The Jews thought that there could never be another king like David. When they dreamed of a golden age, they always thought of David as being king. The prophets often associated this title with the national hopes of the Hebrew people (Isa. 9:7; 11:1; Jer. 23:5; 30:9; 33:17; Ezek. 34:23–24; 37:24; Hos. 3:5; Amos 9:11; Zech. 12:8). This title is ascribed to Jesus twice in the story of blind Bartimaeus (Mark 10:46–52). According

to Mark 12:35–37, Jesus inquired how the Christ could be the descendant of David and still be called "Lord" by David. He did not
repudiate Davidic descent, but he did imply a more spiritual conception of Messiah. Matthew has six additional cases in which the title
"Son of David" was used of Jesus (Matt. 1:1; 9:27; 12:23; 15:22;
21:9,15). Except for the reference in his genealogy, Luke's use of
this term seems to be those taken from Mark. The title does not occur
in the Gospel of John nor in the rest of the New Testament except in
Romans 1:3.

It is apparent that, occasionally, Jesus was greeted by this title, but
he did not use it of himself or welcome it. He did accept the title
since it was rightfully his, but he preferred other titles which better
communicated his true mission on earth. Matthew, the most Jewish of
the Gospels, disclosed a special interest in the title. The belief that
Jesus was the Son of David is reflected in the genealogies of Jesus.
Otherwise, interest in this designation quickly died out in primitive
Christianity. On Gentile soil the title was without interest or significance
or other names were preferred, especially that of "Lord."

King

The title King occurs six times in the Gospel of Mark (Mark 15:2,
9,12,18,26,32). In each case it is used in contempt and derision.
The priests who charged Jesus before Pilate used this term (Luke 23:
2). It was also used by the soldiers in taunting Jesus as he hung on
the cross (Luke 23:37). The title occurs as a term of honor in connection with the royal entry into Jerusalem (Luke 19:38; Matt. 21:5).
It also appears in Matthew in the question of the Magi, "Where is He
who has been born King of the Jews?" (2:2).

The Gospel of John uses the title in six passages that parallel those
already cited. It occurs at least seven times in passages that are peculiar
to the Fourth Gospel. Nathanael marveled at the perceptiveness of Jesus
and said, "Rabbi, You are the Son of God; You are the King of Israel"
(John 1:49). John indicated that, after the feeding of the five thousand,
the people "were intending to come and take Him by force, to make
Him king" (John 6:15). The title "king" occurs in the repeated question of Pilate during Jesus' trial (John 18:33,37,39; 19:3,14–15). It
is present in the protest of the chief priests: " 'Do not write, "The King
of the Jews"; but, that He said, "I am King of the Jews" ' " (John 19:
21).

Jesus claimed to be king of the Jews. Yet, he rejected every worldly notion of kingship and sought no earthly crown. He tried repeatedly to show men the difference in his kingdom (John 18:36). He came to the nation's capital to claim his rightful throne, to reign in men's hearts. The throne he received proved to be a cross.

Word (*Logos*)

Logos (Word) occurs frequently in the Septuagint (Greek Old Testament). It was used to translate a Hebrew word (*dabar*) which expressed the creative activity of God (Gen. 1:3,6,9,14,20,24). This same Hebrew word was used to express God's communication with men, his self-revelation, especially through the prophets. God's *Logos* was the agency through which his will was put into effect. It was not a mere sound uttered through the lips to express a meaning, but a living thing with creative power. It was also the means by which God communicated his purpose to his people.[10]

In some of the Jewish Wisdom Literature, *Logos* and "wisdom" are almost interchangeable. In Proverbs, "wisdom" bears some relation to the created world and seems to have an independent existence in the presence of God (Prov. 8:22–26).

A Jewish contemporary of Jesus, Philo Judeus, used the word *Logos* more than twelve hundred times in his writings which still exist. He used the term with a variety of meanings. According to Philo, the *Logos* gave to the world its form; it gave to men their image of God and even their minds. And the *Logos* led men back to God.

The term *Logos* was used in many Greek writings during the first century. It had many meanings. It was used to describe the cosmic law which rules the universe. It also meant account, rule, reason, saying, talk, subject matter about which one talks, law, statutes, and wisdom. It was an abstraction and a very convenient term for describing any kind of self-expression. It usually carried a double meaning, that is, an idea plus the expression of the idea. It appears likely that Greek thought did much to prepare the way for the use of the term in a Christian context. However, the Hebrew influence no doubt was primary in the concept as it appears in the New Testament.

In the New Testament, *Logos* is found as a title of Christ only in John's writings (John 1:1–18; 1 John 1:1; Rev. 19:13). The idea occurs in other New Testament writings without the title being given. It is probable that John used the term *Logos* because of its familiarity.

John introduced the Christological title *Logos* abruptly in the first verse of chapter 1. His purpose for using this familiar term was to try to explain the person of Jesus Christ. His *Logos* conception seems to have been determined by his previous thought of Christ. For John the beginning of all things lies in the preexistence of the *Logos*. He drew attention to the absolute beginning of all things. In the first sentence he told all that is possible for man to realize as to the essential nature of the *Logos* in relation to time, mode of being, and character. After the first sentence he moved immediately to the creative activity of the *Logos*. In the fourteenth verse he declared that the *Logos* became a definite human being in history. In 1 John 1:1 Jesus was given the title "the Word [*Logos*] of life." The writer then adds that by life he means the divine reality disclosed to men in the incarnate Christ. The appearance on the earth of this incarnate Christ was a fact attested to by eyewitnesses. In Revelation 19:13 Christ is pictured as a conquering warrior and "His name is called The Word [*Logos*] of God."

The two aspects of the nature of the *Logos* which are stated in these New Testament writings are his preexistence and his incarnation. The three functions which are affirmed are creation, revelation (light), and redemption (life). Jesus was never addressed as *Logos* during his life and he never used the title in reference to himself, but he is the fullest possible revelation of God which man is capable of grasping. Jesus was the "idea" of God plus the "expression" of the idea. He is the *Logos* of God.

> Jesus is the Word. He is God's ultimate and final communication to men; he is the demonstration to men of the mind of God towards them; he is the guarantee that at the heart of creation there is love.[11]

Savior

The root meaning of this word in the Old Testament is "helper" or "preserver." This title is used occasionally in the Old Testament to refer to God as the deliverer of his people in time of need (Ps. 106:21; Isa. 43:1–13; 45:15,21; 49:26; 60:16; 63:8; Jer. 14:8; Hos. 13:4). It is also used to refer to certain men who were national heroes (2 Kings 13:5; Neh. 9:27; Isa. 19:20; Obad. 21). In the intertestamental literature the title usually refers to God and generally describes physical deliverance.

In the Greco-Roman world the "savior" was applied to heroes, emperors, and various divinities. Certain kings or emperors were invested with the title "savior" as part of their proper name. Caesar Augustus, in one inscription, was hailed as the "savior of the world." It was perhaps because of its pagan associations that the term was at first avoided by the Christians. It was not until late in the second century that this title came to be one of the acknowledged names of Jesus. From that time on, however, it tended to be used more frequently than the earlier names of Lord and Messiah.

Since the second century, Savior has continued to be the distinctive designation for Jesus. The title was adopted because the concept it carries was inevitable. From the beginning it had been a fundamental Christian belief that Jesus brought salvation, and the belief could not but embody itself in the one word that expressed it.

The title Savior is used only twenty-four times in the New Testament. Eight times it is used as a title for God and sixteen times it is used for Christ. It is surprising that there are only two occurrences of the title Savior for Jesus in the Gospels. It is used by the angel in the announcement to the shepherds (Luke 2:11) and by the Samaritans in reference to Jesus (John 4:42). In spite of the fact that the title appears infrequently in the Gospels, the idea is presupposed on every hand. An excellent example of this is Matthew 1:21 which is part of the account in which the Lord appeared to Joseph in a dream and said, concerning Mary: "She will bear a Son; and you shall call His name Jesus, for it is He who will save His people from their sins."

Among the oldest direct uses of the title "Savior" for Jesus are the two occurrences in Acts 5:31 and 13:23. In Acts 5:31 the title was used in connection with the exaltation of Christ. When Peter and the other apostles were brought before the Council for preaching about Jesus, they said, concerning Jesus: "He is the one whom God exalted to His right hand as a Prince and a Savior, to grant repentance to Israel, and forgiveness of sins." In Acts 13:23 the title was used in the sermon that Paul preached at Pisidian Antioch. While he was speaking of David, Paul said: "From the offspring of this man according to promise God has brought to Israel a Savior, Jesus."

The most frequent occurrences of the title "Savior" for Jesus in the New Testament are to be found in the pastoral and general epistles (2 Tim. 1:10; Titus 1:4; 2:13; 3:6; Eph. 5:23; Phil. 3:20; 2 Pet. 1:1,11). The title is also used for God most often in the New Testament in these epistles (1 Tim. 1:1; 2:3; 4:10; Titus 1:3; 2:10; 3:4; Jude 25). This fact would indicate that the idea of salvation and of Jesus as divine Savior was uppermost in the minds of these writers.

The Old Testament and Hellenism appear to have influenced the use of Savior as a title for Jesus. In the Old Testament God is called Savior. In Hellenism, deities, heroes, and rulers bore this title. Use of the term was especially prominent in emperor worship. In spite of the connotations which the title had in Hellenism, the Christians used it as a title for Jesus, giving it an exalted meaning. To the early Christians Jesus was primarily a Savior from sin and death. He continues to be that for all who place their trust in him.

High Priest

In the Old Testament the high priest was chief among a group of priests. Aaron and his sons were the first priests to be consecrated under the covenant relationship of God to the people Israel (Ex. 28:1). They were to minister to God in behalf of the people under the covenant relationship. They were intermediaries between God and man. Thus the high priest was the chief spokesman on behalf of God to the people. The office was inherited and was held for life.

The title "high priest" as used to describe the Messiah never gained any prominence among the Hebrews. In fact, the evidence for a messianic hope centering around the Messiah as High Priest in the Old Testament is very scanty indeed. There are only two passages in the Old Testament which claim our attention in this regard.

The first of these is Psalm 110, an oft-quoted Old Testament passage in the New Testament. The writer of the Epistle to the Hebrews used it as his main text in his presentation of Jesus as High Priest. This psalm does not say specifically that the Messiah will function as a high priest. The reference rather is to a Melchizedek type priesthood which shall find its fulfilment in Messiah.

Melchizedek means "King of righteousness." He was prince of Salem, which means peace. He was not of the tribe of Levi, thus he was without genealogy. He had no connection with any priestly family, and he had no successor. He was, as the Scripture puts it, "a priest forever." He took tithes from Abraham. The writer of Hebrews had all of these things in mind when he likened the priesthood of Jesus to that of Melchizedek. Christ's priesthood is eternal, unchanging. It provides salvation "to the uttermost" and continuing intercession.

The second Old Testament passage which claims our attention is Malachi 3:1–3, where Messiah is spoken of as coming to his temple.

The reason for his coming to his temple (as explained in verses 2 and 3) is to purify the sons of Levi, so that they may make their offerings in righteousness. This is a probable allusion to the priestly ministry of the Messiah, although he is not mentioned specifically as a priest. His stated function is that of an agent to purify the priesthood.

The intertestamental literature of the Jews contains many messianic concepts. Though there was some evidence to the contrary found with the Dead Sea Scrolls, there does not seem to have been widespread hope for a priestly Messiah.

In the New Testament Jesus never referred to himself specifically as high priest. However, some of his recorded sayings seem to point toward his high priestly work (Mark 10:45; Matt. 20:28; John 17). There also is no evidence that the Gospel writers themselves thought of Jesus as High Priest. The angel's instructions to Joseph concerning the name of Jesus may be construed as an allusion to his high priestly work (Matt. 1:21). Paul mentioned Christ's self-sacrifice and also his office as the one mediator between God and man (Eph. 5:2; 1 Tim. 2:5). It is impossible to conclude from these two references that Paul expressed a highly-developed doctrine of Jesus as High Priest. However, one cannot escape the conclusion that, in Paul's writings, there is at least the idea of such a doctrine.

The doctrine of Jesus as High Priest is developed in the New Testament in the Epistle to the Hebrews. In this epistle there are ten direct references to Jesus as High Priest (Heb. 2:17; 3:1; 4:14–15; 5:5, 10; 6:20; 7:26; 8:1; 9:11). As a title of Christ, High Priest emphasizes the elements of representation and union. Jesus appears in the presence of God as High Priest (representative) for his people. He who appears before God has, through his incarnation, made explicit the union that exists between him and his people. His own life is the sacrifice which Jesus offers on behalf of his people.

The writer of the Epistle to the Hebrews developed the doctrine of the high priesthood of Christ by showing that it was from God that Jesus received both the call and the equipment for this ministry. It is an office which he has held forever. It is a unique and peculiar priesthood, belonging to the order established by Melchizedek.

All of the titles and functions of Jesus have meaning beyond our ability to comprehend. But perhaps none of them has more relevance and comfort than this concept that he is present always to understand us and to "take our part."

Knowing Jesus

If every term used to refer to our Lord were thoroughly investigated and correctly interpreted, it would help us to know what Jesus thought about himself and what others thought about him. The study of his life and ministry and an investigation of these terms reveal important facts about his person and his work. These methods enable us to gain accurate knowledge about the historical Jesus. They show who he was, how he thought, what he said, and what he did.

From the Gospel records we see a person such as the world had never seen before. He was the living type of an ideal humanity—pure and sinless, destined to influence all times, to purify all peoples among whom he is known, and to enable his followers to grow by lifting them toward the measure of his stature.

However, if we knew all the facts about Jesus, this does not necessarily mean that we know him. Jesus Christ is a person and the only way to know any person is to know him personally. There is a fundamental difference between knowing about a person and knowing the person himself. We can *know* personally only those who are our contemporaries. We can know about George Washington, but we cannot know him. Paul probably knew more *about* Jesus than most Christians living today when he began his journey to Damascus; when he finished it, he knew *Jesus*. What a difference it made in his life! Jesus said that this acquaintance with God through Jesus Christ is the essence of and coextensive with eternal life: "This is eternal life, that they may know Thee the only true God, and Jesus Christ whom Thou hast sent" (John 17:3).

Jesus lived nearly two thousand years ago, but he also lives today. He is the eternal contemporary. When Jesus was on earth, he was not exclusively a spiritual man. He had a body of flesh. In the resurrection he became wholly spiritual. He assumed a spiritual body. He is in his total being the spiritual man, the new man, the second Adam.

What does knowing Jesus really mean? It does not mean knowing his titles, knowing facts about him, or knowing theological conclusions about him. It means knowing him in a personal relationship here and now. It means surrendering to his lordship. Our knowledge of God is really conditioned by our knowledge of Jesus. The more we know Jesus, the more we know God; and the more we know God, the more we know Jesus. It is as simple—and yet as profound—as that.

Paul became acquainted with God through Jesus and expressed it by saying, "I know whom I have believed" (2 Tim. 1:12). At an earlier time he expressed the desire to know Jesus better by saying, "That I may know Him, and the power of His resurrection and the fellowship of His sufferings, being conformed to His death" (Phil. 3:10). For Paul and for each one of us who will come to a deep experiential knowledge of our Lord, the "proofs" for Jesus Christ are transferred from the world without to the world within. Then each one of us will want to sing:

> More about Jesus would I know,
> More of His grace to others show;
> More of His saving fulness see,
> More of His love who died for me.
>
> More, more about Jesus,
> More, more about Jesus,
> More of His saving fulness see,
> More of His love who died for me.
> —E. E. Hewitt

1. William Barclay, *Jesus as They Saw Him* (New York: Harper & Row, 1962), pp. 9–13.

2. Kenneth E. Kirk, *The Vision of God* (New York: Longmans, Green & Co., 1946), p. 356.

3. Vincent Taylor, *The Names of Jesus* (New York: St. Martin's Press, 1953), pp. 18–23.

4. Frank Stagg, *New Testament Theology* (Nashville: Broadman Press, 1962), p. 46.

5. Barclay, *op. cit.*, p. 92.

6. *Ibid.*, pp. 43–67.

7. Taylor, *op. cit.*, pp. 38–51.

8. Barclay, *op. cit.*, pp. 229–39.

9. *Ibid.*, pp. 38–42.

10. *Ibid.*, pp. 421–29.

11. *Ibid.*, p. 429.

HEBREW HISTORY

SOME WRITERS, including Josephus, think that Hebrew history began with the call and response of Abraham (Gen. 12). Jewish writers usually refer to the Exodus (or migrations) as the time of the birth of the Hebrew nation. The books of Joshua and Judges show that the Exodus was followed by a long period in which the tribesmen conquered and settled the land of Canaan. This period was one of dim twilight in the history of the Hebrews. The people were often in conflict with the neighboring tribes—Canaanites, Philistines, Moabites, Amorites, Amalekites, Midianites, Sidonians, and Mesopotamians. There even were times when the several separate Hebrew tribes were in conflict with each other.

During this period there also were conflicts between the religious leaders who were endeavoring to establish a theocracy and the political leaders who wanted to have a king like the other nations. Saul was a victim of these struggles. The issue was settled when David became king of all the Hebrews about 993 B.C.

From the accession of David to the death of Solomon about 931 B.C., the Hebrews gave at least nominal allegiance to the house of David. Following the death of Solomon, the tribal kingdom was divided. The Southern Kingdom, Judah, was faithful to the house of David. The Northern Kingdom, Israel, selected other rulers for its kings. The Northern Kingdom seemed to have gained the ascendancy. For about 210 years these two small kingdoms existed side by side.

The period of the divided kingdoms was one of constant change, filled with wars, famines, and invasions. During the latter part of this period, these two kingdoms helped to form a buffer between Assyria on the north and Egypt on the south. Alliance with Assyria meant heavy tribute and the worship of Assyrian gods. Alliance with Egypt meant some independence but war with Assyria. Egypt encouraged these two little kingdoms, along with others, to resist Assyria.

It was during such resistance to Assyria that Israel was invaded by Shalmaneser V in 723 B.C. Shalmaneser was murdered shortly before Samaria fell, and his general, Sargon II (722–705 B.C.), seized the throne and captured Samaria in 722 or 721 B.C. The deportation of the people of Israel was a part of the regular Assyrian policy to reduce the risk of further national risings against the imperial power (2 Kings 17). The foreigners imported by the Assyrians intermarried with the Hebrews who were left. Later these people became known as the Samaritans, taking their name from their capital city.

After the fall of Samaria, Judah survived about 133 more years. During most of this time there was constant threat of Assyrian raids. However, Assyria continued to decline in strength until Nineveh, its capital, fell in 612 B.C. Babylon and Media signed a political alliance against Assyria. Egypt opposed this alliance because Pharaoh Neco could see that the only way to maintain a balance of power was for Assyria to survive. Pharaoh Neco did what he could to help Assyria, but at Carchemish in 605 B.C. Nebuchadnezzar defeated the combined forces of Assyria and Egypt, and the Babylonian Empire was established. (See 2 Kings 23:28–30; 2 Chron. 35:20–27.)

Apparently to assure the loyalty of Judah, Nebuchadnezzar moved south to Jerusalem and was then, or a short time later, acknowledged as sovereign. He took to Babylon some of the sacred vessels from the Temple in Jerusalem and also some noblemen to insure the payment of tribute. (See 2 Kings 24; Jer. 24; Dan. 1.)

In 598 B.C. the pro-Egyptian party in Jerusalem refused to send the annual tribute. Again Nebuchadnezzar marched to Jerusalem and carried more hostages to Babylon.

In 589 B.C. Zedekiah, along with other petty kings, rebelled against Babylon. Nebuchadnezzar's lenient treatment in putting down the first revolt was not repeated. In 587 B.C. Jerusalem was captured, the Temple burned, and the city walls breached. Many of the people were carried away to Babylon while others filed to Egypt (2 Kings 25; 2 Chron. 36).

When Nebuchadnezzar died in 561 B.C., the Babylonian Empire began to decline. A few years later a new power arose under Cyrus of Persia who rapidly overthrew the king of the Medes and ascended his throne, defeated Croesus of Lydia, and then turned against Babylon. Nabonidus of Babylon had deeply offended the religious sentiment of his people by collecting their gods in his capital. Cyrus, posing as a friend of the gods, was welcomed as a deliverer rather than as a conqueror. In 539 B.C. Cyrus captured the city of Babylon and a year later its citadel. The fall of Babylonia not only ended one era in history but instituted a new policy in the treatment of subject peoples.

The victorious Persians reversed the previous policy of repression, humiliation, and destruction. Instead, the Persians allowed their subject people many privileges. The Jews (since the Babylonian exile the Hebrews have been known as Jews) lived contentedly under Persian rule for nearly two hundred years. In accordance with Cyrus' general policy of dealing with subject peoples, the Jews were free to return to Palestine and to rebuild their Temple (Ezra 1–6). A relatively small group took advantage of the privilege, for most of them remained in Babylon where life was by no means intolerable. The Jews who returned to Palestine found that it was easier to get permission to build a Temple than to get permission to repair the city walls.

For nearly two centuries under Persian rule the Jews were, for the most part, loyal to the Persian kings. Judea was annexed to the district of Coele-Syria; and the administration of affairs was entrusted to the high priest, subject to the control of the Syrian governor. The high priest became the political, social, and religious leader of the people. This period saw great development in Judaism. Much of this development was due to ideas which were current in the world at that time. Monotheism gained the day. Both the Persians and the Jews worshiped one supreme God. Jewish exclusiveness manifested itself in a sense of aloofness and separateness. A new national feeling arose and social and religious isolation was practiced. The Jews thought of themselves as clean and all others as unclean.

The law of Moses became the standard of holiness and the symbol of nationality. It became essentially a ceremonial law. Religion was reduced to legalized forms in order to make it more secure against the influences of heathenism. The study of the law called forth scribes and resulted in the development of scribism. There seem to have been four stages in this development: the scribes were (1) first simply copyists of the law, (2) then students of the law, (3) editors of the law, and (4) finally interpreters of the law. The interpretation of the law by the scribes called the people to penitence, prayer, and meditation. Precision in the observance of all the prescribed rituals was made the gauge and measure of piety. The rite of circumcision and the observance of the sabbath became symbols of the close relationship between Israel and God.

The purification bath was added to the Jewish ritual during the time after the Exile. At first these baths seem to have been performed in private; but later in the Maccabean period (in imitation of the Greeks) the baths were taken in public (1 Macc. 1:14).

Recap of the Period

The Persian rulers and their probable dates:

Cyrus the Great	538–529 B.C.
Cambyses	529–522 B.C.
Darius Hystaspis	522–486 B.C.
Xerxes (Son of Darius)	486–465 B.C.
Artaxerxes Longimanus	465–425 B.C.
Xerxes II (45 days)	425 B.C.
Darius Nothus	423–404 B.C.
Artaxerxes II	404–359 B.C.
Ochus	359–338 B.C.
Darius Codomannus	336–330 B.C.

Possible order and dates for the high priests during the Persian period are:

Eliashib	445–430 B.C.
Joiada	430–405 B.C.
Jonathan (Johanan)	405–359 B.C.
Jaddua	359–332 B.C.

It is difficult to make a consistent historical narrative of the events which affected the Jews during the Persian rule. Near the end of this period Josephus related two incidents, both about rivalry of brothers for the priesthood. During the lifetime of Ezra and Nehemiah, the high priest was Eliashib (Ezra 10:6,24,27,36; Neh. 3:1,20–21; 12:10,22–23; 13:4,7,28). His successor Joiada had two sons, one John (Jonathan) and the other Jesus (Joshua, Neh. 12:10–11, 22). According to the account in Josephus, John and Jesus quarreled about the vacant high priesthood and John slew his brother Jesus in the Temple. The Persian general Bagoses had promised Jesus his help in obtaining the position. After Bagoses learned of the murder of Jesus, he advanced to Jerusalem and defiled the Temple by entering it. The Jews sought to prevent him, whereupon he said to them: "Am not I purer than he that was slain in the temple?" Josephus' language is very vague, but he seems to imply that the Temple was closed for seven years, or that a tax was imposed upon every sacrifice.

Josephus recorded another incident which is reported to have taken place near the end of the Persian rule and was caused by the rivalry of two other brothers for the high priesthood. John (high priest mentioned earlier) left two sons, one named Jaddua and the other named Manasseh (Neh. 12:11,22; 13:28). In some way, Jaddua and Manasseh were associated in the priesthood. Jaddua distinguished himself with the elders of Jerusalem by maintaining the strict institutions and observances as interpreted by Ezra and Nehemiah. Manasseh was more liberal in his thinking and acting. He married Nicaso, the daughter of Sanballat, who was the Persian governor of Samaria.

This marriage, which was contrary to the wishes of the orthodox leaders, aroused great indignation in Jerusalem. Manasseh was given the choice of divorcing his wife, who was not a Jewess, or giving up the priesthood. Sanballat offered to build a temple for Manasseh on Mount Gerizim where he might continue to exercise his priestly functions if he would keep Nicaso for his wife. Sanballat, who was an old man, also promised to make Manasseh governor of the territory he ruled. These promises elated Manasseh, and he agreed to Sanballat's proposal. This alliance between Sanballat and Manasseh evidently caused a disturbance in Jerusalem. According to Josephus, many priests and Levites, entangled in such marriages, joined Manasseh and were given money and land as rewards.

The evidence seems to indicate that disagreements arose among the leaders about the marriage laws and that these disagreements led to a schism which encouraged the building of the rival temple on Mount Gerizim. Some of the leaders did not agree with the religious prejudice which led to the policy of religious exclusiveness. There are some who think that it was this division which led some Jews to affirm that sacrifice could only be offered in Jerusalem. This schism, of course, had many antecedents. These two brothers were officiating at the rival temples when the Persian Empire crumbled before the army of Alexander the Great.

HASMONEAN DYNASTY

THE FIRST REFERENCE to the Pharisees and Sadducees, who played such a large part in Jewish life, is found during the reign of John Hyrcanus. Josephus gives a very interesting account concerning Hyrcanus and the Pharisees and Sadducees. After Hyrcanus became king, he called a meeting with the Pharisees, with whom he was on friendly terms. He told them that he desired to please God in every way, and that if he had offended at any point in the observance of the Law, he wanted them to correct him. Most of the Pharisees were afraid to speak their convictions and so, one by one, they praised Hyrcanus for his piety.

However, Eleazar, an elderly Pharisee, told Hyrcanus that he should give up the high priesthood since his mother had been a captive in the days of Antiochus Epiphanes. Hyrcanus became angry and demanded that the Pharisees punish Eleazar. When the Pharisees voted to give him only nominal punishment, Hyrcanus broke with the Pharisees and aligned himself with the Sadducees. This story indicates that at the first mention of the two groups by name, they were already opposed to each other. It also shows the popular hatred for the Hasmonean rulers.

John Hyrcanus died in peace, bequeathing his reign to his wife. However, Aristobulus, the oldest son of the deceased king, seized the supreme power, flung his mother into prison, and starved her to death. He also imprisoned three of his four brothers. Later, because of jealousy and suspicion, Aristobulus had this fourth brother, Antigonus, killed.

Aristobulus I

Aristobulus conquered the Ituraeans to the northeast of Galilee and added this territory to Judea. Those who did not flee were compelled to accept circumcision and to observe the Jewish Law, just as the Idumeans in the south had been forced to do in the time of John Hyrcanus I. This explains why, in subsequent years, the population of Galilee, though predominantly Gentile by race, was Jewish in religion.

Aristobulus died a tragic death and was succeeded by Alexander Janneus, the eldest of the imprisoned brothers. Alexander Janneus succeeded his brother as high priest and went beyond him by officially claiming the title of king which he inscribed on certain of his coins.

Alexander Janneus

Alexander Janneus was a ruthless man. Although high priest, he was essentially a soldier who delighted in war. However, militarily he was too ambitious for his own good. He attempted many military conquests, but his efforts in early years were seldom successful.

By this time the Pharisees had gained an extraordinary degree of influence over the people. Detesting the Pharisees' lofty pretensions, Alexander attached himself to the Sadducees. This caused the Pharisees to hate him.

The trouble came to a head on the occasion of a celebration of the Feast of Tabernacles at which he was officiating as high priest. As he was standing in front of the altar preparing to offer the sacrifice, the people pelted him with citrons which they were carrying for use in the festival and hurled insults at him. The Talmud states that this outburst was occasioned by a contemptuous and stupid action of Alexander Janneus. He purposely poured a water libation over his own feet instead of on the altar as was required by Pharisaic tradition. The people's reaction so infuriated Alexander that he ordered his bodyguard to fall on the unarmed multitude. They massacred six thousand of the Jews.

In 94 B.C. Alexander Janneus' army came to grief in an invasion of Transjordan where the Nabatean King, Obador, would not countenance Jewish intrusion into the areas of Moab and Edom. Most of the Jewish army was destroyed in the field. The Jews, urged on by the Pharisees, broke out in revolt against their ruler. It is reported that in the six-year civil war which followed, Alexander Janneus slew approximately fifty thousand of his own people with the help of foreign soldiers. Near the end of this period, the Pharisees decided to put an end to this indecisive warfare by calling in the help of the Seleucid ruler. Alexander was forced into exile. Six thousand Jews joined him later.

In a complicated three-way military struggle between the Nabateans, the Syrians, and the Jews, Aretas the Nabatean king allowed Alexander to make significant military gains. Alexander moved with such success that when he died in 79 B.C., he ruled over territory almost as extensive as the empire of Solomon. But the days of Hasmonean power were numbered and Maccabean glory was forgotten.

Alexandra Salome

Tradition has it that before his death, Alexander Janneus counseled his wife to ally herself with the Pharisaic faction. By this means she could win the support of the masses and strengthen her hold over the people. The revival of Pharisaic influence and the corresponding curtailment of Sadducean power became the outstanding feature of Queen Alexandra's reign. Her reign is regarded in Pharisaic tradition as a veritable golden age.

However, there were many internal problems during these nine years. As a woman, Alexandra Salome was excluded by the law from the high priesthood. She appointed her eldest, Hyrcanus II, to this office. This did not please her younger son, Aristobulus II. Aristobulus was an able and energetic young man whose obvious ambitions the queen was forced to restrain for the sake of the peace of her reign. Aristobulus was Sadducean in his sympathies and led the opposition against the growing power of the Pharisees. The royal family and the two leading sects were divided. Soon after Salome's death, Aristobulus defeated his brother in battle near Jericho. Hyrcanus willingly retired in favor of his more active brother, and Aristobulus became high priest and king of the Jews.

Aristobulus II

All might have gone well for Aristobulus II if there had not appeared on the scene a controversial figure whose family was to play a vital part in the affairs of the Jews for many years to come. This man was named Antipater (shorter form, Antipas), father of the future Herod the Great and son of the Antipater whom Alexander Janneus had appointed governor of Idumea.

Envious of the popularity and influence of Aristobulus II, Antipater decided to stir up trouble between the two brothers. With the aid of the Pharisees he repeatedly urged Hyrcanus to attempt the recovery of his throne. For a long time the indolent price refused to listen to the suggestions. Hyrcanus was finally persuaded to take action; and, with the help of the Nabatean king, Aretas III, defeated Aristobulus and shut him up in Jerusalem. Within the city itself the priests and their followers remained loyal to Aristobulus, while the Pharisees and the general populace gave their assistance to the attackers.

Suggested Audiovisual Aids

Chapter 1

FILMSTRIP: *Between the Testaments* (73m), 38 frames, color, recording

Chapter 2

FILMSTRIPS: *The Four Gospels* (73m), 37 frames, color, recording; *John's Portrait of Jesus* (26b), 50 frames, color, recording

Chapter 3

FILMSTRIPS: *The World in Which Jesus Was Born* (15f), 52 frames, color, recording; *The World That Needed Jesus* (53s), 38 frames, color, recording; *Holy Night* (66c), 43 frames, color, recording; *The Story of Christmas* (26b), 52 frames, color, recording

Chapter 4

FILMSTRIP: *Jesus Attends the Passover* (57c), 25 frames, color

Chapter 5

FILMSTRIP: *Jesus Begins His Galilean Ministry* (57c), 20 frames, color

Chapter 6

FILMSTRIP: *Jesus Teaches Humility and Forgiveness* (57c), 17 frames, color

Chapter 7

FILMSTRIP: *Visit to Mary and Martha* (66c), 34 frames, color, recording

Chapter 8

FILMSTRIPS: *Jesus' Resurrection* (57c), 21 frames, color; *It Began in Bethlehem* (21c), 50 frames, color, recording; *The Easter Story* (26b), 45 frames, color, recording

Chapter 9

FILMSTRIPS: *God's Covenant Fulfilled in Jesus Christ* (15f), 43 frames, color, recording; *The Gospel of Isaiah* (26b), 50 frames, color, recording

A filmstrip, *The Life and Ministry of Our Lord,* has been released in conjunction with this book. It is suitable for use in preview of this volume, in connection with the class sessions, or as review after the book is studied. The filmstrip, manual, and recording are available at Baptist Book stores for $8.50.

Bibliography

Barclay, William. *Jesus as They Saw Him.* New York: Harper & Row, 1963.
_____. *The Mind of Jesus.* New York: Harper & Row, 1961.
Broadus, John A. *Jesus of Nazareth.* Grand Rapids: Baker Book House, reprinted 1962.
Brown, Handel H. *When Jesus Came.* Grand Rapids: William B. Eerdmans Publishing Co., 1963.
Bowman, John Wick. *The Intention of Jesus.* Philadelphia: The Westminster Press, 1943.
Bultmann, Rudolf K. *Jesus Christ and Mythology.* New York: Charles Scribner's Sons, 1958.
Carver, W. O. *The Self-interpretation of Jesus.* Nashville: Broadman Press, reprinted 1961.
Conner, W. T. *The Cross in the New Testament.* Nashville: Broadman Press, 1954.
Cullmann, Oscar. *Christ and Time.* Translated by Floyd V. Filson. Philadelphia: The Westminster Press, 1964.
Davies, W. D. *Christian Origins and Judaism.* Philadelphia: The Westminster Press, 1962.
Day, Gardiner M. *Christ Speaks from the Cross.* New York: Seabury Press, 1956.
Denny, James. *The Death of Christ.* London: Hodder and Stoughton, 1903.
Dodd, C. H. *The Apostolic Preaching and Its Developments.* New York: Willett, Clark & Co., 1937.
Duncan, George S. *Son of Man.* New York: The Macmillan Co., 1949.

Erdman, Charles R. *Remember Jesus Christ*. Grand Rapids: Wm. B. Eerdmans Publishing Co., 1958.

Filson, Floyd V. *Jesus Christ the Risen Lord*. New York: Abingdon Press, 1956.

Fisher, Fred L. *A Composite Gospel*. Nashville: Broadman Press, 1948.

Flew, R. N. *Jesus and His Church*. London: The Epworth Press, 1938.

Gilmour, G. P. *The Memoirs Called Gospels*. Toronto: Clark, Irwin & Company Limited, 1959.

Grant, Frederick C. *Christ's Victory and Ours*. New York: The Macmillan Co., 1951.

Grant, Robert M. *The Formation of the New Testament*. New York: Harper & Row, Publishers, 1965.

Hooker, M. D. *Jesus and the Servant*. London: SPCK, 1959.

Josephus, Flavius. *Josephus: Complete Works,* translated by William Whiston. Grand Rapids: Kregel Publications, 1964.

Kirk, Kenneth E. *The Vision of God*. New York: Longmans, Green & Co., 1946.

Knox, John. *Christ the Lord*. New York: Willett, Clark & Co., 1945.

————. *The Death of Christ*. New York: Abingdon Press, 1958.

————. *On the Meaning of Christ*. New York: Charles Scribner's Sons, 1947.

————. *The Humanity and Divinity of Christ*. Cambridge: At the University Press, 1967.

Leivestad, Ragnar, *Christ the Conqueror*. New York: The Macmillan Co., 1954.

Manson, T. W. *The Sayings of Jesus*. London: SCM Press, 1949.

————. *The Servant-Messiah*. New York: Cambridge University Press, 1953.

————. *The Teaching of Jesus*. Cambridge: At the University Press, 1951.

Manson, William. *Jesus the Messiah*. Philadelphia: The Westminster Press, 1946.

Marsh, John. *The Fullness of Time*. London: James Nisbet & Co., Ltd., 1952.

Miller, S. W. *Jesus Christ Is Alive*. Boston: W. A. Wilde Co., 1949.

Mowinckel, Sigmund. *He That Cometh*. Translated by G. W. Anderson. New York: Abingdon Press, 1956.

Otto, Rudolf. *The Kingdom of God and the Son of Man*. Translated by Floyd V. Filson and Bertran Lee-Woolf. London: Lutterworth Press, 1951.

Perowne, Stewart. *The Life and Times of Herod the Great*. London: Arrow Books, Ltd., 1960.

Pfeiffer, Charles F. *Between the Testaments*. Grand Rapids: Baker Book House, 1959.

Powell, F. J. *The Trial of Jesus Christ*. London: Paternoster Press, 1949.

Ramsay, William M. *The Christ of the Earliest Christians.* Richmond: John Knox Press, 1959.

Rawlinson, A. E. J. *The New Testament Doctrine of Christ.* New York: Longmans, Green & Co., 1949.

Reumann, John. *Jesus in the Church's Gospels.* Philadelphia: Fortress Press, 1968.

Rhein, Francis Bayard. *An Analytical Approach to the New Testament.* Woodbury, New York: Barron's Educational Series, Inc., 1966.

Richardson, Alan. *The Miracle-Stories of the Gospels.* London: SCM Press, 1941.

Rihbany, Abraham M. *The Syrian Christ.* Cambridge, Mass.: The Riverside Press, 1924.

Robertson, A. T. *A Harmony of the Gospels.* Nashville: Broadman Press, 1950.

Robinson, John A. *Jesus and His Coming.* New York: Abingdon Press, 1957.

Rollins, Wayne G. *The Gospels Portraits of Christ.* Philadelphia: The Westminster Press, 1963.

Rowlingson, Donald T. *Jesus the Religious Ultimate.* New York: Macmillan Co., 1961.

Russell, D. S. *The Jews from Alexander to Herod.* London: Oxford University Press, 1967.

Shepherd, J. W. *The Christ of the Gospels.* Grand Rapids: Wm. B. Eerdmans Publishing Co., 1946.

Smith, Asbury, *The Twelve Christ Chose.* New York: Harper & Row, 1958.

Smith, David. *The Days of His Flesh.* Eighth Edition, Revised. New York: Harper & Brothers, n.d.

_____. *Our Lord's Earthly Life.* New York: George H. Doran, n.d.

Snaith, Norman H. *The Jews From Cyrus to Herod.* New York: Abingdon Press, n.d.

Stagg, Frank. *New Testament Theology.* Nashville: Broadman Press, 1962.

Stauffer, Ethelbert. *Jesus and His Story.* Translated from the German by Richard and Clara Winston. New York: Alfred A. Knopf, 1960.

Stewart, James S. *The Life and Teaching of Jesus Christ.* Edinburgh: Morrison and Gibb Ltd., 1949.

Taylor, Vincent. *The Names of Jesus.* New York: St. Martin's Press, 1953.

_____. *The Life and Ministry of Jesus.* Nashville: Abingdon Press, 1955.

Tilden, Elwyn E., Jr. *Toward Understanding Jesus.* Englewood Cliffs: Prentice-Hall Inc., 1956.

Personal Learning Activities

Chapter 1

1. Identify in a phrase or sentence the following terms.

(1) Aramaic	(9) Pharisees
(2) Alexander the Great	(10) Scribes
(3) Seleucus	(11) Synagogue
(4) Ptolemy	(12) Josephus
(5) Antiochus IV	(13) Apocrypha
(6) Maccabean	(14) Pseudepigrapha
(7) 63 B.C.	(16) Dead Sea Scrolls
(8) Sadducees	(16) Hellenism

Chapter 2 (Fill in the blanks with the proper word or phrase.)

2. The Greek word for substance or content of what is preached: _____.

3. Peter's excellent summary of the gospel story is found in _____ _____.

4. The gospel story that was told by eyewitnesses before the story was written down is known as _____ _____.

5. One possible order of appearance of the four accounts of the *kerygma* (the four Gospels) is: _____

6. The Synoptic Gospels are: _____

7. John is more of a _____ Gospel.
8. Write a sentence about each of the four Gospels, giving at least two facts about the distinctives of each.

Chapter 3

9. List the following information.
   (1) The data which helps in determining the date of Jesus' birth
   (2) The occasion for Jesus' birth
   (3) The major recorded events in Jesus' life between the angel's announcement of his birth and the appearance of John the Baptist
   (4) The events surrounding Jesus' baptism
   (5) The temptations of Jesus and his response to them

Chapter 4

10. Match the terms in the left column with the phrases in the right column.

(1) Judean ministry	headquarters
(2) First two followers	cleansing of Temple
(3) First sign	recognized Jesus as teacher
(4) Capernaum	one year
(5) Passover	Well of Sychar
(6) Nicodemus	miracle at Cana
(7) Samaritan woman	Andrew and John

Chapter 5

11. Select what you believe to be four of the outstanding incidents in Jesus' Galilean ministry and answer the following questions about each:
    (1) What happened?
    (2) What was the response of the disciples?
    (3) What was the response of the religious leaders?
    (4) What was the response of the crowds?
    (5) How does this incident help us to understand the ministry of our Lord?

Chapter 6

12. Indicate what each of these words or phrases has to do with the later Judean ministry.
    (1) The Feast of Tabernacles
    (2) Lighting ceremony
    (3) Adulterous woman
    (4) Seventy
    (5) Neighbor
    (6) Model Prayer
    (7) Feast of Dedication

Chapter 7

13. Locate in at least one Gospel the following incidents or teachings and note the location:
    (1) The narrow gate and straight way
    (2) Warning to Jesus of danger of Herod
    (3) Take up the cross, deny self
    (4) Unfinished tower
    (5) Rich man and Lazarus
    (6) Healing ten lepers
    (7) Woes of Jerusalem
    (8) Importunate widow
    (9) Teachings on marriage
    (10) Rich young ruler
    (11) Christ's approaching suffering and death
    (12) Zacchaeus
    (13) Parable of the pounds

Chapter 8

14. List:
    (1) Each day of Passion Week and give important events of each day
    (2) Four major teachings of Jesus during this week
    (3) At least one Scripture reference for each of the resurrection appearances of Jesus

Chapter 9

15. Select from the discussion in this chapter four designations for our Lord—your favorites—and define each term. Tell what each term reveals to you about him.

The New Church Study Course

THE New Church Study Course effective in January 1970 is based on more than three years of study and design. It offers several improvements in the Church Study Course, which began in October 1959. At that time three courses previously promoted by the Sunday School Board were merged: the Sunday School Training Course, the Graded Training Union Study Course, and the Church Music Training Course. Principles and methods books of the Woman's Missionary Union and the Brotherhood Commission were added in October 1961 and January 1967 respectively.

The New Church Study Course offers increased flexibility in meeting the needs of Southern Baptists. It provides courses of varying length and difficulty, varied formats and types of course materials, additional types of credit, and improved organization of courses.

The New Church Study Course consists of two types of courses: the Christian Development Courses for all church members, and the Christian Leadership Courses for church leaders. Courses are organized into subject areas.

The purpose of Christian Development Courses is to provide courses of study which will help church members grow toward maturity in Christian living and competence in Christian service. These courses offer more comprehensive, advanced, and varied learning experiences in subject areas of a church's educational program than can be provided through curriculum periodicals. Tests and exercises, credits, and diplomas of achievement which help church members measure their progress in developing needed knowledge, understanding, and skills are included in some courses. Units

208

of instruction are provided for Preschoolers and Children. These are designed to reinforce foundational learnings. Materials which churches may use in recognizing the participation of Children in these units are available from Baptist Book Stores.

Christian Leadership Courses provide a comprehensive series of courses organized into subject areas dealing with knowledge, understandings, and skills needed for effective church leadership. Tests and exercises, credits, and diplomas to help leaders measure their growth in leadership ability are included in some courses. The Christian Leadership Courses are the primary source for leadership training materials prepared by the agencies cooperating in the New Church Study Course.

Courses of both types are designed to be effective for individual and class study. Learning aids, study guides, and teaching guides are available for some courses. Credits are granted to Youth and Adults for reading, individual study, and class study.

The New Church Study Course is promoted by the Sunday School Board, 127 Ninth Avenue, North, Nashville, Tennessee 37203, through the departments in the Education Division; by the Woman's Missionary Union, 600 North Twentieth Street, Birmingham, Alabama 35203; by the Brotherhood Commission, 1548 Poplar Avenue, Memphis, Tennessee 38104; and by the respective departments in the state conventions affiliated with the Southern Baptist Convention.

A record of all credits, and diplomas, earned should be maintained in each church.

Detailed information about the course and the system of credits, diplomas, and record keeping is available from the agencies listed above.

Forms for keeping records may be ordered from any Baptist Book Store.

Requirements for Credit

THIS BOOK is the text for course 3208 of subject area Biblical Revelation of the New Church Study Course. If credit is desired for this course through class study, individual study, or reading, the following requirements must be met:

I. Classwork

1. This course is designed for ten (10) hours of class study and carries four credits for such usage. If the course is studied in a class setting of less than ten (10) hours, the following criteria apply:
   (1) Seven and one-half (7½) class hours—three (3) credits
   (2) Five (5) class hours—two (2) credits
   (3) Two and one-half class hours—one (1) credit
   The teacher will indicate the length of the class and the number of credits to be granted on Form 151, Request for Course Credit. For courses in which laboratory experience or practice is desirable, two hours of such guided experience may be substituted as one hour of class time, provided at least half of the required hours are actually spent in classwork.
2. A class member who attends all class sessions and completes the reading of the book as directed by the teacher will not be required to do any written work for credit.
3. A class member who is absent from one or more sessions must complete the required exercises or questions in the "Personal Learning Activities" section on all chapters he misses. In such a case, he must turn in his paper by the date the teacher sets (usually within ten days following the last class). Also, he must certify that he has read the book.

4. The teacher should request an award for himself. A person who teaches a course for Youth or Adults (in any subject area) will be granted the same number of credits as class members. The teacher of an approved unit of study for Preschoolers and Children will be granted two credits in course 6299 in subject area 62. Request award by using Form 151.
5. The director of church training or the person designated by the church should complete Form 151, Request for Course Credit, and forward it after completion of the class to the Church Study Course Awards Office, 127 Ninth Avenue, North, Nashville, Tennessee 37203.

II. Individual Study

1. A person who wishes to complete this course without attending class sessions may receive full credit by certifying that he has read the book and by completing all exercises or questions in the "Personal Learning Activities" section.
2. Students may find profit in studying the text together, but individual papers are required. Carbon copies or duplicates of the answers cannot be accepted.
3. The work required for individual study credit should be turned in for checking to the director of church training or the person designated by the church to administer the New Church Study Course. The form entitled "Request for Course Credit" (Form 151) must be used in requesting these awards. It is to be forwarded by the director of church training or the person designated by the church to the Church Study Course Awards Office, 127 Ninth Avenue, North, Nashville, Tennessee 37203.

III. Reading Credit

1. A person may receive one credit toward the diploma on which he is working by reading this book.
2. Upon completion of the reading, he must complete Form 151, Request for Course Credit. He should give the completed form to the director of church training or to the person designated by his church to be responsible for administering the New Church Study Course.
3. The director of church training or the person designated by the church will see that the request is completed, signed, and forwarded to the Church Study Course Awards Office, 127 Ninth Avenue, North, Nashville, Tennessee 37203.

IV. Awards and Records

Two copies of the course credit award form will be sent by the Study Course Awards Office to the church. One copy should be filed in the church training record and the other given to the individual.